Economics and the
Christian Mind

ECONOMICS AND THE CHRISTIAN MIND

Elements of a Christian Approach to the Economy and Economic Science

Arnold F. McKee

VANTAGE PRESS
New York/Atlanta
Los Angeles/Chicago

FIRST EDITION

Copyright© 1987 by Arnold McKee

Published by Vantage Press, Inc.
516 West 34th Street, New York, New York 10001

Manufactured in the United States of America
ISBN: 0-533-07175-5

Library of Congress Catalog Card No.: 86-090236

Grace does not take away nature, but perfects it.
—Thomas Aquinas

CONTENTS

ACKNOWLEDGMENTS

My special thanks are due Ross Emmett, Bob Faulhaber, Fr. Michael Ryan, John Tiemstra, Anthony Waterman, Bill Wilkinson, and some anonymous referees for comments on part or the whole of my text. Many writers have also contributed to themes discussed, as notes and bibliography testify. Cathy Mendler and Sandy Briand labored on successive drafts.

Books, articles, et cetera, are cited by author, editor or source, and the items listed in the bibliography. Scriptural references relate to *The Jerusalem Bible* (New York: Doubleday, 1966), which is cited by permission of the publisher.

Parts of chapters 4, 6, and 9 have appeared in different form in the *Review of Social Economy* and the *International Journal of Social Economics,* so that permission to draw on the articles concerned (see bibliography) is acknowledged.

It should be noted that, where various points and illustrations refer to "man," "he," et cetera, such terms are to be taken in a generic sense.

Finally, if a work should be dedicated, let this be for Theophilus (Luke 1:3), who will best understand what it is about.

King's College, London, Canada
June 1, 1986

INTRODUCTION

My object in these pages is to relate the Christian mind to economics; that is, my preoccupation is to project attitudes and thought that are systematically and authentically grounded in the Christian religion and way of life on the economy and on the science that studies it. It is perfectly obvious that religion or the absence of it is a profound influence on individual and social life. A total acceptance of God and of what are taken to be His commands will have ramifications on everything we do and think we know. But in Western society we have increasingly compartmentalized our thought and communication. Given our pluralistic society, religion is for those who wish to believe in and practice it, and discussion is best kept apart from economic life and the science that studies it. Moreover, open debate on religion's implications for individual and social living arouses strong passions, so that we have learned to treat it warily, especially our market-conscious media. Why propose, then, to disturb matters by relating Christian thinking directly to how our economic institutions work and to an economic science that most seem content with as a value-free form of inquiry?

One reply is that the Christian religion, like others or any integral philosophy, obliges its adherents to witness to their beliefs in all areas of life and inquiry. In parts of the world such as Latin America and South Africa, religion has a great deal to contribute to the solution of social and economic problems. My own deeper reasons relate to the progressive erosion of the values and attitudes deriving historically (not exclusively) from the Judeo-Christian tradition and underpinning the basic social and economic institutions of Western civilization. Economic freedoms, private property and enterprise, social programs, and the role of government all depend necessarily on certain foundational beliefs in the nature of man and the purpose of life. Accordingly, the disappearance of sufficient consensus undermines the premises of our kind of society. As for the sciences that study social behavior and institutions, equally their work presupposes some code of values to interpret and guide their inquiries. They have no way of creating the premises that give stability to social and individual life, but, provided these premises exist, economics, sociology, behavioral psychology, and the rest may be pursued in a positive or purely factual manner (see chapter 2, section 9) with a good deal of success. If the underlying framework collapses, however, the social sciences cannot solve the problems thrown up, but lose their direction.

Hence it is time for Christians to set aside the compromises and split minds with which we have approached society and the social sciences. There is no longer broad agreement on values with which the Christian religion can basically harmonize, so that there is no choice but to emphasize openly and explore a parting of the ways. Let me amplify these remarks.

1

There is a good deal of evidence that Western society has entered on a decline reaching to the foundations of its life and culture.[1] Our social, political, and economic institutions all show decay; decline of the family, sexual liberties, widespread contempt for law, distress of cities, decadence of democratic governments, decline of the work ethic, exhaustion of resources, high inflation, and insoluble unemployment—these are a few of the pessimistic themes developed in contemporary writing. Too, art, music, and literature seem given over to expressing the ugliness and conflicts of modern life. While one must be cautious with morbid analysis of this kind, especially if one no longer has the energy and optimism of youth, there is a widespread belief that Western civilization and its offshoots in different parts of the world risk disintegration, just as past civilizations have ended. The overall threat of nuclear destruction confirms this anguish.

While surface causes of the breakdown are obvious—the legacy of two world wars, materialism and urbanization, falling population growth, quarrels over distribution, et cetera—at the deepest level arise questions of faith and values. For centuries, despite its vicissitudes and upheavals, European civilization has basically reposed upon Christianity. Its ideals and great social institutions (family, state, church) have reflected this influence, and its economic institutions have presumed basic consensus on such values as personal dignity, essential freedoms, respect for property, faith in a benevolent Providence, and regard for justice and integrity. If the Christian religion has been misused in many applications—for example, colonial exploitation and slavery—those in power and in bondage found in it a center of stability for their personal and social lives.

The disintegration we are experiencing seems to be primarily this: So long as Christian faith and its attitudes of mind and standards of conduct were in place, the questionings of the Renaissance, rationalism and free thinking, individualism, positivism, and many other divergences could be contained and good things they offered absorbed into the mainstream. But now the framework itself and the foundations of faith and values are to all appearances dissolving,[2] at least for a majority of the populations concerned. As Christians see things, social, economic, and moral disorders are linked and the first two cannot be solved merely by institutional reforms.

Further, the clash between the character and direction of Western civilization and Christian life and thought, a theme that has preoccupied commentators and church leaders for a long time, has moved into a phase of growing hostility. Though originally shaped in many of its institutions and ideals by Christianity, the West has drifted increasingly into materialism and indifference to God and religion. The divergence has become conflict, and attacks on Christianity multiply, often in the name of freedom, rights, and humanity itself. Urbanization, materialism, and secular education have been the most obvious forces bringing about these changed attitudes. People leave the countryside, where old ways of life and the closeness of nature keep them within a religious mold, and as they crowd into cities they come under the pressures of urban living and the generally harmful influence of the media. The daily message is, Make as much as you can, enjoy the pleasures of life now as your right, do a little good as you go along, and if there is a God, He surely is content with all this, since nothing more can be expected of you. Meanwhile, secular education, inspired by the modern university and extending now to the first years of elementary school, disseminates the kind of knowledge where God and religion are assiduously left aside as options for those interested. Such an approach, carefully respectful of individual freedoms and beliefs, has formed a generation not merely ignorant of but often hostile to Christianity.

If present-day economies are in trouble enough, in recent years a succession of books and articles has appeared on the crisis of economic science.[3] At first glance, this appears to be confined to macroeconomics: The so-called Keynesian era of analysis and policy is largely ended, and a controversial doctrine of monetarism has partly taken its place. Neither has an answer for the combination of unemployment, inflation, and enormous public deficits, plus their connections with international trade and debt, which plague so many countries. Some declare that the crisis of modern economics is simply that of macroeconomic theory and policy and nothing more. But for others there is a deeper dispute over whether economic science has, through imitation of the physical sciences, become too oriented toward a supposed physical world of economic relations, susceptible to mathematical-type analysis and econometric investigation. If what individual and social behavior truly is—kaleidoscopic, less predictable, emotional as well as rational, and necessarily moral—became the central focus, economics would have to give up some of its pretensions and desired exactness in favor of looser methods and results. The result would be a less rigorous but more truthful science.

More important, the economics that has been elaborated, chiefly over the past century, has presumed certain values and institutions to be in place, such as consumer freedom, self-interest, private property, rationality in choice and action, search for optimal gain and satisfaction, et cetera. On such bases it has created a sophisticated analysis of consumer, producer, investor, and even governmental behavior, accompanied by a wealth of statistical findings and theoretical constructions. But these supposedly solid institutions repose in fact on a certain acquiescence and faith on the part of society, now so weakened as to call them greatly into question. While most continue to support the institutions and values concerned, they function so poorly in practice that deep dissatisfaction with the private enterprise system has developed. Many even conclude that an immensely sophisticated economic science, especially its theoretical presentation in texts and monographs, is increasingly irrelevant to modern society. There is a sort of self-sustaining domain of inquiry where specialists talk to one another, quite simply apart from our actual world, threatened by social breakdown and nuclear destruction.

My particular concern is the clash between Christian thought and parts of economic science, a matter readily agreed to by many Christian economists.[4] Since about World War II, economic science has been marked by a positive approach that pretends to leave values aside and gives attention simply to the "facts." Thus its findings may in principle be adapted to whatever value judgments individuals choose for their actions. In practice, such an ostensibly a-religious approach turns out to be antireligious, since values affect the foundations of economic propositions, give them direction, and assist their reasoning. Consequently, the type of knowledge developed in positive economics can often be linked with Christian thought only by being taken back to its foundations and reconstructed. The determination of just wages, which virtually everybody takes seriously outside of an economics classroom, is a simple example. Since labor is inseparable from the person, it is not just a commodity to be bought and sold in a market like any other.

It is now counterproductive for Christians to continue acquiescing in the conventional presentation and pursuit of economic inquiry and more than time to speak out with active dissent.

3

Now if we have an economy where fundamental institutions and values are undermined and an economic science whose premises and direction are left hanging, how does this connect up with Christian thought? Let me indicate in a preliminary way what is developed in the following chapters.

Christianity is a religion and does not propose directly an economic or social system. It deals with the relations between man and God, where Christ is Mediator and Way, and focuses on good and evil in human conduct, redemption annd sanctification, doing good to others, and conversion of hearts to Christ. It is not immediately concerned with the structure and operation of any political, social, or economic system, and Jesus was not a social or political activist in the Palestine of his day. Yet since Christian teaching aims at a conversion of heart and mind and changed attitudes toward life, it issues in a code of morality that affects human behavior in every area, so that institutions and the very fabric of society are altered. Race, environment, and history must remain an intimate part of this process, so that a Christian society in Europe or Asia or Africa will not present the same external features. Yet in fundamental

xv

characteristics they will be similar, just as Christians of different races and times resemble one another.

In formulating principles of individual and social behavior, Christian thought may call on three chief sources—Scripture, the church, and theology-philosophy. The first offers counsel and directives bearing on conduct, though often needing interpretation in relation to modern economic life. The second has generated a fund of both authoritative teaching and less structured thought on economic affairs, mostly in the modern period but reaching back over centuries. The following pages will, however, give less emphasis to both these sources than many Christians would wish. While the pieces of divine wisdom we get from Scripture are foundational, we cannot easily pass from them alone to a systematic formulation of social principles and critique of economic science, and drawing heavily on church documents creates a reliance on authority that would put many off from my intended applications of religious thought to economic matters.

Hence most reliance will be placed on the sort of intellectual approach represented by moral theology and natural ethics. Forced early into an intellectual stance by the attacks of "pagan" philosophers (cf. Wilken, 1984), Christianity soon developed a systematic account of its central doctrines that, despite vicissitudes, has never ceased to develop to the present day. Christian leaders, councils, and apologists have used the Revelation of Scripture and sought divine guidance, as they believe, to draw up a systematic statement of beliefs, which then issue in norms and directives for behavior in the social domain. This social theology (as it is often now called) is buttressed by a natural ethics of the character and purpose of life discerned from experience and history, itself ostensibly leaving aside religious sources properly speaking. More correctly, from the Greeks, religion almost always supposed a divine ordering of the world, until the modern age relegated God and religious belief to private business.

As complemented by the Christian religion, natural social ethics forms a solid alliance with moral theology for the formulation of social principles that can be led forward to intermediate criteria and applications respecting the political, economic, and social domains. We shall spend a good deal of time on the methodology of getting to applications, pointing out that the certainty and obligation of principles steadily give way to diversity of options and conflicting opinions for practice. For instance, determining the degree of culpability in crimes or children's behavior and the punishment and damages justly awarded is not precise business, but to do our human best is the reality of translating moral principles into practice.

If the thrust of this account of Christian social principles is to examine the foundations and shape of institutions in a basically free economy, its complement is a critique of economic science, calling for the incorporation of values and a modification of its pervasive liberal individualism. Equally, aspects of its methodology are questioned, particularly Platonic abstraction and mathematical modeling, and a case made for "moderate realism" in economic theorizing. A crucial difficulty is that the present conception and methodology of economics simply blocks off the entry of Christian values and thinking. How could this be otherwise when modern social sciences simply omit the place of religious belief in understanding and knowledge?

4

Evidently this book is written by a Catholic Christian,[5] whom many would also typify as traditional or conservative. Hence its account of the Christian mind and economics risks turning off many readers, including Christians whose views differ on points of doctrine and ensuing attitudes. Concerning this, I offer three comments by way of explanation.

To dispose of an initial question, it is not my position that Christianity in general and Roman Catholicism in particular are the only valid route to God or to sanctifying personal life and gaining eternal salvation. In what is inescapably a realm of conjecture, there is today widespread opinion that all genuine religion leads to God. It is the belief of my communion that Jesus, whether so acknowledged or not, is the only mediator between God and man and that all who approach the Father enter into some form of solidarity with the church established by His Son. All surely agree, too, that God alone judges authenticity and what we here below uncertainly perceive as "good will."

But after recognizing the different premises that govern perceptions and conduct in modern pluralistic societies and readily accepting whatever convergence they may have with the Christian church, my aims preclude setting out from mere broad agreement on human values. While nobody can be indifferent to the appeal and good sense of such a procedure, it has to be left aside, for the reason that my entire purpose is to present an integrally Christian approach to economic questions. Just as humanists, Marxists, free thinkers, and others write logically and unrestrainedly from

xvii

their viewpoint, basing their case on freedom of thought and the right to be heard without prejudice, these pages aim to present what their author regards as an unadulterated Christian approach, equally having its claim to be heard. Hence those who are not Christians must grant its premises as working hypotheses, to extend that initial sympathy essential for appreciating any novel line of thought.

A more formidable problem arises from the divisions among Christians, including liberal and conservative Roman Catholics. One solution might be to define a preferred approach and defend it as required, which would require apologetics and cause my economic concerns to be sidetracked repeatedly. A second is to adopt a reasonably common Christian view on essentials, while avoiding recourse to the position of a specific denomination. This is the compromise attempted, despite its awkwardness. The good side is its ecumenism, deemphasizing divisions; the weakness is that a particular perspective will thrust itself through here and there. To take one example, it will be asserted (in chapter 3, section 3) that man is finally social because he is made in the image of a triune God, social in His essence. This immediately posits the divinity of Christ and the doctrine of the Trinity, both dissented from by many Christians.

One upshot of these difficulties is that no formal definition of the ''Christian mind'' can be attempted. My only foundation is that the principal or essential tenets of the Christian religion, totally accepted and lived, give rise to certain premises of thought and a characteristic approach that impinge in sufficiently clear ways on the institutions and working of the economy and on economic science. To go further, giving a tighter statement of assumptions and drawing logical inferences would result in a narrower perspective, making the approach used less accessible. For instance, many Catholics base themselves on papal statements of social principles, other Christians rely on a neo-Calvinist (e.g. Vickers, 1982) approach, and others adopt particular biblical interpretations (e.g. North, 1973). But, while building in a stronger base, such more specific premises narrow the appeal considerably.

5

If the above indicate my preoccupations, the program of work is as follows. Part 1 sketches the foundations and leading attitudes of mind that characterize Christian thought (chapters 1 and 2). This will seem an undertaking unnecessary to many and strange to others, but in fact a large proportion of Christians and virtually all non-Christians (in most Western countries, at least) do not properly bring to mind what is involved in an authentically religious approach to economic life and science. Too much has been forgotten. Modern Islam is rather clearer on the holistic attitudes religious persons must adopt toward all aspects of human life and the learning that studies them.

Given this background, part 2 sets out in chapters 3 and 4 principles that flow from this respecting a few leading institutions of society and then the economy at more length. What is the nature of society and the purpose of economic life, and what basic guidelines should be in place? Since a primarily reasoned approach drawing on natural law thought has been employed, chapter 5 comments on direct reliance on Scripture and other modern approaches. Then chapter 6 applies the principles outlined to the problems of fair wages and inflation, to illustrate how social ethics links up with economic analysis.

Naturally the elaboration of economic science is closely bound up with the structure and operation of actual economies, so that the clash with Christian thought extends to it. The aim of part 3 is to point to certain premises and procedures that are at variance with the Christian mind and to the path of harmonization (chapters 7 and 8). The clash is illustrated with the somewhat technical example of welfare economics and the more straightforward one of government in the market economy (chapter 9). My overall position is that the Christian mind is much more comfortable with a reworking of economic science that incorporates values and promotes individual and social welfare in a rounded sense, though the idea of a specifically Christian version is rejected. The conclusion develops the case for a social economics representing the recasting suggested.

Evidently this extensive program tries to cover too much—an initial outline of Christian attitudes toward reality and scientific knowledge, an account of principles applying to the institutions and operation of the economy, and a critique of economic science, plus many examples of linking up Christian thought with both. Yet omission of part 2 would render the comments on economic science less justifiable and comprehensible, and leaving out part 3 would leave economic science unchallenged on its high ground. Many valuable discussions of a Christian approach to both remain in a void, since they fail to deal with the methodology of getting from principles to applications or to tangle with economic science.

Finally, a word on presentation. A numbering system within chapters is used throughout, where each section deals with a specific topic, so as to give a sense of direction. Next, academic readers will quickly notice that this book is not intended to be a work of detailed scholarship, in that many topics raised could be examined in greater detail, digressing on sources and controversies. Interdisciplinary work causes one to range over many fields and topics, each the subject of specialized study, painting a large canvas and summarizing to the neglect of nuance and qualification.

Indeed, a purely intellectual style of argumentation is not possible, since this would falsify the Christian approach necessary for my task. Reason and logic have their unquestioned importance, but they must be complemented for the concerns of this book by faith, respect for Scripture and traditional authority, and prayerful guidance of the Spirit. Many of this book's assertions cannot be "proven"—for instance, that the collapse of the Judeo-Christian framework of values is a disaster for society and positive social science, that much current economic theorizing is irrelevant to our most important social problems, or that integral Christian thinking projects such and such a view. Indeed, there is often not space to introduce the kind of evidence that might at least persuade. Later, of course, we shall note that commonly accepted proofs based on induction and logic (see chapter 8, section 6) have acknowledged limitations; but religious argumentation is even more subject to an inability to convince, owing to differing interpretations of evidence, disputes over appeals to authority of the church and Scripture, and entry of faith. Positions adopted inevitably strike some as dogmatic and others as illuministic. Christians, perhaps more so than nonbelievers, are heavily critical of views not coinciding with their own. Yet time has a way of separating true from false prophets, and the fruits of good and bad social principles are where my case must rest. What dechristianized societies have become and the gaps in what positive social science holds out for their betterment are both extremely clear.

Finally, to whom are these pages addressed? To a variety of readers, including those chiefly interested in religious socioeconomic thought, past and present students of the economy and economic science, and those having a professional interest in both. The first group may be dissatisfied with my outline of Christian thought and its social content and be put off by technical material. The second may be puzzled by the constant linking of religion and economics and questioning the methods of economic analysis. The third will be unhappy with the perfunctory treatment of theory that the other two groups struggle with. This is surely the fate of interdisciplinary work, which draws together knowledge from different fields, satisfies specialists in none of them, and leaves most wondering at what is put together. But addressing exclusively any of these groups would deemphasize essential parts of the argument—namely, the validity of a religious approach to the economy and economic science, the need to discuss applications, and the epistemological clash with parts of economic science.

But so much for introductory remarks. However finely planned and prepared, the proof of any pudding lies in the eating, and we must set to work.

Economics and the
Christian Mind

Part 1

THE CHRISTIAN MIND

INTRODUCTORY REMARKS

To bring out the approach of the Christian mind to economic thought and science, it is now essential to begin with a brief account of what it means to be an authentic follower of Christ and how the committed believer may be expected to think about economic behavior. Until recently one could presume widespread understanding of Christianity in Western countries, but this is increasingly less the case. The former cultural, devotional, and values background has largely given way to secular humanism with many pluralistic attitudes, so that the inner substance of Christian belief and piety is no longer generally appreciated beyond superficial facts.

Further, posing central Christian beliefs directly as premises has a startling impact on how the mind shaped by religious belief will approach the working of the economy and reflection on it. Materialistic and secular pressures coming from society, the universities and the media are such that it is very difficult for committed Christians to set aside compartmentalized thinking and find the mindset that their religion requires towards daily experience and what the various sciences have to say about it. Hence let me recall in two chapters a few fundamentals of Christian belief and consequent attitudes toward reality and knowledge.

Chapter 1

SOME FOUNDATIONS

Within the space that can be given to beliefs and doctrines serving as starting point for the Christian mind, only three matters will be touched on—the centrality of God, discipleship of Christ, and role of the community or church. It is not my intention to embark on theology properly speaking, even less critical comment, since the proper context for both is elsewhere. Instead my plan is to outline a few foundational beliefs of Christianity, including some suggestion of its devotion. Emphasizing the latter is based on a personal conviction that a purely intellectual approach, introducing disagreements and criticisms (e.g. Munby, 1956, I), only distracts attention from the necessary confrontation. The truths believed in by the Christian mind and the piety it feeds on are deeply opposed to the prevailing approach to economic life and study of it customary in the universities; but this will matter only for those whose intellectual perception of the Christian religion is made alive by faith and prayer.[1]

1

Every committed Christian acknowledges God as the centrally important fact of his own life and that of society. Whether God may exist and whether agnosticism and atheism are viable attitudes are obviously essential issues for discussion, and proofs for His existence have been debated for centuries.[2] All this I leave aside, however, to insist that God is necessarily the focus of Christian life and thought. It is not possible to leave Him in the background, unmentioned in any deep consideration of reality and the sciences that probe it. Doing this, however necessary or convenient for communication with non-Christians or believers with split minds, will only introduce falsity. Indeed, to contemplate any aspect of reality with no reference to God is for the Christian not an authentic attitude toward reality at all.

Yet this acknowledgement is not mere intellectual assent, nor is it some remote or fearful relation. Instead the Christian approaches God in a *personal* way, as a loving Father who has an intimate regard for his welfare, as Jesus frequently emphasized (Luke 12:6–7). Consequently the Christian attitude is different from that typically found in Oriental thought, say the remoteness of God in Buddhism or the animism that pervades Hindu religions. Even more obviously, it is quite distinct from the intellectual concepts of theology and philosophy. While most of these reflect aspects of God, they are not at all the same thing as the reality of a personally caring Father as taught by Christ. God for the Christian is an experience touching his entire being, not a mere proposition of the mind.

Consequently a gap opens between the Christian mind and intellectual, cultural, and artistic discussions that do not take God into serious account. The Christian can understand rejection or contestation, but silence toward what is the most important issue to be encountered in life is intolerable. Most unfortunately, the habit has arisen in most Western intellectual circles (not all) of omitting God and religion as topics too sensitive and controversial to form part of public discussion of social issues. If this attitude is understandable, since we all desire to communicate easily with our fellows, the result is to leave an all important area uncovered. The interminable discussions on art, literature, and modern living in the media, serious and popular, must for Christians remain incomplete if they do not include proper reference to the Source of all beauty and welfare.

Going further, the Christian thinks neglect of God in human living and the laws regulating it is thoroughly dangerous. Not merely do we falsify the basis of debate, but we incur divine punishment. That we have a just, caring Father demands our attention, so that acting as though He does not exist corrupts human hearts, leading to personal and social disasters that could be averted by the long-standing means of prayer and reparation. The warning that divine love and patience eventually give way to anger has been given repeatedly in Christian experience.

2

The purpose of life as the Christian sees it is to serve God or, to say the same thing in a more uplifting way, to live it for His glory.[3] Like all creation, we live out our days primarily to manifest the glory of God and obey the Will of the Father, as Jesus taught. While this idea is initially strange, it means that we realize what we most authentically are by being transformed into a life of praise before God, as confirmed by the witness and writings of mystics over the centuries. If "heaven" consists in knowing God as He knows Himself, it would indeed be odd if this earthly life did not consist in approaching Him as much as may lie within our power, aided by grace.

If to glorify God is the purpose of life stated at the most general level, this primary goal gives every secondary aim its focus and is at the root of the moral code that must govern detailed living. Our vocation, state, and work in life will provide fulfilment only if made part of this overall intention. Such notions as humanistic or creative self-actualization[4] make sense only as related to the primary purpose of life and its moral nature. You fulfill yourself in God, and any attempt at self-realization while leaving Him aside is a deception leading to self-destruction. Accordingly, the goals stated in economic texts, such as maximizing consumer satisfaction, producer efficiency, welfare, et cetera, find their justification and direction only insofar as they are subordinated to the primary aim of life itself. Mere materialism and concentration on rising standards of living disfigure men and women.

3

One of the deepest problems that has always preoccupied mankind is the coexistence of good and evil. Alongside all that is good and beautiful in this world flourish many horrifying manifestations of evil. Also, it is not merely the guilty who cause harm and suffer the consequences. Much is due to natural forces or chance, and the innocent and whole societies may suffer frightfully. Children are born deformed, the innocent are maimed, and one nation seeks to annihilate another. As a result, many feel they must reject the possibility of a benevolent God who may not cause, but at least allows, such evil to occur. Anger at God for permitting evil is not infrequent. Many are torn between joy in the goodness and holiness of God and yet bewilderment at what He permits or may even appear to send.

This immense and difficult mystery, which causes so much anguish for those immediately hurt and those who see God's allowing evil as an insuperable obstacle to hopes for surely bettering the world, is beyond my scope. Suffice it for present purposes to say that Christians accept the fact of an active force for evil and believe that God sent His Son, or some sharing of Himself in human form, to redeem mankind from sin. It seems to be the eternal wisdom that sin and wrongdoing must be compensated for if love and holiness are to overcome them; and those whose hearts are strong and generous enough are called to imitate the sufferings of Christ to share in his atonement.

But the social sciences rarely, if ever, address the problem of evil in the terms and with the approach commonly adopted by the Christian mind. Instead they are pervaded with a strange belief in the perfectibility of men and women. What people want or do is typically accepted as "good;" some obvious lack of good consequences is referred to as dysfunctional, socially unacceptable, opposed to conventional mores, or inefficient; and the remedies offered are more education and research, improved production and distribution, and the like. A Christian, however, has a very different approach to the fact of evil and its causes, consequences, and remedies. He does not belittle in the slightest immediate and necessary cures proposed, through medicine, psychiatry, education or adequate income, but he knows their limitation. Christians cannot forget that one of the principal reasons given by Jesus for failure of the word of God to take root and flourish in people is the snares and attacks of the evil one (Matthew 13:19). Education and psychiatry alone cannot overcome the sources of wrongdoing and may become its instruments.

4

There are two fundamental reasons for serving God, the attraction to goodness that is basic in our nature and the consequences of turning away. "Heaven" has been conceived in elaborate ways; the quintessence, however, is to "see" God, to know Him directly and fully and to rejoice in this everlastingly, which is an overwhelming prospect for all who contemplate it and strive for the goal in the traditional ways commanded. Individualists—who figure so prominently in economic theory—need not apply, since Heaven does not consist in God and *me,* but in an essentially social God and *us* (cf. chapter 3, section 3). Hell, on the other hand, is a decidedly menacing idea, not talked about in polite circles and conveniently treated as unscientific knowledge. Whatever it may contain of devils, flames, and so forth, again the essential reality is total separation from God, in complete hatred of goodness, of oneself, and others, and all this in utter loneliness forever. Such an agony is far greater than whatever physical sufferings may be involved.

This height and abyss of human destiny is again recalled, not with apologetic or controversial aims, but merely to emphasize in a matter-of-fact way that the Christian mind cannot treat heaven or hell and the paths that lead to them with some sort of equanimity. Instead, the choice each person makes has tremendous consequences. Moreover, individuals are powerfully influenced for good or evil by their family and social situation. God alone judges personal guilt, but belittling the role of the group in leading some of its members to destruction is totally foolish (and unscriptural). Now you will not find problems of individual and social sin raised in social science courses or textbooks or learned journals. These are unscientific, controversial questions to be pigeonholed by the compartmentalized mind, for discussion when and where it may be appropriate. But integrally Christian thinking views the consequences of righteous or evil living as the greatest question in individual and social life, not to be passed over in silence and posing the truest issue of self-fulfillment.

5

The most distinctive side of Christianity as a religion is the belief that God fulfilled an ancient promise to the Jewish people by sending His Son among them. The first followers of Jesus hesitantly learned to understand and then accept him as God in human form, come to redeem mankind from evil and proclaim a spiritual kingdom. But given the ideas and controversies that burst in at this point, let me restrict myself to just two points, namely the divinity of Christ and his sovereignty over the world, including the economic domain. (See section 8).

Whether Jesus was (and is) divine, how one should understand the title Son of God, how the concepts of sonship and paternity should be clarified, whether the New Testament contains glosses affirming the divine nature of Christ but not spoken by Jesus himself, et cetera, are ancient and yet contemporary controversies. The theological storms of the third and fourth centuries fill us with wonder still, the central issues have often flared up over the centuries, and the last hundred years or so have seen the debate carried to learned textual study of the Scriptures and professorial theology. Many writers have urged that the traditional doctrine be reexamined or at least reexpressed in contemporary terminology, so as to be more acceptable to present-day experience and knowledge.[5] On the other side, the vast majority of Christians have retained their belief in Christ as God, sometimes casting aside scholarly commentaries as subtle forms of betrayal, while not a small number have taken refuge in agnosticism, unable or unwilling to make up their minds on what is, after all, the most momentous question life puts to us all—did God become man and teach us directly about our present and future?

This issue is raised not to debate it, but to insist that the very possibility of an effective Christian approach to social and economic questions falls to the ground if one does not stick unequivocally with the traditional doctrine of the divinity of Christ. After all the explanations, clarifications, and reformulations, if one does not accept that Christ and his teachings are divine, one no longer has sure ground on which to take one's stand. (i) The divinity of Christ is essential for many Christian doctrines proclaimed and believed in over the centuries, such as the Trinity, the Incarnation, the Eucharist, and the redemption of man from evil through divine satisfaction. (ii) In simpler terms, Christians have always held that the Gospels record the words of God speaking as man to them; to relegate Christ to the status of merely a great prophet, like Muhammad, destroys the Christian religion. (iii) Jesus taught that he comes to dwell in the hearts of followers gathered in his name, providing a source of guidance and inspiration that they have regarded as the center of Christian living. The conclusion is that without faith in and acceptance of Jesus as God, Christianity falls to the ground and along with it any possibility of an effective Christian social thought. These things are perfectly evident to those who are not Christians.

6

But let me pass from this affirmation to a glimpse of the deeper reality. Being a Christian does not consist merely in being baptized, professing certain beliefs, praying privately and publicly, et cetera, though these and other things are essential. The difficulty is that they may be superficial. One way of going to the heart of the matter is to say that the authentic Christian has come to know Christ, to love him before all else,

8

and to seek to do in all things the Will of the Father.

When we say we "know" somebody, this usually means an aware-ness of who he is through our senses or what he is through dealings over time; but such knowledge may not go deep. Instead, knowing somebody in the deepest and truest manner consists in loving him, since love creates what is truly known and raises that person up to authentic importance in one's mind. Accordingly, knowing Jesus means an awareness of who and what he is through love; since he is the Son of Him Who is love, knowledge and love converge in one thing. Further, loving Jesus consists centrally in doing the Will of the Father, exactly as the Son showed in his earthly life and beyond this eternally. We encounter the mysterious realm of obedience, authority, fidelity to what we must do, and acceptance of what happens to us.

If this is not the place to enlarge on this great convergence of knowl-edge, love, and obedience, of which all Christians are deeply aware, two consequences are worth stressing for my purpose. An authentic Christian intellectual, worker, or activist has a first loyalty to Christ and to the Father, implying a readiness to practice obedience to rightful authority. Without this, one is adrift, allied to attitudes and activities that are a perversion of discipleship. This does not at all preclude protests against human abuses, struggling for justice, et cetera; but the latter are conse-quences of following Jesus, not in first place. Then, being a Christian thinker requires one to adopt the perspective of Christ, if only to the imperfect degree possible for all of us. This does not mean that we abandon our ordinary occupation or leave aside conventional scientific methods. But our intellectual work takes on an approach and set of values contrasting with much that has common acceptance in the social sciences and other university work. A Christian, for example, must interpret his-tory as part of the great contest between good and evil where Christ intervened decisively for the redemption and salvation of mankind. The rise and fall of nations, the march of armies, and economic and social and political changes are only superimposed on this primary theme.

7

Next, what the Christian seeks to believe, what he has to say of his interpretation of life and knowledge, never come alive without the Spirit of God. To know and follow Jesus authentically, one must be "born again," passing through the "metanoeia,"[6] and seeing all things differently. It is a very common experience to listen to a young person play Bach in a technically correct way that nevertheless almost totally lacks understanding of Bach's thought and musicality, or to hear the difference between a schoolboy's recitation of Hamlet's soliloquy on life and death and its rendering by a gifted actor. In the same way, the teachings, prayers, liturgy and rites, attitudes, et cetera, of the Christian religion are all dead things unless vivified by the Spirit of God. They may have a deep intellectual interest and beauty, but they come alive only in the hearts and minds of believers. The cathedrals of Europe are only (magnificent) piles of stone without the worshipping faithful.

Which is to say that nobody can grasp the full meaning of how the Christian mind relates to modern intellectual knowledge unless he is changed by the Spirit of God. Without this, the comparison between Christian and non-Christian attitudes is only an intellectual curiosity, to be debated and then filed away like any other item of information. It is to be hoped that those who do not understand the Christian viewpoint will respect it, if only for its idealism and its strength over two millenia; but they cannot attain the identification necessary for full understanding, since only the Spirit conveys this. They remain on the outside, peering in through a misted window. But this reference to the Spirit of God as sine qua non for Christian enlightenment is not elitism or smugness; it is simple fact that without this light and confirmation, believers cannot understand the things of God or endure.

8

Coming to the second point (from section 5) respecting Jesus as the center of Christianity, his followers have long accepted him as Lord over the material as well as the spiritual world, so that this clearly extends to the economy. Initially the sovereignty of Jesus was taken in primarily a spiritual sense, to judge from New Testament affirmations and the famous scene before Pilate. The emergence of Christianity as a secular power in the late Roman Empire culminated in the extraordinary claims made by Innocent III over the temporal realm in the high Middle Ages, and theocracies of one kind or another have appeared in different places. Today, where Christians have rebecome a troubled minority in most Western countries, it again seems strange to assert the lordship of Christ over societies that largely disregard God. Yet this remains a central belief (Ephesians 1:20–23), plus the assertion that one day this temporal world will be entirely judged and perhaps ended (Matthew 25: 31–46).

The transcendent sense in which Christians regard Jesus as king of material as well as spiritual life may be conveyed by recalling the description he gave of himself as "the Light of the world" (John 8:12) and as "Way, Truth and Life" (John 14: 6). Taking these words literally, as they must, Christians conclude that Jesus is unmistakably sovereign of the world and of economic life. Given the centrality of God and Jesus as Way, economic life becomes part of an ordered world intended to conform to this, and an economic science that disregards this has a kind of falsity equally true of a history or physics or whatever that at some appropriate point does not acknowledge and take into account the dominion of Christ. Further, if Jesus is Light and Truth, all knowledge and science must somehow link up with and lead back to this Logos. If they veer off with no apparent connection, no matter how amazing their achievements, they can be only partial truth and knowledge, incomplete or distorted and misleading in basic respects. In sum, the lordship of Jesus helps give direction fruitful for human welfare and away from harmful and irrelevant avenues. Biology and physics yield ready examples: Alongside beneficial work, disquieting experiments proceed on human birth or cloning, and ever more extraordinary ways are evolved of exterminating people.

Anyone who contemplates the history of philosophical and social ideas, to take just these domains, must be struck by their wanderings. Especially since the so-called Enlightenment ("le siècle des lumières" puts it with more irony), many brilliant minds have put together systems of thought to explain and guide human life and social relations, wildly impractical in relation to reality, frequently contradictory, and of no interest to anybody except a few specialists (cf. McDonagh, 1982, chapters 2–3). The human mind seems to have a limitless capacity for fantasizing on the theme of social betterment. In the social sciences there is a bewildering stream of research topics and intellectual inquiries that briefly flourish in academic journals before being forgotten, a large amount of them generated by the necessity of publishing. The vast energies of the sheer numbers engaged systematically in "research" and the intellectual life pour themselves out necessarily in a multiplicity of directions, whereas the energies of Christians who realize what they are about should be channeled in the service of the Master.

Next, to say Jesus is Life means, most directly, that Christ represents eternal life for all who believe in his name, death and sin will have no lasting victory, and he will one day raise them up (John 11: 25). This may signify less for those young and in good health, but for others who have looked closely at death it takes on an overwhelming sense. To focus more mundanely on social and economic affairs, consider the daily working of the economy, where many thousands of goods and services are produced and consumed in an amazing demonstration of achievement. Beneath it what truly matters is the men and women caught up in this vast process, and the key question is what gives meaning to their daily existence.[7] When they look into their hearts, they know that all material things are transient and the satisfactions of today and tomorrow will be insubstantial memories. What is enduring has to be found elsewhere; for Christians, the presence of Christ alone conveys lasting meaning to the tasks that otherwise signify nothing in the scale of eternity.

9

The third foundation for Christians is the religious community or church. The followers of Jesus instinctively and necessarily gather as a group for worship, they believe the Trinity is present among all who come together in his name, and they are commanded to love and serve one another. Indeed, they "see" Christ in their brothers and sisters. They accept the authority of their leaders, for whose guidance as divine delegates they continually pray. It follows that Christians have a radical loyalty to their church, which they accept as repository and fount of teaching and guidance, even if they must make a sometimes heroic distinction between its ideal as the Body of Christ, without spot or stain, and its imperfect human and institutional forms. But if many aspects of church come rushing in for comment—historical, legal, organizational, liturgical, et cetera, and they are all interconnected—only a few remarks will be made here on the place of Scripture, the role of tradition, and the teaching authority of leaders.

First, the church has continually preserved, communicated, and drawn upon the writings of the Old and New Testaments. (The latter was written by some of the church's first members). Without being rendered alive by the believing community, such writings are no more than historical books, like others that survive from past religions or are created

12

by new sects. But as recreated by the living church, they become the Word of God, speaking to men and women today as in the past and future. Initially, there is a great deal to be learned concerning the human modalities of that message, since the various parts of the Bible were written at widely different times in quite different styles. Skilled interpretation is often required to help detect correct or probable meaning. Further, quarrels abound on interpretation: Many Christians hold to degrees of literalism, plus a belief that the Holy Spirit will guide them in a personal way. Catholics normally rely on the interpreting church or community, in addition to personal prayer and enlightenment. There are, unfortunately, some Christians (and others) who rely exclusively on their intelligence and end up understanding nothing of significance, since the Bible is not meant to be read like a treatise. No matter what the topic (history, poetry, wisdom, prophetic remonstrance), the author sees and writes of human events in the framework of a divine plan.

After all the scholarship, however, the bottom line is that a Christian has to take Scripture as the Word of God, with something to say for himself and society and, indeed, for all his intellectual work and attitudes. Beyond the immediate context, through it God is in some way speaking to him today, as to men and women of the past and future. The Bible read in the evening somehow connects up with the psychology or economics studied in the morning, even if in so indirect a way as influencing values and personal integrity. Quite naturally, church statements on social questions abound with quotations from the Old and New Testaments to support the principles of economic justice and applications discussed.

10

Second, the manner in which the church respects and draws upon its tradition of teaching and guidance over two thousand years is quite vivid in the Catholic mind, not so clear to the Protestant viewpoint, and perhaps obscure to modern fundamentalists. Essentially, over the course of centuries the Catholic church (now termed Roman) has faced hundreds of doctrinal, theological, pastoral, liturgical, and disciplinary issues and difficulties. Solutions of some kind have been found, involving definitions of belief and position, and in all this vast process, the church has perforce believed in the basic guidance and support of God and His Spirit, as promised by Christ to his followers. This is not to claim a record of error-free results or infallibility in the many positions taken by church leaders and councils; all that is a nuanced matter. But what does remain is a vast legacy of tradition. It is not possible for Catholic Christians to set aside what the church may have decided in the past on important questions, especially theological and pastoral, as though some doctrine of progress makes that of only historical significance.

What matters for my purpose, however, is not differences on the significance of tradition or modern disputes on its nature but its use as a source for the Christian social thought outlined in part 2. While the focus of the Christian church has been primarily on religious and liturgical matters, a surprising volume of comment on social and economic life can be put together from the earliest times.[8] Many early church fathers were forced to comment on a wide variety of temporal affairs, from which one indeed gains a sense of Christianity being extended to the social domain. On record are much better writings, from the High Middle Ages to the present, where we still draw on the works of theologian-philosophers. Then, over the last hundred years, as the church turned its attention to the social qustions, the record of official and semiofficial writings and endeavors of many Christian social reformers has constitued a source of knowledge that no Christian thinker facing the problems of modern societies and the social sciences can neglect.

11

One of the most difficult aspects of the church for outsiders, and not a few insiders, is the authority of its leaders. This matter ranges over every aspect of the church's life and the activities of its members, there is a history extending back to the origins of the Christian church, with many checkered episodes, and there is a strong clash between the positions typical of the Catholic church and of Protestant groups. While there are explanations and qualifications, finally no church community can survive without the exercise of some form of teaching and guiding authority, so that the differences within the divisions of the Christian church are a matter of degree, of how and where authority should be exercised, but not of the principle itself. The Christian community necessarily believes itself to participate in the authority derived from God Himself—there is no other sovereign source, Jesus remains continually with it, and it enjoys the guidance of the Spirit in all that is fundamental.

Catholics have a hierarchical view of the church: Certain individuals are raised up to be supervisors or bishops, and they are assisted by ordained elders or priests. The whole is presided over by the Vicar of Christ and successor of Peter. Accordingly there arises, and one must recall the constant stream of prayer for guidance of leaders, an obligation to be attentive to the teachings and admonishments of those members of the community empowered to teach by their office, so that the accumulations of this plus their study constitute a precious source of knowledge for members of the church.[9] Consequently Christian social thought is, in important respects, subject to the teaching authority of leaders. Presumably they will limit themselves to principles or basic truths, where they may speak in an authoritative way; and if they venture into the realm of human judgment and prudence where principles link up with applications, they will acknowledge room for divergent views. Yet even here their views should be heeded, since presumably they are guided by the advice and the prayer of the community.

The reverse of the coin is that those who systematically turn away from legitimate teaching authority have put aside one of the characteristic notes of the authentically Christian mind. Is it possible to observe the centrality of God, to accept Jesus as the Way, Truth, and Life, and then to rebel against the authority of the community that Jesus promised to sustain and guide? Of course, leaders can drift close to error, presumably in matters temporal and involving the realm of prudence and practical judgment, and from time to time members of the church are called on to point this out courageously. Such exceptions aside, the authentic Christian normally accepts the authority of the teaching community as expressed through its leaders.

*   *   *

If the preceding pages are a very inadequate account of a few central Christian beliefs, they nevertheless indicate the premises posed as the mind informed by them reflects on current economic institutions and behavior and the systematic account of them given by modern economic science. It has been correctly said that the interpretation of this world and its history proposed by Christianity is wildly at variance with those offered by secular authors, popular and serious, and modern university sciences. The believer interprets his own life and that of society as a vast conflict between good and evil. God, Christ, the heavenly host, sanctification, and the like are on one side and Satan, the world, hell, and destruction on the other. All our daily experiences and events have one

15

kind of interpretation talked about in the media and analyzed by academic disciplines, but another in a transcendental world reaching beyond what we see and know immediately into that constructed and sustained by hope and grace. The Bible and all it implies are about one kind of world, our secular literature about another, where only faith makes the connection.

This is indeed the sort of contrast aimed at in this chapter, reflecting the conviction of believers that the transcendental Christian interpretation of human life is reality and will endure, while that proposed by secular knowledge is incomplete and false in essential respects.

Chapter 2

APPROACH OF MIND

Given the premises of the previous chapter, let me infer some attitudes of mind that should characterize Christian thinking about the search for knowledge represented by scientific disciplines, especially the social group. If the Christian makes the fatherhood of God the center of his life, accepts totally the Lordship of Jesus to the point of being ready to surrender all things, and is nurtured and fashioned by fidelity to the community of his church, what orientation of mind will dominate his intellectual work? Surely, were he to leave aside the separation of mind and the compromises that may be necessary for communication in a pluralistic environment and personal advancement, he will think and speak out as one having a radically different interpretation of reality and human life and behavior. This is as true as when Paul set aside "philosophy" (1 Corinthians 2).

But the purpose of what follows can only be to set up a few signposts, indicating how integral Christian thinking diverges not merely from agnostic and atheistic attitudes, but also from the indifference and silence on religious aspects that characterizes so much "scientific" work. To go further, sketching the life of prayer, the pursuit of holiness, mental discipline, and much more reflecting Christian habits of mind is beyond my scope.

1

Saying initially that the Christian intellectual is totally committed to truth and to an accurate appreciation of reality only invites debate on what each may signify, since people of all backgrounds would so commit themselves. "Truth" may be taken in two senses, the first being correspondence between some statement and the facts it intends to represent. But it is the second aspect that concerns us, namely, our understanding and interpretation of reality, including the consequences for moral behavior. The extraordinary affirmation of Jesus, "I am the Truth," and the infamous question of Pilate both indicate this sense.

Various sciences have sought to answer what reality may be, each in its specialized domain. They subdivide phenomena from many points of view, each giving its account of what it learns. Quite apart from the bewildering task of integrating these perceptions, however, each "answer" peters out in taxonomic labels or further questions. Modern physics has pursued its analysis of "matter" into little understood particles or forces, with no finality in view, and nobody understands the relation between physical elements of the brain and the abstract concepts it manipulates (Fourastié, 1981, p. 165 seq.). What the social sciences call reality is partly subjective physical and psychic states that they and the physical sciences never succeed in analyzing completely and partly evolving institutions that reflect and mold individual and social behaviour.

After such immediate partial responses comes the deeper problem of what meaning shall we attach to whatever is definitively perceived to exist. What *is* finally and what is *final truth* we can recognize and utter about it (cf. Kolakowski, chapter 2)? To respond summarily, for the Christian ultimate reality is God and truth is Jesus ("logos" was John's term). This has nothing to do with pantheism, but means that all our attempts to understand reality and truth about it and how we should live given our understanding of them remain incomplete until we close the circle with the divine link. All that we validly learn about the composition of matter, or how the body works, or what makes up the universe is not false, but remains partial information and never finally put in place, so long as it does not link up with what faith, prayer, and grace have to tell us concerning the divine dimension of all reality. We reach a transcendent viewpoint, where all that exists in time must be referred to the eternal, all that we know and experience become relative, and God is finally truth.[1]

To comment on one further aspect of "reality," some philosophers and psychologists have concluded that since we can be sure of the existence of only what our senses and intelligence perceive, our subjective knowledge of reality is all we may be certain exists outside of ourselves and our experience of it is all that counts.[2] We are not entitled to affirm more about a supposedly objective reality than our subjective perceptions of it and should order our lives in consequence. Before such views, the Christian must put himself firmly on the side of moderate realism (see also chapter 8, section 1), opposed to all forms of nominalism. He accepts that reality exists externally to himself and that his subjective knowledge of it is only part of what is to be known, determined by his particular interests and by general limitations on human modes of knowledge in this life. He accepts the fact of a God toward Whom his being tends, and he is painfully aware of his being restricted to knowledge of Him furnished by analogical concepts and infused perception through grace. Not unsurprisingly, our knowledge of virtually everything else is similar: We can never know the totality of ourselves, birds, stars, or whatever, and our limited knowledge of their aspects comes partly from the concepts we use as approximations to the reality in question and partly from a certain direct intuition of things familiar by use and experience (cf. section 5). Acknowledging these limitations on knowledge, the Christian is an objectivist, rather than a subjectivist, and accepts his inability to have other than a limited grasp of all reality, including himself. This situation will only be remedied when, one day, he comes to see God and perceive reality with completeness.

2

The Christian intellectual does not merely seek truth in various domains; he is also faced with the necessity of fitting it all together, at least in some tentative way. Essentially he has an integrative quest, beyond all the specialization that is so necessary. The practical vehicle of this must be some philosophy of knowledge in a broad sense, offering a structure of concepts and thinking that can ''put things together.''

Specialization has long been a key to progress in science. Not only do we mark off broad domains for isolated study, but within each discipline numerous subsciences arise. The advantages are obvious but the disadvantage across and within disciplines is the immense difficulty of linking up so many disparate findings, due to time and effort, terminology, manner of thought, lack of common values, and an approach to knowledge into which the parts may be fitted. In economics, not even the most brilliant mind can grasp in a holistic way the work pursued in dozens of specialized fields. Taking the whole spectrum of scientific work, a sort of bedlam exists, where specialists are little able to communicate with one another and have no time for the effort necessary to see the whole and, perhaps, little interest in it.

The integration in question calls for an approach to knowledge involving a framework of thought and concepts (and eventually an epistemology) capable of synthesizing at a fundamental level. This must be broader than the studies actively pursued as the philosophy of science and social science, which are generally not marked by the wideness of integrative effort in question and typically disregard the religious domain. They are concerned more with methodological analysis, offering a "critical" approach to the various sciences, especially the physical, as systems of knowledge. While successive doctrines of verification, falsification, falsifiability, confirmation, corroboration, et cetera, have flourished as criterion of what is truly science before coming under attack in their turn (see note 5), a Christian must summarily comment that since these doctrines typically leave aside values and the religious domain as "meaningless" subjective knowledge and neglect transcendental aspects of reality, they are incomplete.

In the area of the social sciences, as will be illustrated in part 2, integration is at least easier to set in motion, since man and his behavior are the immediate focus of the inquiries in question and Christian thought. The latter moves from faith and revelation to compose a theology that itself must be aided by a philosophy to comprehend reality and the signification of concepts and patterns of thought. There arises an interpretation of life that can link up with what economics, sociology, psychology, anthropology, and history (to speak only of these) each establish concerning behavior in their specialised domains. For instance, worker productivity or the entrepreneurial spirit can be validly studied by each discipline, but to fit the findings together it is essential to include the dimension of morality and human evil.

Integrating the knowledge of science with Christian thought, however, is not solely an intellectual task. If one approached it as such, one would risk creating at a new level the analyses and disagreements that presently render synthesis impossible. Instead, "putting things together" requires also a faith and a willingness, an effort of the heart, to seek unification and on which the intelligence can build as servant. Essential aids are prayer and grace, since these invoke the help and resolution of difficulties provided by the Spirit of God, seeking the vantage point of truth itself. Further, the Christian intellectual has an obligation to pursue this work. Partly for himself and partly for his community, he must face up to the task of linking together in some way, at some level, the truths of religion and his field of inquiry.[3] Jewish scholars are often accused—the more candid accuse themselves (cf. Silk, 1976, p. 6)—of going along with prevailing fashions in society and intellectual work to achieve success, while segregating their orthodox faith and practice. Many Christians do the same. Some Islamic countries seem clearer on the need to bring the various parts of life into closer harmony with religious beliefs, even if this has been marred by some fanaticism.

3

The supposed clash between the knowledge proposed by "science" and that based on religious faith is some three centuries old and has lost a good deal of its thrust.[4] Physicists no longer have so much confidence in their ability to arrive at final explanations of reality and assist human betterment and have learned humility respecting their search for the "laws" of the physical universe. Meanwhile, religious doctrines and explanations have evolved from simplistic presentations and interpretations (the account of creation in Genesis, for example, or of what the soul and heaven may be). In the post–World War II period, the clash between the social sciences and religious belief has become more important, as the former continue to imitate the methods and claims of an older concept of physical science and seek to reduce religion to mere social practice or self-persuasion. In face of this vast topic, strewn with controversies and important writings, let me merely reaffirm that the Christian mind respects all legitimate scientific knowledge and methods of inquiry and yet keeps religious faith in first place, necessarily and absolutely. It also asks that such knowledge be aware of its limitations and not pretend to be more than it is, equally in its techniques of inquiry and verification.[5]

From the time of Newton to perhaps 1920, physics conceived of the world as a kind of intricate machine, to be patiently understood by the two engines of mathematical logic and experiments set up to verify hypotheses coming from induction and inspiration. Now we no longer believe in the universality of its findings and laws, seeing them rather as dependent on factors to some extent contingent, particularly time. Apparent contradictions and even impossibilities (antimatter, for example)

21

can no longer be ruled out if a new environment, improvised today but perhaps normal eventually, may call them into existence. It is perfectly evident that by the latter twentieth century the physical sciences still cannot finally explain either matter or life or solve the problems of human deliverance. Each hill climbed and each valley explored only reveal new heights and depths, and in the process the means have been acquired of destroying civilized life on our planet. The attempt to understand matter dissolves into the mysteries of "particles" and "waves," signifying different responses to tests, where science relives an old lesson that its role is to explain *why* effects follow causes, not *what* either may be.

But rather than dwell on the epistemology of modern science, let me address the supposed conflict with faith, which turns partly on methods of investigation and partly on findings. Classically the physical sciences have relied on observation and experiment, focusing on the facts and supposedly hard data and pursuing a rigorously positive method. Today there has been some shift, at least at the working face of science, to confirmation in terms of logical coherence rather than objective verification by isolated experiment. The question is not so much to fit in place the pieces of a gigantic jigsaw, itself a grand design, as to perceive that they could fit many grand designs or perhaps none at all (cf. Prigogine and Stengers, 1984). Christian faith, on the other hand, with its recourse to Scripture/Divine intuition/church authority uses a radically different method to seek its kind of knowledge and arrives at findings that cannot be demonstrated by the techniques of experiment and rigorous deduction conventionally accepted in science. In consequence, either route pursued uncompromisingly ends in a standoff. While Christian thought is indeed prepared to link up its knowledge with that of science, harmonizing to whatever extent possible, the physical sciences themselves reply that the postulates and findings of religious faith lie beyond their possibility of cognition. The conclusion for the Christian is that they will wander forever, never finding the promised land of their aspirations, since analysis of facts and cause-effect relations is not the road to it.

Interestingly, following on important studies of the methodology and epistemology of the sciences and "paradigms" according to which we understand their progress and findings, we are very aware that faith in the ordinary sense of undemonstrable belief underpins them (cf. chapter 8, section 6). "Faith" may, of course, be taken in several senses. It may imply simple acceptance of statements on somebody's authority, and as such is a component in all teaching, though the implication is that what is conveyed may be demonstrated or argued satisfactorily. Or it may refer to the intuition and will that carry many a successful discovery or achievement to success through an apparently illogical path or overwhelming obstacles. Many people recover from illness through strong belief. In another sense, it has been justly observed that all knowledge ultimately reposes on faith (Polanyi, 1958). Some belief in the ultimate goodness of what is or in its intelligibility or in the universality of observed physical laws must underlie the interpretation and understanding of the phenomena we arrive at.

But it is faith in the religious domain and the sort of questioning it may involve of scientific findings that are the sources of conflict. Two things require to be affirmed from my point of view: First, after all the clarifications, concessions, and qualifications, for the Christian mind, religious faith on essentials and its implications maintain their place unshakably and await elucidation of apparent scientific incompatibility. Time has been rewarding in this respect (the emergence of parapsychology and a new cosmology being examples). Second, final understanding of reality, at least that measure of it possible for the human mind, supposes religious belief. While the interpreting intelligence plays its role in expressing and refining faith in God and His Son as ultimate reality and truth (and it is only at this point that all relativity ends), ''unless you have believed, you will not understand.''[6]

4

If a chastened physical science and a more confident religious faith are living at least tolerantly with one another by the 1980s, the conflict with the social sciences, which have too often copied the goals, methods, and precision of their physical cousins—at least this is true of economics —remains strong. It is a commonplace that economics has remained too much modeled on nineteenth-century science, approaching the economy as a complex machine to be unraveled by patient deduction and verification and insufficiently as also the creation of contingent human behavior, relative to beliefs and goals as well as time and place. Much sociology believes religious faith, doctrines, and practice are only the product of the social environment. Some psychology offers a doctrine of self-realization, even a program ''beyond freedom and dignity'' (Skinner, 1971) and certainly better than the illusions of religion. Let me comment on one central issue raised for Christian thinking by the social sciences.

"Reductionism" may be described as the practice of limiting causes for some whole effect to just those that an observer considers necessary and sufficient to explain parts of it (cf. Barbour, 1966, pp. 6, 294). One is easily into the familiar business of defining the criteria of what one is prepared to accept as sufficient and necessary causes for phenomena, shutting out what does not meet standards set a priori and often gratuitously, as the history of knowledge shows. Modern reductionism is really a product of specialization, causing us to see phenomena predominantly from a particular optic, exaggerating the causes discerned. Examples are familiar: A psychologist may tell us that the believer only persuades himself there is a God Who listens to his prayers and watches over his needs, his acquiescence in the Will of God enabling him to interpret everything as divinely intended for his good. The exultation of the devout, singly or in groups, is merely a type of hysteria and religious ecstasy is self-hypnosis. The only reality is the psychic phenomena and there is no need to introduce so-called divine inspiration and grace.

Modern sociology is usually defined to be centrally concerned with social processes and interactions—though within this broad field there are differences enough on the character of social behavior and the orientation of inquiries—and the sociology of religion begins usefully enough. It perceives correctly that the church—in belief, prayer, liturgy—constantly exhibits the interacting influences of social relations. It is a community validly studied for its formative effects on members and the whole. Many sociologists go much further, however, and interpret theological beliefs and religious practices as essentially and only the product of individuals interacting with one another and community.[7] The doctrines and institutions believed in are created through social processes, albeit reflecting ill-understood human needs and drives that science will eventually clarify and dissipate. Perhaps most Christians will concede that there are elements of truth here: A community and its institutions are to some extent projections of what their members believe in, and peer pressures do affect what theologians and liturgists write. Faith does to some mysterious extent create what is believed in, as Jesus taught (Mark 2: 23). But it is another thing to conclude that the practice and thought of religion are *solely* the product of community reactions, denying explicitly or implicitly that God and His grace play any part. It is everyday Christian experience that Jesus manifests himself powerfully and unmistakably in community celebrations, as he promised, in a way distinct

24

from all human contributions, individual and mass.

Confronted by reductionist hypotheses, the Christian mind will make prudent use of them to cut away falsity; the great number of reported visions and religious experiences would produce bedlam if all but very few were taken seriously. Illuminism (Knox, 1950) does produce some fevered brains (which God surely treats indulgently). But after this the Christian asserts the place of faith and prayer and takes a holistic, generous attitude toward accepting Divine Providence and intervention. "Nothing but" attitudes repel him, not merely for their arrogance and ignorance—of which the flaws in supposedly scientific explanations are recurrent witness—but also for their rejection of God's benevolent work for humanity. The whole of life is not merely the sum of its parts reduced to specialized analysis and explanation, and at the stage of putting things together "fidens quaerens intelligentiam" (faith seeking understanding) is the Christian's guide.

5

In most phases of life, the intelligence is an excellent servant but a bad master when wholly in charge. Formally, it is a faculty or power of the mind enabling it to perceive, to reason, and to understand, too often identifying wholly with ratiocination, or the procedure of deducing conclusions from premises. In the tradition of Christian thought, on the other hand, we come to "know" by three methods—direct perception, ratiocination properly speaking, and connaturality (cf. Maritain, 1942, chapter 3). In the first case, we directly "see" some truth, such as the goodness of life or that a thing cannot both be and not be at the same time. The second is the most familiar aspect of intelligence, always ready to overwhelm and confuse with its brilliance. In the third we know by becoming likened to the thing known. The obvious example is coming to know something of God through the life of grace; a lesser is the ability to "see" more deeply the greatness of Bach as the result of musical formation.

"Critical intelligence" is a virtue greatly prized by the university-trained mind, meaning that in the search for truth and falsity one must constantly reexamine arguments and findings and pick over concepts. Which is important, but in the case of the social sciences (where verification is often not available) mere dissection easily turns into a vice. It is indeed typical of university-educated people to be unable to conclude respecting ultimate truth for human life and behavior and what must be done in consequence, since so often they are unwilling to introduce the framework of moral principles and faith necessary for synthesis. Rarely do graduates emerge from their studies with a coherent view of the world and a philosophy they can use to guide their lives; almost exclusively they have been taught to pull things apart. But religion itself shows the worst examples of the perversions arising from exaggerated intellectualism, where excessive analysis of doctrine, the liturgy, church, virtues of Christian living, and the rest easily blot out their substance in favour of the externals of concepts, phrases, gestures et cetera. These must be just so for the narcissistic intelligence, when love finally is the only way to know God (chapter 1, section 6), since this is His life.

Setting intelligence aside would be absurd, leading to an uninformed, confused illuminism; giving oneself up to an exclusive intellectualism in religious matters leads to the deceptions of formalism. Hence the Christian seeks a middle path through the guidance of the Spirit, believing that God enters in some mysterious way and that a sort of union—weak, imperfect, and liable to upset—begins even in this life. Christ promised exactly that (John 14:23), so that his followers acquire a type of knowledge and understanding that is different from unaided reason. Such a form of knowledge is not directed toward scientific discoveries or intellectual or artistic attainments as such. Rather, it consists in an understanding of what matters about human affairs in God's eyes, so that it conveys a special character or interpretation to what we perceive or do. The religious background of Bach and Elgar did not help them to be better musicians, but it did lead to an unmistakable religious quality in much of their music, something that Beethoven only infrequently obtained and Mozart rarely. (Remember that "spiritual" is not the same as "religious.")

6

Freedom is a universal aspiration, despite the constraints of personal limitations and societal customs, and is so powerful an intuition, so noble a quality, that one readily concludes it is God-like. But it may also aspire to total liberation, even from the sovereignty of God, and herein lies its ancient danger. For another reason, freedom is immensely important in that it is closely connected with the yet more God-like quality of love, apparently since the capacity to choose freely is the prerequisite for what is truly love. Others must be loved for their own sake, as an act of choice on our part, without which love is a constraint and false. God, too, requires our act of choice and respects even to self-destruction our unwillingness to respond.

Even the most elementary experience teaches us that freedom cannot consist in total liberty to do as we please. This leads to the tyranny of bad habits, so that there is no escape from the need to exercise physical, mental, and moral discipline. Christians have always understood by freedom the ''glorious liberty of the sons of God'' (Romans 8: 21), meaning that it is most truly realized by obedience to the Will of the Father. This translates itself into the requirements of morality in the broad sense and then into the supererogatory demands of moving ever closer to God in this life as a preparation for the next. The paradox is that in its fullest exercise, freedom rejoins a kind of divine slavery, where we realize our liberty totally only by abandonment of it to God, Who is all the goodness finally signified by freedom.[8]

To descend from these heights, freedom implies for the Christian a readiness to accept both its responsible bounds and all legitimate authority, since the latter has to be from God (Romans 13: 1–7) if it is not to consist simply in the power to compel. Jesus taught unremittingly that obedience to the Father was essential. Can His followers do otherwise (including obedience to delegated authority)? But this need to obey raises, of course, the issue of abusive exercise. At what point may a Christian actively dissent and even rebel to correct it? The worst problem for the modern intellectual is the constraint imposed on his liberty of inquiry and expression coming from church authority, so often set in its ways and fearful of challenge. The non-Christian may have no reason to take notice of this, but the Christian can experience deep tension when his work leads into sensitive areas. There are no easy answers, where the hard thing is to distinguish legitimate protest from questioning due to a restless temperament, egged on (so Christians believe) by the forces of evil always tempting us. All this taken into account, the authentic Christian intellectual recognizes the legitimacy of authority, placing its ordinary and supererogatory demands on him. The alternative is to reject, and there are ancient stories (Genesis 3: 16–19; Revelation 12: 7–9) driving home that unwillingness to practice obedience leads away from God to destruction.

Can this restriction on freedom of act and inquiry be reconciled with today's urge to be ''true to oneself''? To realize oneself is a first duty, since to seek to be other than ''me'' would be hypocrisy. Like all quasi-truths, this quest for "sincerity" has its important side. It is perfectly true we must respect what we and others are and intellectual and moral positions held with deep conviction. It is perfectly possible for Christians of two denominations to hold differing interpretations of certain sayings of Jesus and to persist loyally in them; presumably God accepts this. But talk of authenticity is often an excuse to cling to prejudice. In the New Testament Jesus is frequently seen telling the crowd to change their hearts and act differently, but never telling them to persist in wrong ways, however "authentic." Instead he taught his followers to seek depth in practicing the Law and the revisions he brought to it. He frequently attacked hypocrisy, in that sense stressing genuineness, but the standard of truth to guide the latter was made clear. What Jesus asked of his followers was fidelity to his teachings and to the Father, and in that way self-realization would take care of itself (cf. chapter 1, note 7).

7

Christianity, as distinguished from the actual behavior of Christians, has from Roman times (Wilken, 1984) been accused of hostility to "this world." If this is interpreted to mean opposition to materialism and commercialism, many in modern society may sympathize, but if it goes on to imply indifference or lukewarmness to technological and scientific progress, that sympathy runs out. Jesus, the apostles, Augustine, and other writers may indeed be quoted as condemning "the world and the flesh." Yet the sense is more correctly taken as the latter pursued for their own sake and not directed to God. Later some important Protestant thinkers, reflecting Old Testament attitudes, treated a certain worldly success as reflecting the worthy Christian life. This Protestant ethic is alleged to have been a basic factor in the rise of capitalistic accumulation, perhaps also that of modern science in the seventeenth century.[9] Today all shades of Christians are prominent in scientific, technological, industrial, and artistic achievements and are often no less distinguished than others for their materialism.

Let me single out just one issue, the goodness of "this world." One can usefully begin with the *City of God*, which Augustine wrote to defend Christianity against charges that neglect of the old Roman gods and customs brought about the disaster of Alaric's sack of Rome (A.D. 410). In his fiery manner, Augustine ranged over a vast canvas and a thousand

28

pages of modern text before ending, perhaps from sheer exhaustion. His first ten books are a polemic on the worthlessness of the pagan gods and beliefs, so that the fall of Rome could not be attributed to Christianity; and the following twelve books develop and contrast the cities of God and earth. There is a theory of history implicit that is scarcely prominent today but recurs in Christian thought. Augustine centers it on God's plan for the redemption and salvation of mankind, prefigured in the Old Testament and accomplished in the New, and on the continual struggle of the two cities before the final triumph of Christ. While the interpretation of the *City of God* has been much discussed,[10] it is very possible to read out of it a general condemnation of the *civitas terrena*, even if the more correct contrast lies between life according to the flesh and life according to God. Much of the fascination of this great work for our day lies in Augustine's attempt to reconstruct a vision of a Christian alternative to the Roman world and order that was crumbling around him, just as our own appear to be disintegrating. To do this he put on, wholly and unremittingly, the optic of Christ, using Scripture, faith, and grace.

Aquinas gave the essential answer to Augustine's polarization with his "gratia non tollit naturam sed perficit" (grace does not take away nature, but perfects it).[11] Interpreted for the question at hand, it means that this world and life—material things, progress, our bodies, the evolution of history—are all good, as indeed they are in God's creation; but faith and grace draw them away from the tendencies toward evil resulting from that great primal turning away from God we call original sin and redirect and sublimate them towards goodness. This remains the basic reconciliation of the modern Christian mind with "this world": All that composes it is good, but it is capable of misdirection and evil, and authentic religion converts all things to the service and glory of God. The redemptive role of Christ, to which his followers join themselves, is the channel of this grace.

At various times Christian writers continue to condemn this world and the flesh. Carried away by the abuses of the societies they observe, they call on God to destroy what is unclean and to purify with His vengeance. Thus Christians have often appeared in the role of unjust, excessive critics of a world that, according to their own faith, a benevolent God creates and sustains. Setting aside past errors of judgment, where the equivocal attitudes of some church fathers toward sex and marital questions are the greatest embarrassment, the Christian today must unhesitatingly accept all the work of God's hands as good, condemn the evil that intrudes through human temptation and failure, and join himself with Christ for the conversion and transformation of the "world." This life will always exhibit struggle between good and evil and stand in need of perfecting by divine favor.

The Catholic church has often been accused of inhibiting "progress," scientific and material. In the late Middle Ages, it probably delayed the birth of modern science, many times checked initiative and thought with its binding codes and authority, and as late as 1907 condemned "modernism"[12] Such accusations are, of course, a large topic, where the truth of charges requires to be patiently disengaged. It is correct that at various times the Catholic church, as distinguished from most Protestant groups, has shown lukewarmness, even hostility, towards scientific and material progress, though God alone can set in the balance the religious goals and achievements sought against the earlier improvements in human welfare that might have occurred. Today, under the impulse of humanism, the need for rapid development in so many backward countries, and the aim of enhancing the social justice of property and wealth distribution, there is more danger that many in the church set economic and political goals before religion properly speaking (cf. chapter 5, section 6).

8

It will be useful to conclude by commenting on two prevalent attitudes in intellectual work that contrast sharply with the Christian mind, namely, the values of secular humanism and the methods of inquiry of logical positivism.

Like socialism, humanism can be interpreted in so many ways that anybody wishing to discuss it must begin with an approximate definition. Today secular humanism broadly denotes a code of values reflecting realization of all the potentialities of men and women, setting aside in particular the restraints of religion and any arbitrary power and regime. It allies itself with statements of human rights and affirms liberty of thought, expression, and action; it normally calls for their responsible exercise within the framework of some social contract, since group living must restrict absolute liberty; it welcomes progress and education, to reduce the ignorance that inhibits freedom and self-realization; it rejoices in the overcoming of disease and improving of social conditions and it usually rejects supernatural doctrines and supposed interventions in favor of rationalism and science (cf. Kurtz, 1980; Lamont, 1965). Thus, if you have a mind to, secular humanism can be traced in a long line through Western thought to the Greeks, skirting around any religious figure and even linking up with some non-Western thinkers. It tends to go a little berserk before fundamentalist or illuministic religion, with its emotional faith and appeal to divine inspiration. Taken in a more moderate way, humanism is a widely prevalent code of values and way of thought among university-trained intellectuals.

Numerous attacks have been made on secular humanism by Christians objecting to its values (cf. Holmes, 1983, chapter 2), radicals linking it to protection of vested interests, and general critics seeing it as favoring libertarianism, in fact. As a doctrine it must depend finally on a secular faith and undemonstrable premises concerning the goodness of human actions and rights. Even sympathizers see it as a closing off of life from the transcendent and spiritual, which are the hope and transformation lying beyond the drudgery of the mass of people. Glorying in the achievements of humanity in the pages of some article or in a television program is light-years away from what men and women go through in their daily lives.

Turning to another polar position and neglecting the imaginary humanism of communist and other authoritarian societies, Christian humanism has been discussed as a sublimation of the secular version. Historically, the teachings of Christ were at the origin of the emphasis placed on the worth of each person in Western civilization (cf. Troeltsch, 1931, p. 55; O'Brien, 1920, p. 12) and his followers steadfastly opposed mere absorption of the individual into the community or the state. Christian thought has always dwelled on the development of the human person in its incomparable richness, refining the concept of many virtues and admiring their role. Many men and women of different backgrounds have been held up as "saints," models for all. In modern times, Christian social activists have championed the poor and oppressed. Thus, bringing this transcendental approach to the human person and values to bear on modern issues of the political, social, and economic orders, one may draw from "integral humanism" a general program for social justice, as notably Maritain (1936) suggested.

Not to pursue this large topic, however, what requires to be said is that if the values of Christianity are left out of the picture, those of secular humanism lose their foundation and sense of direction. They sidetrack one from fundamentals and give rise to wrong goals. To be "fully human"

31

could mean different things according to the code of morality used as guide. "Needs" could give rise to any number of competing physical and social demands unless rooted in some valid philosophy of the person. "The glory of God is man alive," said Irenaeus, but he added "the life of man is the vision of God" (*Adversus Haereses,* IV, 34–37; cf. I Corinthians 11: 7). Mankind without God vanishes ingloriously one by one, leaving only dust. The conclusion is that while the Christian intellectual will be ready in a pluralistic society to accept and applaud the values of a prevailing humanism to whatever extent possible, he must distance himself from them in essential respects and give his full allegiance elsewhere.

It is frequently observed that Christians who abandon their faith and the practice of their religion (the first generation) guard the standards of morality and conduct inculcated into them. Their children (the second generation) do not have the same roots, however, and are often confused as to the sources and content of their parents' code, and later generations retain nothing of the first's beliefs and practice. Similarly a country that loses its Christian formation originally guards much of the code of personal and social morality associated with it, but then steadily leaves it, as one may see in Europe and North America today. Equally, secular humanism is a highway diverging from the religious principles that gave it most of its values and leading only to growing decadence from them. Its hostility to the religion that initially inspired it is a perfectly natural development, even if this means the eventual destruction of all that is of value in humanism. This kind of outcome is the special aim and pleasure of the father of all lies.

9

Positivism is a doctrine encountered respecting physical science, the social sciences, and philosophy. Centrally it holds that facts and hard data alone are the proper subject of scientific investigation; verification (for some, falsifiability or simply confirmation) of events and conclusions must be possible through observation, experiment, or logical necessity; and metaphysical, ethical, and theological statements cannot be the object of science, properly speaking. A long history of the concept of positivism may be traced before and after its popularization by Comte in the mid-nineteenth century. Rather obviously, Christian thought rejects the limited notion of science involved and its restricted methods of investigation and verification, since positivism taken strictly dismisses religious knowledge, experience, and moral obligation as necessarily uncertain and probably illusory.

Positivism in science may as an attitude of mind be traced to (at least) the first Renaissance thinkers who confronted the physical universe as phenomena to be understood in themselves, for their own sake,[13] in contradistinction to the religious mind, which would instinctively interpret physical phenomena as the handiwork of God pointing to His designs. Of course, the first researchers of physical science often combined religious faith and practice with their work, with this petering out by the nineteenth century. By the middle of the twentieth, a total divorce between the worlds of science and religion became normal, while a new breed of "cosmologists" sought to elaborate explanations for all world reality from the point of view of science (cf. Toulmin, 1980, part 2). But there is hope for the rebirth of some concerted enterprise between science and religion: After their long neglect, even natural theology and religion (i.e., based on reason alone, excluding Revelation) may well rise again to challenge the domination of positive science as we contemplate its incapacity to arrive at final explanations of its universe and the fearful weapons it has created.

Respecting the social sciences, "positivism" was introduced by Comte (*Cours de philosophie positive,* 1830–42) to denote his approach to science and philosophy. Observable relations and quantitative empiricism characterize the first, and the second should equally be concerned with such positive knowledge, eschewing metaphysics and theology. The era of the latter had been succeeded by that of the sciences. Comte believed in a science of man (calling it sociology) to mold and reform social life, and in a later aberration he visualized a religion of humanity. Today positivism in the social sciences is somewhat modeled on that of physical science, more so in its earlier conception as knowledge to be gained by unraveling the vast machine of the cosmos. The elimination of values as part of their inquiries was more controversial since human behavior is so impregnated and shaped by them. Dissecting individual and social behavior without attention to ethics struck most people as foolish (which it is), leading to ethical relativism (which it does). The outcome for social positivists has not been to deny the role of values, which would have been absurd, but to lead rather to compartmentalized thinking restricting their role to modifying "scientific" conclusions. The great weakness of positive social science, apart from contestation of its approach and method, has been its failure to predict even with rough acceptability, so that it has never commanded the respect accorded physical science.

The logical positivism ("logical" reflects emphasis on logical analysis) of philosophers is a fascinating story not to be recounted here.[14] A group of Viennese thinkers concluded that philosophical inquiries should be modeled after the physical sciences, accepting only demonstrable knowledge and rejecting the nonverifiable tautologies of metaphysics and ethics. This celebrated approach swept away many great questions of the past (the one and the many, human destiny, et cetera) and reduced philosophy to "critical analysis" (which not surprisingly also appeared to do away with the need for philosophy as a special form of inquiry). Clever analysis of language led to the conclusion that the only meaningful statements are those that are verifiable or observable (a proposition itself unverifiable and a tautology). Today metaphysics and ethics are back in fashion and the tide of positivism has receded sharply. A version of philosophy that declared that much of the noblest human discourse of the past and present is "meaningless" clearly overreached itself.

For the Christian thinker, the story of positivism is that of a man who drank too much. He discovered an excellent wine, strong-bodied and rich, which inspired a fresh view of philosophy. But as he drank more, strength became extravagance and confusion, and after lurching about, he collapsed before an indifferent world caught up with its own preoccupations. What "facts" and hard "data" may be is not as precise as so easily imagined, conventional methods of observation and verification turn out to have unsuspected limitations, and a certain faith and influence of peer thought are strongly present in the seemingly most objective of intellectuals. Finally, as in the case of humanism, science without God ends in barrenness.

*   *   *

This review of a few Christian intellectual attitudes points to many divergences from those encountered in modern university work: The authentic follower of Christ sees final truth and reality in a particular way, seeks to integrate all knowledge, draws on sources of knowledge inadmissible to many, guards religious faith in first place before science, resists the reductionism that excludes the religious domain, rejects mere intellectualism as the interpreter of life and religion, respects but restrains liberty, and regards the world as a place of confrontation between good and evil before its final transformation. Secular humanism and positivism are two prevalent codes of thought and behavior before which the Christian is especially on his guard.

While all this is elementary enough and immensely clear as one reflects on the matters in question, it does pose a problem for pluralism. Modern society, growing rapidly toward a world community of some sort, will doubtless continually hold out differing philosophies of life, so that, as a practical matter, Christian intellectual attitudes must, in all charity and forbearance, be presented with some restraint in the common endeavour of daily work and communication. My concern has been to emphasize their distinctive character, to counteract the danger of their being denatured and overwhelmed by current fashions of thought and behaviour. After their assertion, it is to be hoped that compromise and tolerance will be found on both sides. Typically, it is secular humanist and positivist thought that is much more arrogant and uncompromising in intellectual and academic circles than that based on religious premises.

Part 2

CHRISTIAN ECONOMIC THOUGHT

INTRODUCTORY REMARKS

If through its reflection on all reality the Christian mind arrives at a distinct interpretation of life and knowledge, obviously it has a particular view of the nature and purpose of the economy. It not merely analyzes institutions and their working objectively like everybody else, but goes on to judge them in relation to its premises. My purpose in part 2 is to outline how Christian thought conceives of the economic order (meaning the organization, pattern, and operation of economic institutions). It often speaks of the economic, political, and social "orders," believing that God intended some proper pattern for life and that following His law will move society toward it, ideal though it remain. Which does not imply there is a single model of a "Christian economy," even as ideal. It makes no sense to suppose that this would present the same institutional features and working in different countries, given their varied history and character. Instead Christian thought holds out confidently certain principles, acknowledging that they may receive varying modes of implementation. Obviously it does the same thing in other domains: there is no single model of ideal living, but only principles and virtues reflected in different ways.

Since the development of Christian social thought is recounted in many sources, let me briefly comment that a large part of its reflection on the economy has been associated with the Roman Catholic church.[1] Its leaders, in particular successive popes, have felt the need to issue carefully composed statements on social issues, so that a considerable body of social teaching is to be found in encyclical letters and episcopal declarations. Their premises derive from the natural law (see chapter 3, section 6), Scripture, and revelation, and traditional positions extending back to the early church though concentrated in the modern era. If for the period following *Rerum Novarum* (Leo XIII, 1891) to World War II, the church experienced a need to justify its right and duty to speak out on social questions,[2] criticism is now heard rather of its failure to take positions. Then, beyond what might be termed more or less official statements, there are layers of commentary by individuals, seeking to extend and interpret principles in relation to different problems. While this has only the authority and persuasiveness of its authors, there is some consensus on applications. Nobody can fail to see, for instance, that Christian principles call for extensive reforms in landholding and employment opportunities in many Latin American countries.

There is a smaller volume of Protestant socioeconomic thought[3] and only little in other world faiths, though some Islamic nations have set out uncertainly along the path of integrating modern economic life and religion. While Protestant thought is commonly believed to have exercized powerful influence on economic behavior, it has not until fairly recently become an important critic of economic institutions and policy. Some think the Reformers opened the doors to materialism and eventually the combination of productive methods and science that gave rise to industrialism, through their relating godliness with economic industriousness and lessened strictures on profit seeking.[4] From about 1950, Protestant churches and councils have indeed been making up for lost time in constructing a social message, but they have not yet put together a well synthesised structure of socioeconomic principles plus their implications for reform.

After Vatican II, a turning point in which the Catholic church relaxed its authoritarian structures and modes of thought somewhat, a certain drawing together of Catholic and Protestant social thinking has been noticeable. Doors have been opened and receptivity is evident, even if two steps forward seem followed by one backward. Catholic thought has toned down its neo-scholastic style, opened itself to some modern philosophical and theological currents, and adopted a more scriptural approach, while Protestant thought is in some quarters aware of the hazards of unqualified biblical reference and the strength of a systematic approach to socio-economic questions.

To provide background for my properly economic concerns, chapter 3 summarizes basic Christian social principles, chapter 4 extends them to the economy, and chapter 5 sets out alternative approaches to both. If my sympathies lie mostly with the concepts and reasoning of what may be called modernized scholasticism, since they link up more readily with the critical analysis typical of economic writing, it is essential to discuss approaches (chapter 5) that place more immediate reliance on Scripture and draw more directly on the urgent injustices present in so many countries to formulate intermediate criteria. Then chapter 6 examines two applications, wages and inflation, to illustrate the crossover from ethical principles and the falsity of omitting the moral dimension in policy discussions.

Chapter 3

SOCIAL PREMISES

While Christian social thought may be extended to the entire life of society, it is usually restricted to the economic, political, and social domains. *Social* is sometimes used to include all these and sometimes limited to institutions outside those commonly accepted as economic and political. More important, a loose distinction exists between social "principles" (or "doctrine" or "teaching") and "thought," where the latter includes their applied discussion (cf. Dorr, 1984, p. 213). Actually, it is convenient to treat Christian social thought as comprising several stages. Initially there are principles respecting the nature and purpose of life, where some are universal, holding for all forms of society, and others suppose a certain development. For example, whereas everybody is entitled to minimal nutrition, some level of education for all is now indispensable if a democracy is to function effectively. Second, principles must be led forward to applications by developing intermediate criteria: What are decent living standards in Peruvian or Canadian society today, or what education is appropriate in Afghanistan and Japan? Clearly a certain relativity enters. Third, both fundamental and intermediate principles merge with the detail of specific applications by complex processes that I shall illustrate a number of times.

My purpose, then, is to state a few leading principles of social life[1] to serve as foundation for the following discussion of the economic domain and applications. If it is sadly true that Christian social thought has had relatively little impact in Western countries, owing to the decline of Christianity and the relentless secularism imposed on the educational system, this chapter will make clear the neglect that exists.

1

What is man, in the sense of wherein lies his worth or value? Such a question cannot be answered by physical or positive social science, which is equipped to explain only why effects follow causes, not why a human being merits esteem. To get started on social principles, one must instead find a source of human rights. One beginning point is our universal intuition of the value and dignity of human life, an insight that leads us to perceive in the lowliest as in the greatest of human beings and achievements the immense worth of humanity.[2] The fact of human disabilities, failures, or suicides only reinforces this. Christian thought goes on from this to declare that each human being is a creature of God, uniquely loved for his or her own sake, and intended for union with Him forever. Further, God so loves all men and women that He sent His Son to free them from the dominion of evil. The purpose of their lives is to glorify God by following the teachings of the Son, so as to enter now into the preparatory stages of eternal life. Can merely humanitarian or philosophical reflection compare with this as source for the worth of man?

Given such a concept of the "person," a traditional concept summarizing human dignity, a sure basis is established for rights and obligations. If life is to serve God, now and in eternal union, unmistakably one has rights to the means necessary for every legitimate domain of personal development and obligations to furnish them to others. A number of authorities have drawn up declarations of human rights, founding them implicitly on various moral approaches, where we have been able to agree on much of the outcome if not the logic.[3] The Christian can to a degree acquiesce in such statements, while founding them on the Source of rights and authority.

2

Human rights are a modern preoccupation. Though implicit in scriptural and older theological writings, it is really since the rise of modern government as the creature of human arrangements in pluralistic societies that it has become necessary and fashionable to spell out their detail. They may be classified in different ways, where a useful distinction lies between natural and civic rights. The latter derive from specific laws dealing with modern circumstances (say, unemployment insurance or parking in designated areas) and amount to a projection of basic rights into the areas concerned. "Natural" rights include those to life and security of the person, marriage and children, certain minimal living standards, various freedoms, absence of discrimination, and so on. Since all human beings are equal as persons in the sight of God, in a proper sense all possess equality of basic rights. But since as a practical matter all are not equal in their talents, capacities for work, and circumstances, their translation into applications does *not* call for equal detailed realization (so that Christian social thought has generally rejected arguments for equal income and wealth distribution, cf. Vickers, 1982, pp. 110–11).

Evidently individual rights can at some point be so exercised as to endanger the welfare of self and others. Do I have the right to take my own life? Should my rights extend to proselytizing homosexuality? May I bomb the place of businesses whose dealings I reject as immoral? Clearly such questions cannot be solved simply by laws and democratic procedures, since the latter can be unjust. Instead the Christian leads them back to divine law. While this does not dispose of all the issues (should women enjoy the right to the priestly vocation?), without such a basis, human rights come to depend *only* on some common intuition of men and women and notion of social contract, a state of affairs much more open to abuse.[4]

Rights imply correlative duties. If we have the right to life, we must take ordinary means for its preservation; or if we are in need, others have the obligation to assist us, within the limits of what is reasonable. If some rights and duties are imperative, others are optional—say, the choice to marry. The obligation of the Christian to help satisfy the rights of others follows directly from the commandment to love others as himself and the threat of retribution (Matthew 25: 31–46). In fact, Christian thought contains a terrifying affirmation of human dignity and rights. Literally everyone is God's special creature, and nobody may despise him, judge him, or cast his claims off. The practical side can pose many controversial issues, such as our duty to cooperate with welfare programs by consenting to the necessary taxation or the limits of personal sacrifice in giving to the poor. Conscience and prayerful enlightenment usually find the answers.

3

After this stress on the worth of the individual, man is social by nature and a common good of the group requires to be taken into account no less than individual goods. The community side of life is studied by many disciplines, and we have acquired a wealth of knowledge about our physical, psychological, economic, and other needs and relations. Christian thought goes on to insist that man is by his very nature oriented toward the good of others, egotism is self-destructive, and any individual's good is properly realized only in relation to that of others.

Why? Many reasons may be adduced: Each person is born into a family, he cannot live or develop on his own, the universal experience of individuals and societies attests to his gregarious nature, and arguments in natural philosophy may be constructed. But the Christian also turns to God as explanation for the necessity of society: The doctrine of the Trinity obtained through Christ teaches that there are three Persons in one, the Son proceeds from the Father, and the Spirit is their loving union. Theological and philosophical attempts to cast these relations into human terms such as consubstantiality, coeternal nature, the concept of Persons, et cetera, are not my concern; there is a mystery that can only be penetrated slightly by human terminology. What matters is that God Himself is social (cf. Hagerty, 1976 and Maritain, 1947, pp. 46–48), directing Himself *ad alterum* in some mysterious way; so that man made in His image is necessarily both individual and social, finding in his relations with others the completion of himself. This social orientation and interpretation of life pervades Christian teachings concerning redemption, church, community, need for works of charity, and more.

Hence, his individuality and exceptional cases of solitaries[5] notwithstanding, man is meant to spend his life in society, which may be described as a stable union of persons committed to some common end. A lasting period is in question, and shared lines of commitment and action are required relative to goals. Provision for some authority and for methods of solving disputes is also implied in the notion of collective action. One may contrast society with a chance collection of individuals (say, at a railway station) and their good as a mere addition of individual goods (everybody catching his train). Instead a true society is a communion for ends that both include and yet contain something additional to individual goods.

Christian thought has generally distinguished three "perfect" societies—the family, the church, and the state—implying that each offers a fulfilling degree of common life, action, and goals, beyond which there exist many lesser societies, such as local and regional communities, ethnic groups, and labor unions. The stable union of parents and children called the family has always been presented as the primary cell and bastion of Christian life. It has been cherished as the cradle of the virtues of good living, where from infancy children should learn every instinct required for it. Consequently it has always been defended fiercely, and urgings, counsels, and prohibitions may be quoted from the earliest times to the present.[6] As for the church, Catholic Christians identify it with the Body of Christ, perfect and spotless, though making a necessary distinction between the ideal reality and its temporal incarnation always journeying, often in disarray, toward it. This quite extraordinary society comprises not merely its members engaged in the combat between good and evil in this world, but also the heavenly host and those expiating their sins before joining them. The church one sees is only part of a transcendent reality (cf. Maritain, 1970, p. 37 seq.). But though the family and the church are essential topics in the widest sense of Christian social thought, the state is our concern.

4

The third perfect society is not as clear-cut as the other two, since over time it has been identified with tribe, kingdom, country, et cetera. Neglecting these historical and evolutionary problems, we shall simply take the state to be the second temporal community, which complements fully (though not absolutely) the initial providing for individuals' needs by the family. For several centuries it has been predominantly identified in the West with the nation, a grouping primarily based on language, culture, and common government, even if in many instances several communities constitute the state in question. In our own day, supranational communities have come to exist, so that we may be moving, if the world survives nuclear destruction, toward forms going beyond the nation.

A great deal of controversy exists concerning the origins of the state, partly as historical fact and partly as to why and how this sort of union has come to exist. Aristotle saw it as an extension of the family, village, and clan to the city. Certain church fathers and theologians, usually in addition to seeing society as a consequence of man's social nature, accepted the authority and compulsion of the state as necessary to control the fallen nature of man. Calvin extended the latter idea to make a principal purpose the protection of religion as a public institution and the repression of idolatry. Social contract thinkers like Hobbes and Rousseau saw the state as a human compact of convenience for the protection of human liberties. Drawing on Hegel, Marx visualized the state as molded by an inner dialectical or conflict-resolving process, finally withering away in ideal communism.

Christian social thought has generally adopted the approach of Aristotle (cf. Rommen, 1945), while grafting on a divine plan shaping and ennobling the character of social life. To comment on a few characteristics of this view, in the first place the state is ideally a communion as opposed to a mere grouping of individuals, families, and lesser communities. Its members cannot direct their activities only by self-interest and exclusively selfish ends, service and care for others being essential. Since the human person cannot live or develop in isolation, there is a necessary projection to others for self completion, and divine injunction clarifies what nature tells us. Consequently a communion of mutual interest arises in addition to individual interests, a middle ground between the extremes of anarchy and the totalitarian state. Obviously this ideal conception provokes some extraordinary contrasts with actual societies, which resemble warring factions with incompatible goals, sometimes seeking the annihilation of one another. Can ideal and reality be reconciled? The essential reply of Christian thought to this kind of problem lies in its continual presentation of this life as a struggle between good and evil, where the ideal is held out.

Second, the central goal of the state is the common good, which both includes individual goods and circumscribes them for mutual benefit, while gathering them into something different from their mere sum. The obvious analogy is that of the body, the good of which includes and yet is greater than that of its parts taken individually (cf. I Corinthians 12: 12). Clearly such a concept of the common good makes little sense if one does not first take society as a communion, since otherwise it is a mere agglomeration of individual goods in a Paretian sense (cf. chapter 9, section 2). Then, if one asks concretely what is the common good, the normal reply is to describe its economic, political, and social components in any society; so that again we are dealing with a general principle that requires to be led forward to its applications in the case in question. If there are no facile answers to specifying the common good, it is also true that a healthy and just state of society is easily distinguishable, just as bodily health and welfare are clear enough after the business of medical and psychic definitions.

Thirdy, it is characteristic of Christian thought to regard the state as bodylike or organic,[7] in the sense that the different parts of it have different functions, where each must be respected and all contribute to the good of the whole. From this derives the much emphasized principle of subsidiarity,[8] holding that superior and stronger parts of the body politic must respect and leave in place the proper functioning of lesser parts. The consequences are dramatic: Ordinarily government may not nationalize private industry nor may large enterprises simply proceed to swallow up smaller, without serious justification. Excessive takeovers and vast conglomerates clearly run counter to subsidiarity; small is beautiful (Schumacher, 1973), and it merits protection.

Fourth, the state has legitimate authority going beyond its apparatus of law, the juridical system, penalties, et cetera, and deserving acquiescence. In Christian thought all authority is derived from God (see chapter 2, section 6), and its reflection in the home, society, enterprise, institutions, et cetera, demands respect. The concept in question equates itself with service—to be in charge is to serve—not mere power. Ideally those who possess authority use it as delegated by God and those who obey guard their freedom, since they consent (which, in passing, is the way communism also answers the problem of freedom). In this way, tensions between authority and obedience find their resolution, assuming its legitimate and moderate use, its respect for the dignity of those affected, and the decision of the latter to acquiesce with goodwill. There is a massive contrast between this concept of the authority of the state in Christian thought and the aggressivity to it so characteristic in societies today.

Clearly Christian thought takes a different position from some sociological thought that speaks of society, the state, the public good, and authority as theoretical entities, where our experiences of politicians, bureaucrats, and power are the only reality. Not so. The latter are immediately encountered, but beyond them lie the meaningful realities of society as community and the common good as the welfare of all. Community is composed of individuals, but is also something beyond them, as we all experience at great patriotic or religious occasions, even at sporting events.

5

A consideration of social principles usually goes on from society and the state to deal with leading institutions of the economic, political, and social orders—property owners, labor unions, democracy, the judicial system, the family, education, and so on. Accordingly, in chapter 4 we shall take up a number of economic institutions. But for the remainder of this background chapter, let me turn to law and the social virtues, since these regulate the behavior of individuals, groups and government and, in effect, the working of all institutions (themselves patterns of human activity, shaped over time by law and custom).

Along a traditional approach, law may be defined as an ordinance of reason for the common good promulgated by whoever has charge of the community. It consists of prescriptions for the good of society rather than of this or that individual, it must be publicized and declared in force, and the appropriate authority must be responsible for such action. To quote Isidore's (d. 636) well-known remark, "Law shall be virtuous, just, possible to nature, according to the custom of the country, suitable to place and time, necessary, useful; clearly expressed, lest by any obscurity it leads to misunderstanding; framed for no private benefit, but for the common good" (Madden, 1930, p. 48). Evidently, the sense of law invoked has theological overtones and differs from an approach that tries to find authority, legislative power, obligation, justice, et cetera, in only social process and contract.[9] Instead, God is the fundamental source in the Christian mind.

Setting positive secular thought aside, law must for the Christian be taken in a sense going beyond that of civil law to refer to the entire plan of God's creation, which may be called the eternal or divine law.[10] This may be considered to have three divisions: regularities implanted in animate and inanimate nature (instinct and physical laws), moral injunctions sensed through conscience in human beings, and specific commands recorded in the Old and New Testaments. By the "natural law" Christian thought has typically meant the second or a restriction of the more general sense of the law of nature, denoting that part of it that God has implanted in the human heart and mind as moral command. Aquinas called it a "human participation in the Divine law,"[11] and longstanding tradition has interpreted it to mean the sense of God's commands given us by our nature, leaving aside faith and revelation. Parents have from such a concept of the natural law the right and duty to oversee the education of their children, and it is wrong to cut off one's hand or kill another. Thus in the wider sense of the law of nature, we are subject to the overall plan of creation, needing food or suffering electric shock, but as rational creatures we are called on to have some share in God's own role, perceiving His law in ourselves and in community. Subsequently, what the natural law may tell us is confirmed and enlightened by knowledge based on faith, Jesus' teaching on monogamy being an example.

Taken in this sense, the natural law has long been a controversial topic,[12] since it is linked to belief in God and is interpreted to impose a divinely planned morality upon behavior. Its history reaches back beyond medieval thinkers to Roman and Greek origins and forward through seventeenth-century discussion (notably Grotius, d. 1645) to the present. It usually receives speedy dismissal from those who reject religious faith and discuss social issues from the positive facts of behavior alone. Legal texts briefly notice it as a quaint relic of the past. Among Christian writers, reliance on the traditional concept of the natural law has been mostly identified with a neo-scholastic approach to the moral theology and social thought of the Catholic church, though after the changes of Vatican II not a few writers underplayed it as out of touch with modern philosophy and misused by conservative thinkers and church authority.[13]

6

Leaving aside these debates, three points will suffice for my purpose. Firstly, the natural law must remain one essential foundation for Christian social principles, which suppose the concept of a human nature common to men and women created in the likeness of God and the ability of all to perceive what is right and to direct their actions accordingly, albeit as assisted by the wise and enlightened.[14] This obligation to act justly, arising from a true perception of what they are and the purpose of life, is in effect their awareness of the natural law. Granted today the concept of a human nature has been fragmented and confused by the many sciences bearing on behavior and granted it is essential to supplement use of the natural law by theological and scriptural argument, plus the magisterium of the teaching church, its place must still be guarded in Christian thinking.

Second, admitting to the fact of a natural law implanted in us is not difficult for most people; its practical implications are the area of conflict. That we have the right to marry is evident, but whether this denotes a single partner and for life are other questions. Does one's right to have children extend to entire control over their education? The upshot is that

49

in spelling out the content and detail of the natural law we are engaged in familiar problems of advancing from general principles to applications and of accepting the role of community and of authority in this. Just as civil and religious authorities help define and limit individual and social rights, they must also protect and guide the human participation in the divine law in question. The conditions under which marriage may be annulled or the care of children by incompetent parents suspended are obvious instances. Still, while there can be a great deal of disagreement over the practical implications of the natural law, this is not a reason for discrediting it.

Also, as in the case of rights that depend on the concept of the person and the end of human life, one must admit to a certain evolution in perception of requirements.[15] For example, tribal customs show diversity that is not simply to be ascribed to ignorance or evil influences; so that if they are to be regarded in the main as reflecting in some instinctive way a divine plan, careful attention needs to be given their circumstances and history, so often given superficial interpretation in anthropology. Or slavery and distinctions based on race and color may have seemed reasonable to people of past times and still are considered so in some areas today, and the world has had to evolve before the injustice of these things imposed itself as a reality.[16] But whatever qualifications and distinctions need to be introduced respecting this evolving perception of the natural law, such facts do not militate against its existence and importance.

Third, as the most controversial area, positive civil law—be it the result of legislative process, long entrenched custom, tribal practice, et cetera—must in some sense finally repose on the natural law (while bearing in mind the problems of evolution and perception). To some extent this is undoubtedly so, as instanced by the traditional listing of crimes in Western legal codes. But saying one can be led back to the other does not mean that all positive law is somehow implicit in the natural law or required to be discerned therein. As Finnis justly remarks (1980, p. 28), founding positive on natural law sitll recognizes the creativity of legislators who have to deal with transnational corporations, international law for sea and space and a thousand unforeseeable problems of evolving societies. In any event, any opinion that the underpinning of natural law may have faded from view in modern society is soon corrected by disputes over noisy stereo systems, industrial pollution, or spending on armaments. Recourse is instantly had by disputants to what they perceive as human instincts of what is right and just. Denying that some concept of natural law underlies positive law, as it is and as it should be, is rather odd for ordinary folk.[17] It is like a debater's defense of atheism, which so often evaporates the moment danger to life appears.

7

The role of law in helping shape the just society has been greatly exaggerated in the modern era. Liberal individualism repeatedly affirms that social consent and the political process must decide what should be legislated and beyond that individuals are free to do as they please. Nothing more can be expected in a pluralistic society. To this Christian thought resolutely opposes the view that virtue, both individual and social, has an important place in shaping behavior. It is another way of talking about the morality that both supports just law and extends beyond the limits of what it is prudent to legislate. Hence the role of the social virtues in helping mold the just society must be stressed. (Personal virtues, such as temperance or fortitude, are rather concerned with enhancing individual behavior, a matter far from irrelevant to social welfare, but another topic.)

While *virtue* has unfortunately taken on a certain prudish sense, the concept merely signifies a good habit or customary way of acting. Common examples are fortitude, compassion, and love, and contrasting vices are weakness, hardness of heart, and hatred. A virtue is a quality of soul or spirit properly speaking (or whatever our nonmaterial essence should be called), flowing through to inform physical characteristics of mind and body (cf. Carrel, 1961, p. 59). Somehow goodness of soul is apparent in eyes or hands as well as in the speech we mostly attend to. It extends beyond the merely natural and humanitarian; for the Christian, what is virtuous in men and women ascends to God through prayer and union and is shaped by the Spirit. In this way, virtue stays alive and does not become formalistic behavior degenerating into hypocrisy. While a listing of its different forms is important, one should not be carried away by classificatory business; really "every virtue is a diffraction of [the] infinitely rich simplicity [of God] upon a potentiality of man" (Guardini, 1967, p. 8). The virtues are simply names for the aspects of God that we strive with divine assistance to impress upon ourselves.

Christian social thought has always stressed the importance of the social virtues, in that certain good habitual ways of thinking and action are essentially directed toward others, such as love of neighbor, liberality

51

or social charity, or patriotism and good citizenship. Their special characteristic is love and service *ad alterum*. Even if most virtues have at least some effect on others, here we are thinking of those with specific impact on relations between individuals, between individuals and groups, and between both and the state. Among them justice is preeminent, since it is par excellence the virtue concerned with the rights of individuals in relation to one another and the community, along with correlative obligations. Yet it is far from being the whole of the matter, and in particular love or social charity is the connective force in social bonds. It is an old teaching in Christian thought that social peace is founded on the two pillars of justice and charity;[18] the first removes the elements of friction, and the second supplies the creative sources of union. Justice without charity becomes cold legality, giving rise to as much hostility as it may remove.

8

To recall a familiar approach, justice may be defined as a constant and perpetual will to render everyone his due.[19] It is a virtue or good habit residing *subjectively* in the person as a quality and reflected *objectively* in his actions. Justice has traditionally been termed a cardinal virtue (the others being prudence, temperance, and fortitude), since it is a prime regulator of our relations with others. Essentially social, it is fulfilled by an external equality between what is due and what is rendered, so that it is possible for an action to be just independently of the motives of the doer.

For the Christian, like all virtues, justice is finally an attribute of God, the source and explanation of all righteousness in which we share in imperfect ways, and its measure is the divine law or God's plan for all creation. This marks a parting of the ways. If the source of justice and its reflection in rights and duties are sought elsewhere, in *only* intuition, humanistic instincts, social contract, or the will of a despot, et cetera, there is no sure or lasting point on which to take one's stand. No individual can be the justifying source of his own rights and duties, so that no group or purely human source can serve better. Instead, history shows that great movements or revolt against individual or social cruelty have always made their appeal not merely to the deepest roots of human nature, but also to some objective source and standard of right and wrong.

In the writings of Solzenitsyn (especially his *Gulag Archipelago*), the rejection of Soviet tyranny by so many men and women is repeatedly shown to spring from deep inner moral consciousness—divinely implanted, in the author's view.

The kinds or aspects of justice[20] are neither as simple nor as clear a matter as one might wish. Justice may be taken in a narrow or strict sense denoting equality between obligations and what is rendered, or instead in a more general sense of all that is right. To begin with the first, commutative or exchange justice concerns the rendering of what is exactly due in contracts, explicit or implicit. We have a deep instinct that what is agreed on should be exactly rendered, and our courts and industrial and commercial system insist on this. The obvious problem is to know exact equivalence, typified by the question of just price. (See chapter 4, section 11). The principle is clear enough, with the difficulties lying rather in applications. This is exactly the same, of course, as the question of finding particular realisations of injunctions to love our neighbor or respond truthfully to questions.

Distributive justice, the second narrow form usually distinguished, requires special care. Aristotle and medieval writers used it in the sense (with which I concur) of a fair sharing out of common burdens and benefits. The formation of community gives rise to the latter, and distributive justice consists in equivalence between what is due to each (as burden or benefit) and what is granted or imposed by the central authority. In the modern context taxes and public expenditures are very largely in question, though there is also the sharing out of offices, privileges, civic recognition, and the like. Distributive justice as a virtue resides in those responsible for allocation and, in my approach, "contributive" justice (below) covers the response of those obliged to pay taxes and otherwise contribute to community obligations.[21] The obvious problems are to determine the sort of equality (same absolute or proportionate or progressive/regressive shares?) that should obtain in modern society and the relation of distributive justice to the celebrated question of just distribution of income and wealth. The following chapter (in section 12) takes up these matters.

9

The notion of social justice, despite its endless repetition and popularity, poses considerable difficulty as soon as one asks what obligation it places on whom to do what. The term appears to have arisen about 1850 (cf. Hayek, 1976, vol. 2, pp. 63, 176–177) in connection with the social question that set in with advancing industrialism and concern for the position of the poor and disadvantaged. The loosened hold of an older ethics facilitated the practice of linking *justice* and *social,* and eventually Pius XI used the new expression in *Quadragesimo Anno* (1931). This was followed by much discussion as to whether he had wished to discern a new category of justice or merely apply a modern name to an old concept, with the latter view prevailing. In recent years, ''social justice'' has been used with fairly free interpretation by many writers, some equating it with justice in distribution and others, more correctly in my view, applying it primarily to the structure of economic institutions, on the ground that their right formation and functioning are essential to secure economic justice in practice.

To fill in some background, Aristotle remarked (*Nich. Ethics,* Book 5, chapter 1) that there is one sense in which justice is a general virtue, taking in the whole of virtuous behavior. This is seen easily enough by extending the concept of righteousness toward others to its fullest sense, where everybody receives what is due in the completest way. One can thus visualize total righteousness, to call it this, as including the practice of all the virtues in so far as they extend to *ad alterum* relations. In this widest sense, general justice can have no operative requirements itself, neither specifying nor requiring particular actions. The concept only reflects other virtues, and obviously we still use it in this sense (''Joseph was a just man,'' Matthew 1: 19). Then Aquinas identified ''general'' with ''legal'' justice (a term he used more frequently), by which the Scholastics meant the concept of justice that reflected the divine and natural laws (in their moral sense) and should be translated into positive or state law to whatever extent appropriate. The significant shift from ''general'' justice is that specific requirements have now been introduced, falling primarily on lawmakers but in effect extending to all (as we would now insist) for the entire fulfillment of the natural law in its social implications.

So if we propose to identify social with general justice in Aristotle's sense, we have one kind of problem, in that at present all commonly believe social justice calls for specific action to reform social institutions. If we identify it with legal justice in the medieval sense, we have others: ''Legal'' now means courtroom justice, but social justice must today be used in such wider senses as denoting the framing and reform of positive law, the building up of desirable institutions throughout society, and the necessary contributory actions of individuals and groups.

The solution is to hold that social justice may be taken in two senses: It may be identified with general and/or legal justice, as explained and with the qualifications and difficulties noted; or it may be taken in a narrower sense to refer to the obligation of lawmakers and then all participants in society to contribute to its requirements, which is appealing, but raises the question of whether a third form of narrow justice is being distinguished, where equivalence must arise between obligation and act. My position is to accept this: Modern circumstances do require recognition of a third form of strict or narrow justice, which should be called contributive justice.[22] This problem did not arise so much for medieval and Renaissance theologians, since they did not have to visualize the sort of contributory action essential in modern democracy.

Coming to the obligations of social justice—who is called on to take what action—when we take the concept in its wide sense, we are only repeating the obligation of all to conform to the natural law and the practice of all virtue. But in the narrower sense we are asking, What is the formal act of social (contributive) justice? Some years ago, Ferree (1951) concluded that social justice is precisely aimed at the organization of our acts into such institutions as will promote the common good and allow particular justice and the other social virtues to operate effectively. Cronin (1956, p. 76) went on to describe social justice as "a virtue which inclines the individual to seek the common good, and particularly directs him to seek in an organised fashion an economic society whose laws, customs and institutions are directed towards the promotion of the common good." What is being slurred over in each approach is the question of equivalence between obligation and act that is typical of strict justice. For my part, the equivalence does exist and is to be worked out in the same sort of fashion as in the case of distributive justice (cf. chapter 4, section 12). Even if in both cases equivalence is less well defined and the obligation less specifically laid on each individual than in the case of commutative justice, in situations in which many individuals and group leaders find themselves today, obligations do arise to act in the interests of social welfare and failure to act is an omission in social justice.

* * *

Social justice is accepted readily by people of all backgrounds as the ideal code and goal of community. Many equate it with "distributive justice," meaning by this some equitable distribution of income, wealth, and general economic and social benefits loosely added in. But this interpretation simply does not fit the history and analysis of what social justice may properly mean. A celebrated attempt (Rawls, 1971) sought so make it the result of social contracting by individuals, relying on an intuition of primary goods (liberty, equality of opportunity, income, self-respect) and rationally framing rules to secure maximum mutual advantage for all.[23] Quite apart from the proposal to erect agreement for mutual benefit into an entire theory of good social relations, leaving religion aside and taking no account of evil, Rawls's central weakness is his putting forward social justice as the sole basis of the good society, when two millenia of Christian wisdom have held out love as the creative and connective force. Justice removes the obstacles to peace by satisfying rights, certainly, but love breathes life into social bonds.

Or a von Hayek (1976, Vol. 2) dismisses the concept of social justice altogether: There are only individuals with values, rights, and responsibilities, and social justice is a mirage, since nobody can pin down its substance and requirements precisely, which is a view dismissing much of what Christ taught as unrealizable (what are the *exact* things that should be given to God and which to Caesar; how *precisely* shall I love my neighbor?) and is an obvious enough outcome of Hayek's extreme individualism. Hayek might consider that the detailed applications of individual rights are often not precise business either. For the Christian, however, social justice in the wide sense, and objectively, summarizes the end result of the ideal or "right" economy toward which we must continually strive despite constant failures. Taken subjectively to reflect virtue in those who act righteously *ad alterum,* it is ideal Christian behavior for the common good. The passage from first principles to middle criteria and on to applications, especially social, is often hard slogging, but the goal is no mirage.

Chapter 4

ECONOMIC PRINCIPLES

One may come at the economic principles put forward by Christian thought in several ways, such as an elaboration of rights in the economic domain, an investigation of economic justice, or an examination of institutions and their working in the just economy. Economic rights call for their fulfillment in terms of goods and services needed, operation of the work place, reception of public goods, et cetera. Economic justice (social, distributive, contributive, commutative) consists in each person receiving what is due, so that as virtue it directs the actions of individuals, groups, and government, and as end result it reflects the realization of rights and duties. Then institutions are the place of immediate contact for all with economic life, so that their formation and working are critical for welfare. While the three approaches converge, it is convenient to shift from one to the other according to the topic under consideration.

When one speaks of the economic principles that flow from social thought, it is easy to assume some given structure of economic institutions is implicit in them. Christian thought may be supposed to project some model of the economy, albeit ideal, fitting in best with the way of life taught by Christ. Let me again (cf. part 2, introductory remarks) correct this: Social thought primarily gives rise to broad principles of economic life that must be translated into institutions varying from country to country and era to era. If we but reflect that Christian life has existed for two thousand years in many different circumstances while fundamentals remain intact and a similar spirit underlies institutions, it is obvious that concrete details will vary a great deal. Yet in its historical context a feudal economy may be as legitimate a vehicle for the functioning of Christian ideals as the private enterprise economy.

In keeping with my aim of presenting an overview of the Christian mind and the economic order, the following outline of principles is only a selection from what could be extended greatly.[1]

1

If every human being is created in the image of God and has His service as the overriding purpose of life, from this condition flow economic rights implying that all are entitled to the material requisites of physical and mental health.[2] Moving towards application, in the case of the advanced economy of today such rights include minimum standards of health, habitation, and education and these with a certain provision over time.[3] A minimum of health implies adequate diet, availability of medical care, protection from excessive environmental pollution, and sufficient recreation. Habitation deals with living space per person, building and materials standards, sanitation disposal, and adequacy of air and light. As for education, it has become necessary for virtually all to have elementary schooling, and the more advanced the country the greater the case for required education up to, say, fifteen or sixteen years of age.

But if such minimal standards of living reflect fundamental human rights, what of the implication that such should be the case for all people at all times? Quite apart from historical and contemporary situations of tribal and primitive life, achieving even rudimentary minima for the steadily increasing billions of the world's population presents staggering problems of production and distribution. My comment on problems of this sort, which arise repeatedly in universal statements of human rights, is again (cf. chapter 3, section 6) that a certain relativity attends their realization. Decent minima are not the same in the Roman and modern eras, in India and Canada, in tribal and city living today. One can only affirm that basic material welfare must be assured in whatever society, after that judgment enters. It would be absurd to assert that superior minimal standards in one environment must be copied in another.

Then rights imply obligations (see chapter 3, section 2). If its members are entitled to basic minima, society has the duty of assuring them through the operation and management of the economy, underdeveloped or affluent. If the advanced economy is not functioning in such a way as to furnish sufficient health, habitation, and education to all, far-reaching obligations arise for the owners of property, those who direct enterprise or who operate the financial system, and governments that supervise and stabilize the economy. Those who control property must employ or invest it appropriately, enterprise must be conducted for the welfare of all employees, and the financial and distributive system must cooperate in the work of ensuring minimum welfare for all.[4] While many aspects of economic reality come crowding in at this point—the excessively materialistic character of society that pushes living standards continually higher, dangers of bankruptcy for enterprise, abuses of social security, and so on—all this is an applied debate lying beyond the affirmation of basic rights and obligations.

2

The second fundamental aspect of economic rights is free exercise of our faculties of mind and body, so that in choosing our work we may use our physical and mental powers as we wish (within the bounds of law and morality, naturally). Many constraints limit our choices—necessary training and abilities, oversupply or lack of demand for many occupations, legal restrictions, customs, et cetera; but beyond them basic liberty remains.

An obvious consequence of each person having dominion over his own powers is that certain institutions arise in the free economy. Consumers may buy what they choose, whence consumer sovereignty derives its legitimacy and influence over what is produced; all human work may be freely withdrawn, which justifies both labor mobility and strike action (though the group character of the latter needs further consideration); freedom of enterprise takes its justification; and competition results from individuals pursuing the same objective on differing terms. These four matters will receive further discussion; for the moment they are merely stressed as consequences of economic freedom.

Any advocacy of liberty requires emphasis on its limitations. (See chapter 2, section 6). Since Christian thought is both personal and yet social, it does not acquiesce in the excessive expression and protection of rights known as economic individualism (see chapter 7, section 7), which in fact entails violence toward others. Given the purpose of individual life, the exercise of all freedoms must enhance, not endanger them; and given the social orientation of each person and the need to respect the good of others and the common good, individual use of physical and mental powers is limited by the rights of the community.

59

At the other extreme, equally, the Christian ethic does not acquiesce in the excessive curtailments of authoritarian regimes. Instead it pursues the middle road of defending economic freedoms while constraining them within right morality and the law which presumptively reflects this.

3

Do basic rights include individual ownership of property? To dispose of some preliminary points, *property* normally signifies things external to the person, such as land, fixtures, et cetera, plus intangibles like goodwill and trademarks.[5] If it is commonly extended to include one's body and faculties (where the lordship of God makes our possession more clearly a trusteeship), what matters in economics is the means of production, the ordinary source of wealth and power. Their ownership signifies centrally rights to control, enjoy, and alienate by sale or testament. The Soviet people may constitutionally own the means of production, but control is the essence.

It is easy to state the central Christian view of property: God gave dominion ("entrusted" is the more correct idea) to man over all creation (Genesis 1: 26–30), as confirmed by the universal practice and intuition of societies. Everywhere and at all times men have felt empowered to use all lesser life and inanimate matter for their own needs and benefit (if within customary and moral limits). But Scripture clearly gives the earth to mankind for its *common* welfare, so that it must be divided up by human arrangements to permit individual and group control. Hence the question arises whether individual property rights determined in this way are still "natural," reflecting the force of human nature and the natural law (see chapter 3, sections 5–6), or depend purely on historical or social contract decisions, so that societies are free to decide on forms of common ownership as they choose. In the latter case, extreme socialist doctrines could be held as legitimate human arrangements.

The ancient question of common ownership versus private has seen thought and practice sway from one extreme to the other. To judge from New Testament allusions (Acts 4: 32–37), the early Christians practiced communality to some extent, doubtless with private ownership widely intact. In time, community of property became largely the preserve of religious orders, though the feudal system remained well removed from exclusive ownership as we now understand it. Aquinas left a classic statement (*Sum. Theol.*, II–IIae, Q.66, 1–2) covering the basic principles of private versus common ownership in Christian thought. If the earth exists in common for the welfare of all and is by human arrangement divided up, private ownership is necessary for human living; for men are more industrious about what is their own, greater order results if one person has charge of particular things rather than everybody having charge of everything, and greater peace will reign if each has his own. While these points may be contested, they are still the usual considerations adduced to support the desirability of private property. Aquinas concludes with the Christian reconciliation of individualism and socialism, "Man ought to possess external things, not as his own, but as common so that he is ready to communicate them to others in their need." In sum, our exclusive rights to property are tempered by the duty of assisting others and using it, not merely for our own good, but also for the benefit of others and the community. Stewardship is a common latter-day expression of this.

But now to the awkward point: If human arrangements intervene, can individual ownership of property be taken as sanctioned and even required by the natural law, more simply human nature? My own and a common reply is that what is natural, man's dominion over external things, has been carried a step further to specify that individual ownership is also natural. This may be based on three considerations: practical reason judging that individual ownership is best, as above; evidence from the widespread evolution and practice of societies; and Scriptural citations (e.g. the commandment not to steal a neighbor's property [Deuteronomy 5: 21] and perhaps as an inference from certain parables of Jesus [Matthew 20: 1 and 25: 14]). To take a parallel, man by nature has the right to marry; then monogamy is the additional natural rule specified by Jesus, which one may also argue is required for the best welfare of spouses and their children. Then if the history of property owning has witnessed, as the world still does, to common and group as well as individual ownership and to different concepts of possession and control, such situations are presumably still evolving toward the normal ideal of morally responsible personal ownership.

Hence my interpretation of the long-standing assertion in Catholic social teaching "man has a natural right to property"[6] is that each person has the capacity to exercise control over external things and should normally exercise it by owning significant items. If he has this by nature, such rights and the corresponding obligations of others to respect and help realize them are part of the natural law. It is not to be concluded that everybody must own a house or land or the means of production, but rather that each person has the capacity to own such and that it is desirable and normal he own some minimal external property. This is a reflection of personal dignity and permits at least some independence, in contrast with the slave or serf. Such a general principle, despite the difficulties of interpretation and implementation, remains the bulwark against wrong-headed doctrines of common ownership and communality.

A further problem arises concerning the sources of entitlement by which the world possessed in common is divided up. One long-standing argument made prominent by Locke (c. 1690; 1963, Book 2, chapter 5) though implicit in Scripture (man is to subdue the earth [Genesis 1: 28] and is entitled to a fair wage [1 Timothy 5: 18]) is that personal work is the key source of individual ownership.[7] Individuals are entitled to the fruit of their labor and to a fair share in the benefits of enterprise, so that their earnings build up possessions. One may also note other sources, some picturesque and debatable: clearing virgin lands (often contested occupation occurred in fact), conquest, inheritance, divine right, social contract, et cetera. The more interesting point, not emphasized by Locke but critical, is that labor is always social and inheritance and contract are social arrangements, so that the claims of others to share in the benefits of private property—in justice, through state taxation or the requirements of charity—are never extinguished.

Sharing the benefits of property with others is covered by the operation of virtue and law. Justice has even been interpreted by some as giving those in dire need a right to the surplus of others.[8] Whether this is so in strict justice is debatable (may a starving person help himself up to his need for food in a store?), though such rights in social (general) justice are clear and are generally reflected in redistributive programs. While it seems unworkable for civil law to spell out such rights as strict claims, social security programs widely reflect the justice of sharing incomes and property. Then charity goes beyond the unclear limits of the rights and duties of justice. Mother Teresa has made this terribly clear, urging all to give to the poor not from their abundance, but even from their own needs.[9] No Christian can ignore the far-reaching demands of charity except at peril not merely of salvation but the living nature of his faith.

In sum, to assert a natural right to own and enjoy property is not to defend exclusive rights to control it to the detriment of others and the common good. Quite apart from the case for society sharing in the benefits of property, it is only too clear that abuses by individuals destroy the effective exercise of property rights for all but the few and create social upheaval.

4

If all have the right to use their talents and property with responsible freedom, it follows that private enterprise has an entirely legitimate place. But while its universal emergence in societies is evidence enough of its naturalness—let an authoritarian regime that has tried to extinguish it relax for a moment, and backyard producers and markets spring up—the significant questions in the modern economy concern its restrictions for the good of individuals and society and what place should be given communal and public enterprise.

As far as Christian social principles are concerned, one may only assert the right of individuals to engage in enterprise for personal benefit and the general desirability that some reasonably large number in a free society do so. This follows from the rights outlined and from their relation to self-realization and social welfare. Then many qualifications arise: For instance, private enterprise in any prominent sense clearly supposes a certain evolution of society from communal forms of property owning; tribal or nomadic communities are not ready for it to any significant degree. Next, private enterprise destroys itself when unrestrained individualism leads to irresponsible competition, excessive takeovers, and eventual destruction of widespread ownership of the means of production. Freedom to use one's talents and property as one wishes is a strong yet fragile thing, demanding the protection of morality as well as law.

The actual forms of enterprise raise particularly difficult questions concerning the modern corporation. Single proprietorships and partnerships are straightforward, but the corporation is not. It may range from small to giant size, with the latter somewhat justified by economies of scale and the requirements of defense production; limited liability and continued life make it a better proposition for large capital raising; and its size permits employment of specialized equipment and personnel. Yet the divorce between ownership and effective control, the limited responsibility and exposure to risk of paid management, and the sheer complexity of corporate organization and interrelations, not to mention unending scandals, raise serious questions concerning the scope that should be left the corporation in the modern economy. Many observers conclude the need for close social control. For my purpose, however, the actual forms of enterprise and their problems are applied questions lying beyond the immediate case for widespread private enterprise.

There are also communal undertakings focusing on mutual service, such as cooperatives; nonprofit undertakings of the sort found in education, health, and social service; and public enterprises, whether profit or non–profit seeking (say a national airline or a transit system). Some think private enterprise should be largely replaced by them, given its abuses in practice. More relevant questions for social ethics are what place should be reserved for the forms of communal enterprise that require extensive public subsidization (say private hospitals or homes for the aged) and what should be the limits of public undertakings. The answers largely depend in practice on the limitations of private enterprise (the market system is said to "break down" (cf. chapter 9, section 9), through failure to take social costs into account or through the need for, say, monopolized supply by utilities) and the principle of subsidiarity (see chapter 3, section 4), which requires government to respect the place of lower tiers in the economy. The success of non–profit-making forms of enterprise usually turns on the dedication of those concerned or assistance coming from benevolent foundations or government subsidization.

5

The case for private property and enterprise having been stressed, even more important is the right of everybody to find work. In modern societies, a large segment of the population do not possess the means of production, a condition aggravated by mass migration to cities, or have the capacity for successful enterprise in a highly competitive environment, so that employment is indispensable to furnish a livelihood for oneself and dependents. Further, men and women should broadly be able to find suitable work for their talents and abilities, even if this cannot be spelled out precisely as a right and must be heavily qualified by the circumstances of any society and misplaced personal aspirations.[10]

This right goes very far, since it places an obligation on those concerned (cf. chapter 5, section 10) to satisfy it. Enterprises may not simply dismiss or lay off employees lightly, nor may governments avoid their role of intervention and stabilization. Evidently one must take into account the viability of the enterprise, the safeguards provided by unemployment insurance and welfare schemes (so easily taken advantage of by both employees and employers), the abuses that unions may engage in, and more. Beyond all this, however, the fundamental right of all to be provided with work must be recognized.[11] The existence of unemployment can be given some justification only through the need to preserve economic freedoms in using work and property. A necessary price is a certain dislocation in employment, aggravated in many economies by excessive mobility of labor and an economic system that has deemphasized the kind of enterprise loyalty seen in modern Japan. However, unemployment as a passing experience for many is one thing, but as an excessive and permanent condition it represents a wrong deeply productive of individual and social malaise.

6

Turning briefly to the rights of those who work to combine and to withhold labor, modern unions rose in the nineteenth century as workers sought to join together for mutual protection and benefit. Typically the climate was one of suspicion and repression, as the propertied classes feared (not incorrectly) civil upheaval, given the background of the French Revolution and social unrest in the first half of the century; and old laws and presumptions against conspiracy were invoked to prevent effective organization. Step by step, in various countries at different times unions gained the right to organize openly and then take action to achieve their ends. The latter involved chiefly the power to strike and to prevent employers simply engaging other workers from the unemployed and immigrant labor. Leo XIII's *Rerum Novarum* (1891) recognized the legitimacy of unions and (implicitly) strike action for just cause, in opposition to right-wing Catholic thought.

Today there is general recognition of the right to combine in labor unions, which flow from the natural tendency of individuals to band together in associations for mutual benefit. Consequently it is wrong to prohibit this and effective action to obtain the goals that are the very purpose of association. Clearly these rights do not extend to abusive actions harmful of the true interests of members and the common good: breaking the terms of a labor-management contract, sympathetic strikes and secondary boycotts, and violence to those crossing picket lines are practices commonly outlawed. More controversial are union rights to insist on membership by all working in some plant or to exact dues by checkoff; here a question of contributive justice arises concerning the obligation of individuals to support socially beneficial organizations, the usual complication being the political affiliation of unions, to which many object.

Unions are a classic case of the need to exercise freedoms and rights responsibly for the common good. Most go quietly about protecting and furthering the interests of members, but a prominent few cause a great deal of disruption. The dangers are real, since unions are subject to the abuses of vote-catching and partisan leadership, an adversary mentality typically prevails in relation to management, and too fragmented organization leads to a certain inability to respect the welfare of the enterprise and society. Quite apart from the fact that many firms have to deal with multiple unions, jealous of the relative position of their members, across society unions are almost inevitably swept into a leapfrogging process to improve wages and benefits that ends by harming everybody. The consequence is that forty years after the end of World War II, unions have in the West lost a good deal of public sympathy and even encountered legislation restricting union shop practices and other old privileges.

But after these remarks on the place of labor organization, which at least recognise its importance after previous sections discussing private enterprise, this vast topic must be left aside for the detailed discussion it requires in the context of different countries.

7

If rights to the free exercise of human talents and exploitation of private property have been defended, what of their natural accompaniment of motivation by gain? ("Search for benefit or wealth" would accord better with Christian thinking.) The most obvious right involved is entitlement to the fruit of one's labor or a share in the benefits of enterprise, and extension of this to gain seeking is acknowledged as the mainspring of the private enterprise system. Those who organize economic activity of any kind do so in expectation of net returns. Those who hire out their physical and mental capacities also do this for reward and easily switch employers for more. On the other hand, such aims are criticized by protagonists for cooperative and communal organization, who declare service for others the best and only defensible motive and the search for mere gain abusive.

Yet motivation by gain or benefit, whether in enterprise or hiring out one's talents, is entirely defensible, even if its abuses can be pushed so far as to undermine the institution itself. Nobody can deny that such motivation is so close to human nature as to be considered a natural instinct[12] and that the energies released for economic advancement are enormous. In the latter twentieth century, the more socialist economies are heavily outclassed by private enterprise societies. (Compare North and South Korea or Taiwan and China.) It is difficult to imagine how many democratic societies with rising populations could maintain their standards of living without the energies unleashed by individual search for gain—all of which is not to deny some necessary circumscribing through morality and social regulation, since the beneficial side so easily degenerates into the greed that breeds social violence.

The most suspect area is the search for profit, where a good part of the trouble derives from faulty analysis. One (too) simple sense is the difference between sale proceeds and costs; the accountant refines both and for taxation purposes the result must again be modified to reflect the treatment of inventory, depreciation, et cetera, required by law; and the economist has his own concept insisting that all implicit as well as explicit costs be taken into account. But the latter approach raises its own problems: From the whole of what may be described as net return to property are marked off any rents or interest on property employed, determined usually as normal or average return and leaving profit (if any) as pure excess. When so defined, the moral problems do intensify as to whether enterprise may legitimately seek it and whether those who control property have exclusive rights to benefit from it. One may indeed argue that price should not be so set as to give rise to an excess profit, though its emergence due to unexpectedly large sales, weakness of competition, et cetera, does not call its legitimacy into question. However, after taking account of difficulties such as these, my principal point remains intact that motivation by gain and in particular the search for profit, understood as a normal return on capital, are legitimate institutions.

8

Turning to consumption, a further aspect of economic freedom is the right to choose what one pleases, so that consumer sovereignty determines what is produced and thus the allocation of resources. Such a view of the production process, flowing from consumer to producer, fits in well with individualism and its liberties, even if it is much exaggerated in the modern economy, where advertising is so important and consumers are subject to changing fads. According to one well-known thesis (Galbraith, 1967), much production is undertaken in advance of consumer wants and the latter are created by the media. Both views contain a measure of truth.

However, given that consumer sovereignty does exercise important determination over the allocation of resources and that this follows from basic freedoms, it should both be used responsibly and assisted. Ideally, informed consumers would choose goods and services that accord with morally upright living (even if many may be classed as neutral), forcing producers and advertisers to observe ethical criteria. Quite unrealistic, undoubtedly, but what better answer is there to pornography? Then government would support responsible choice, as it frequently does, by quality controls, prohibition of fraudulent advertising, and the like.

The alternative is state planning of production, at one extreme authoritarian and arbitrary and at the other presumptively responsive to consumer indications. Some older writings (e.g., Lange and Taylor, 1939) supposed that a socialist economy with the means of production state-owned and -directed could also respond to consumer sovereignty in the manner of private enterprise. History has shown that such views suffered from an excess of imagination. While the planned version may indeed try to improve quality, design, conception, et cetera, of goods, bureaucratic failures to respond effectively are only too clear in present "socialist" economies. In any event, the wholly planned economy, denying consumers effective powers of exercising their preferences, runs counter to basic rights and freedoms, a matter to which consumer frustration in communist countries testifies.

9

We reach an important conclusion: Clearly if all have the right to use their talents, own property and engage in enterprise and choose goods and services with the kind of freedom indicated, competition and the market will result as economic institutions. The consequence of economic freedoms, surprising to many and scandalous to others, is that the market process of determining prices and the allocation of resources will prevail, and competition is part of it. The implications are that changing supplies of and demands for goods, resources, and factors may adjust prices, causing inventory pressures and under (over) full employment and requiring possibly painful adjustments. Thus the basic position, even if law and virtue (notably justice) must regulate the freedoms in question and resultant institutions.[13]

Many Christian social thinkers and others criticise or reject the market as an institution and, somewhat more vaguely, the entire market economy. They focus on sellers' and buyers' taking advantage of one another's weaknesses, the deceits of commercialism, and the harm done by those seeking power. Despite all that may be said in favor of the market and the energies it engenders, they find its abuses overwhelming. By the ''market economy'' critics apparently include a good part of the central institutions and working of private enterprise—to some undefined degree the free use of property, the private enterprise system itself, motivation by gain, and competition in any extended sense of the term. In its place they propose some version of the socialist economy, meaning tight restrictions on private enterprise and an extensive degree of state intervention and control or at best a vast extension of cooperative enterprise. The contradictory side is that, if Christians, such critics must support basic freedoms to control property, utilize one's talents, and engage in enterprise, since their absence would be an affront to the dignity and liberty of the person.

Of course, in that always tortuous passage from principles to applications, circumstances may justify temporary suppression of market freedoms, but, supposing a normal situation and appropriate safeguards, the Christian social thinker who follows through on the implications of human rights has no choice but to support the market and competition as institutions having some appropriate place in the just economy. The case reposes not merely on personal freedoms but also on demonstrable achievements for the common good. The effects of competition on suppliers of goods, resources, labor, finance, et cetera, are clearly salutory. If some individuals and enterprises are hurt by fair competition, this has to be accepted as a necessary consequence for overall welfare. There are, incidentally, church statements that may be quoted in support of the market process.[14]

Obviously, competition must be restrained by law and morality. The first sets the regulatory framework, and the second includes the domain into which law cannot properly go. A notorious example is the difficulty of regulating antirestrictive practices successfully, since at some point the law is trying to define what "undue" competition may be, or maneuvers and devices "unduly harmful to the public interest." Courts have trouble with such definitions, and an improved social and business morality is an essential part of the solution. Also, as in the case of property owning and enterprise, the absence of ethical criteria in the operation of market institutions will only result in their destruction, through the loss of public acceptance.

10

Any statement of Christian economic principles must include an account of the place and role of government. After the general account of the state given in the preceding chapter (section 4), what remains to be dealt with is the different conception of government arising with respect to contemporary economic thought and some applied questions concerning its growth. Since chapter 9 takes up these matters, their discussion may be deferred.

One other set of rights close to consideration of the state, however, concerns the free movement of people, goods, and capital across national boundaries. Let me make at least a few comments to widen this discussion of economic principles to the supranational context. The nation-state is now about five hundred years old, and many newcomers have joined the older group as different peoples assert their sovereignty. But so-called nations, often grouping quite disparate races, cannot blind us to the fact that all compose an international society, a whole human race on planet earth, where part must assist part and resources are finally meant for all. There is ultimately no human power entitled to claim exclusive possession of land and resources when others are sufficiently in need. This does not open the door to unlimited movement of people, resources, or capital, since all societies do have the right to ensure their integrity and well-being, but it does imply that at some point there exist limitations to claims over territories and resources.

What reasons justify exclusive possession of a territory cannot be defined in any finally satisfactory way. Duration of control, long-standing conquest, proclamation of sovereignty backed by force, and divine promise are commonly advanced reasons that have their weaknesses. Finally,

70

for the Christian, God gave to the whole human race an earth that is divided up by human arrangements. Accordingly, since all human beings have basic rights to decent minima of life, at some point they may exercise a radical claim to share in the land, capital, and wealth of others. It follows that, in need, people do have the right to immigrate and there is no theory of the nation or country that can validly exclude them. There are many qualifications, of course: It must be a question of actual need (and not merely the desire to participate in a higher standard of living), the recipient society does retain the right to protect its welfare against too large numbers, and excessive entry of too disparate people may generate dangerous social problems. This said, it remains true that countries should extend some welcome to other peoples in need.

Foreign trade raises venerable disputes over the longer-term advantages of freer movement in goods and services over immediate benefits from duties, quotas, and a host of devices. Normally the debate is conducted in terms of national interest: Is domestic prosperity enhanced by moving toward free trade or by stopping short, with some degree of protection? Beyond this, it must be pointed out that all countries have the right to trade with one another, having their goods accepted and having access to foreign commodities. Why? Because the world is an international society, where each part has the right to earn its livelihood by selling what it produces to others, exactly as within a society. The general benefits are those of specialization and exchange, as obvious between countries as within a country. Of course, some sensible arguments exist for protection, temporary or permanent; it is the principle that interests me of the right of a country to benefit from trade and its duty not to shut itself off from others. How industrious, low-cost Asian exporters should be treated, the problems of the European Common Market, and the goals of international trade agencies are further applied questions.

Much the same reasoning applies to the movement of capital across national borders. The donor country should permit it, assuming its own welfare does not require prohibition, and the receiving country should be willing to accept the likely benefits for its own population. Planet earth thus helps its various peoples, and the cause of peace is strengthened. Our experience of the transnational corporation highlights the qualifications and abuses that arise in practice where a company, usually identified with one country but perhaps in another, sets up plants in less developed countries to exploit their resources while returning insufficient benefits to the local populace. Worse, its strength and multilocation are such that it slips through the control of any national government. If the placing of adequate controls on international movement of capital is intensely difficult in modern circumstances and exercises the best of minds and technical devices, since nothing is so nervous and ingeniously mobile as money, nevertheless the movement of capital across national boundaries is a right to be protected for its benefits to donor and receiver countries.

11

Thus far some basic rights related to the economic order have been outlined, where their exercise shapes institutions and creates obligations for society. As pointed out at the beginning of this chapter, the entire topic of fulfilling economic rights can also be approached from the angle of specifying the requirements of justice, since this consists in each member of society and the whole receiving their due. Hence this discussion may be continued by giving some examples of how the divisions of justice should be reflected in the institutions and operation of the economy. To begin, commutative or exchange justice (see chapter 3, section 8), requires that equivalents be rendered in explicit and implicit contracts, since each party has the right to receive what has been agreed. The giving of what is due constitutes justice in the action (as opposed to the active virtue in the doer). Voluntary contracts (cf. such ''involuntary'' exchanges as theft or personal defamation and the need for restitution) include transactions at all levels of production, exchange, and consumption and all sales of factor services. The applied problem for justice is how to determine equivalents as closely as possible, so that to get to the central issue let me comment on the famous question of just price. (The other most relevant application, just wage, is discussed in chapter 6.)

Price is a concept that is both simple and extremely complex. While some prices are set in bargaining or auctionlike situations, in the industrialized economy the vast majority are determined in a tortuous production and distributional process leading to the final buyer. Their formation summarizes the entire working of a given economy, identifying the economic system and its relative efficiency. Economic science naturally conducts an elaborate examination of price setting in production and marketing, so if we turn to the applied side of just price, we encounter exactly the same complex determination and discussion. It is now absurd to expect some simple formula of the sort used by the medievalists and later canonists—general consensus, need, labor cost, or public reguation (O'Brien, 1920, chapter 3)—to be a simple answer. In a few instances, ''general consensus'' may be an apt description, but this is hardly a useful summary for the vast majority of prices which issue from modern industry and commerce.

To clarify the question of just price, three sorts of approaches should be distinguished. What did medievalists mean by the concept, how may we link up their meaning with later economic theory, and how may we directly come at the reality of just price today? The third is my concern, but first a word on the others. Notably Aquinas declared (*Sum. Theol.*, II–IIae, Q. 77, I) that it is sinful to sell a good for a higher price (*pretium*) than its value (*valor*) or worth (*quantitas*), though potential loss *(damnum)* of the seller or benefit (*utilitas*) of the buyer may occasion legitimate difference. But what the medievalists may have understood by this worth is a question interesting historians of economic thought and it should be left to them. Next, relating the question to later price theory, some have concluded that conflict exists and others that determination of price in the theory of the firm reflects it accurately enough.[15] That is, the ideal set by the perfectly competitive firm would correspond closely with the prices of imperfectly competitive firms derogating more or less from it.

In elementary microeconomic theory, price is taken as determined by supply and demand in market situations and supply then analyzed as part of the theory of firm. In the extreme case of perfect competition (firms are small so that none can affect market price, and product is identical so that a buyer has no reason to prefer one seller to another), one may argue that the ideal conditions supposed will produce most efficient output at lowest cost and price and minimum profit. One may also link this case with the operation of Paretian criteria for a socially optimum economy (cf. chapter 9, section 2). But an immediate difficulty is that perfectly competitive firms do not exist in reality, so that just price become unknowable and unattainable in practical situations. It appears contrary to good sense to adopt a concept that is impossible of realization, leading us to abandon any attempt to know the excess demanded from us by unprincipled sellers. Then there are the general criticisms made of the theory of the firm (cf. Lipsey, Purvis, and Steiner, 1985, chapter 16): one has to suppose demand known (so as to equate the famous marginal cost and revenue), one supposes cost efficiency as given and profit maximization as the supreme goal, and operation over time is neglected. My conclusion is that it is much better to use the alternative cost-plus approach (where the firm adds a markup to cover return on capital, et cetera, as is widespread practice in industry, trade and finance) to determining price; it is not only better theory but accommodates the ethical problem of knowing just price much more easily.[16]

Setting aside this discussion and coming directly at just price in modern economies, one must adopt a more general approach extending beyond the too absorbing theory of the firm. We have to begin more broadly by saying that exchange of equivalents is the correct general principle, after which come the two stages of filling in intermediate criteria and determining prices in actual situations. In a few areas of the economy, prices are set auctionwise (say the stock exchange or cattle sales); in a great part of it, cost-plus pricing is usual; in other sectors prices reflect what is regarded as a fair income (professional fees, for example); in others government subsidies are important (many agricultural prices); and so on. In all this competition plays a large role, income distribution is a crucial consideration, the returns to labor as against property are disputed, state intervention is frequent, and sheer chance and good luck matter. Price determination reflects the entire working of the economy, so that the detail of determining just prices is as complex as that. What is required is that moral criteria must influence the workings of complex markets at every stage. Producers, suppliers and buyers must constantly admit and observe ethical criteria in their dealings, even if compromises will frequently resolve opposed convictions.

To put the matter another way, just price is the principle that stands inviolate in all exchanges and contracts, like the dignity of human labor or the duties of employer and employee to fulfill their obligations. Then intermediate criteria intervene, related to the pricing sector in question: Surgeons' fees will have reference to the existing social valuation of such services, or the pricing of public utilities will be affected by private sector standards of return on capital and the case for wide availability of the services in question, or furniture prices will be affected by the prevailing character of competition. Third, particular just prices must then be decided in all applied instances, as accurately and honestly as possible. The difficulty many analysts erect for themselves turns on the question of value: They regard actual prices as moving around some intrinsic value, so that the possibility of knowing just price reduces to knowing this value.[17] Such a concept of intrinsic worth involves not merely cost of production and subjective estimation, but also worth in the widest senses of welfare. These things matter, of course, but just price is simply actual price corrected for unethical accretions and exclusions. This is economic value, and what the latter may mean when further senses of welfare are introduced is another matter. There is a just price for heroin on the street, even if such transactions should not occur.

Now, if the prices established in many instances reflect judgment calls, disputes, and compromises, with effects that ramify backward and forward, the possibility of establishing sufficiently exact justice in the millions of prices involved at every stage of production and exchange is not at all futile. Exactly the same sorts of problems present themselves in other social relations. To say just price is unknowable is to say that justice in all our dealings with one another is unknowable, which is absurd, certainly from a Christian point of view, which continually stresses the need for individual responsibility and divine assessment of our actions. Somewhat of a parallel is offered by the working of the free economy or, say, the plant or animal worlds. It is incredible that free agents could somehow coordinate their actions for the production and distribution of millions of commodities or that the billions of related events necessary for the flourishing of plant and animal life occur, yet these things are accomplished. Similarly the morally directed actions of a vast number of agents can realize commutative justice in practice; this we have to believe, since, like all virtue, justice *is* realizable and knowable everywhere it is in question.

12

By "distributive justice" it is very tempting to understand a just distribution of income and wealth, but several difficulties stick out. The first is that justice in income distribution depends on exchange of equivalents in all wage contracts, plus fair taxation and return or at least availability of public goods (education, social security, et cetera), and effective institutions, so that commutative, distributive (in my sense), and social justices are all involved. The second drawback is that justice is primarily a virtue, so that if you interpret distributive justice as requiring all concerned to take specific action to ensure equitable distribution to everybody, an impossibly complex role for narrow justice is created. Hence it is better taken with the meaning already given (see chapter 3, section 8), so that just distribution is the outcome of the three narrow forms of justice as well as its widest sense (social charity and more enter). It is the *result* of pervasive moral behavior by the participants in the economic process.

Sticking with my preferred sense, at the stage of basic concept distributive justice requires a fair sharing out of community benefits and burdens among members. When a group of individuals form a communion properly speaking (cf. a labor union or a crowd at an airport), certain common goods and burdens arise, and justice calls for equivalence between what is due to or from each and what is received or levied. In the modern economy, public and merit goods (cf. chapter 9, section 9) and the means of financing them are chiefly in question, though many other "goodies" are shared out. Evidently, the obligation to practice such a concept of distributive justice falls primarily on those in authority in any community. For their part, citizens have the duty of complying with the presumptively just laws of government and contributing to the working of the institutions necessary in social justice for community welfare.

Coming to the stages of sharing out the burdens of government revenue and the benefits of public goods, there is the initial matter of their overall size, itself a reflection of what is taken to be the role of government in the economy. Government activities are conventionally analyzed as modifying the allocation of resources, altering distribution, and stabilizing the short-run path of the economy; later (in chapter 9, sections 7–8) we shall refer to the philosophical bases and choices governing them. For the present, those decisions must be taken as given and determining the overall level and purpose of taxation and public goods. There are, in addition, old discussions concerning the taxable capacity of a country (Stamp, 1922), newer criticisms of excessive welfare costs, and assertions that leaner government facilitates a more productive economy. Then recent developments in overall revenue and expenditure concern financing enormous national debts and military spending (in some countries). But, leaving aside these wider questions of size and role of government, let me move to my main concern.

If distributive justice regulates the sharing out of the burden of taxation and the benefits of public goods, what will be the basic shape of the distribution? What form of equality applies between what is due and what is received or levied? Must this be flatly equal or instead some form of proportionately equal share? Somewhat the victim of the mathematical mysticism of his day, Aristotle declared (*Nich. Ethics*, Book V) the proportionate equality in question to be geometric. Toning down the mathematics, Aquinas (*Sum. Theol.* II–IIae, Q. 61, 2) held one type of proportionate equality would be appropriate in an aristocracy, another in an oligarchy, and a third in a democracy (where he doubtless had the philosopher's concept in mind).[18] In modern mass democracy, where each person has an equal say in electing government and where accumulation of economic power subverts the system, it seems appropriate that taxation be levied in an approximately equal manner and that public goods be equally available to all (though not necessarily received equally—for example, a childless couple have no need for school services). Given this presumption, the Greek-medieval problem still remains concerning the nature of the equality.

Faced again by the question of moving from a general ethical concept to its applications, we may introduce certain well-known criteria in public finance, namely the ability to pay and benefit principles. Both imply equal burden or sacrifice, where the problem is to determine an equality rule. Taking income as the tax base, for instance, should the same or a proportional or progressively larger amount be taken as it rises? Economic analysis yields no solution (cf. Musgrave, 1959, pp. 98 seq.) so long as one adopts a strictly subjective view of utility, since the last dollars taken from a millionaire may hurt him more than the same amount taken from lower income receivers. So the ability to pay criterion has to ride rough-shod over such difficulties. Income dollars are roughly taken to reflect comparable utility to income receivers, and more of them steadily decline in their subjective worth. In consequence progressive tax rates achieve rough equality of burden, even if the exact degree of progression remain a complex and imprecise matter. Then the benefit principle (tax should be paid in proportion to benefit received) is of much reduced importance in modern society, given our emphasis on redistribution and welfare outlays.

Many intricate matters remain concerning equitable sharing out of the tax burden, such as direct versus indirect modes, influenced by the case for having all make some contribution to financing public outlays (to appreciate that welfare is not a free ride), and effects of taxation on savings, investment, and productivity. While it would take too much space to explore these questions, it is this analysis that pins down more closely the approximate equality of the tax burden. Government can only effect this in some imprecise manner, even ideally and leaving partisan-ship aside.[19] Such problems, as repeatedly said, do not make the reali-zation of justice a hopeless task, since they are simply the reality of how social principles pass into applications in the affairs of a free society.

As for the allocation of public and merit goods, and again starting from the position that there exists some fund to be distributed, a fair share for all involves partly an actual allocation of goods and services, as in the case of say police services, and partly their availability as required, say, unemployment benefits. Within this actual and potential distribution, efficiency criteria and such principles as proportional and progressive allocation of benefits to the needier have to be explored. Everybody is entitled to the same share in defense and protection of property, but welfare recipients will normally be entitled to different levels of benefit.

When one first studies the question of what may be just distribution, it is tempting to think of it as an objective, identifiable state of affairs corresponding to such criteria as one may have decided on, such as elimination of inequalities, discrimination, poverty, et cetera. Instead it is most usefully described as such a sharing out of income and wealth as reflects the operation of just principles of distribution, where my own version of them has been indicated sufficiently. It is not as though there is a single determined outcome, reflecting the equilibrium or maximization that is so often the term of reasoning in positive economics. An economic system may be constituted in many ways and evolves steadily, the functions exercised by government change, taxation and public spending alter in consequence, and countries rise and fall in relative prosperity. In consequence the attempt to pin down the exact modalities of just distribution is a here and now exercise, essential but transient. It is much more useful, as a long-term position that one can maintain, to understand by it the full reflection upon distribution of the operative virtue of justice in individual, community and governmental actions, ideal though this must remain.

13

As remarked in chapter 3, section 9, social justice may be taken as equivalent to the old concept of general justice, to mean the seeking of what is right in all one's social dealings. With some care it may also be equated with the medieval concept of legal justice, understanding by this not merely positive law but the wider fulfillment of the natural (moral) law. Used in this sense, social justice would be primarily reflected in the establishment of just laws, regulations, and order in all social domains, not merely governmental but including unions, enterprises, nonprofit organizations, clubs, et cetera. Its end result, therefore, is the setting up of just institutions and their proper operation, not that this implies identical structures in so many disparate societies. Taken next in a narrow sense, the obligations of social justice include the duties of all individuals and groups to *contribute* to the right structure and functioning of institutions so as to enhance the common good. The awkward point, if we make of contributive justice a third strict case (after distributive and commutative), is the need to designate a sufficiently exact equivalence between contribution and obligation. As said, it is now necessary to conceive of justice in this sense.

Narrowing our focus to the economic order, what appear to be the chief requirements of social justice? Curiously, there is an enormous amount that requires to be said but it is with great difficulty put into any simple classification of topics. The problem springs precisely from definition. Social justice, used in the widest sense to mean right order throughout the economy, becomes a catchall extending to its entire organization and operation. You could take any convenient classification of institutions (say production, distribution, exchange, consumption) or subclassifications (say primary, secondary, tertiary industry, and then subdivided) to discuss the implementation of social justice. Their formation and operation would be the primary focus, since institutions mold and convey the benefits and harm of human behaviour. Banks, consumer associations, social security arrangements, or whatever could be examined and the role discussed of legislators and all who participate in their design and functioning for the common good. If instead you take social justice in the narrow sense of the contribution required from all in the situations in which they find themselves, again you open up for consideration the entire economy, now from the side of individual obligations.

Take the working of a modern automobile factory. Commutative justice necessitates the payment of fair wages and benefits to all employees; distributive justice calls for some fair sharing out of common burdens and benefits, within the enterprise and organizations attached to it (unions, clubs, et cetera), such as administrative work loads, bonuses, privileges; and contributive justice requires all to assist in the successful working of committees, the solution of group problems, and the like. Going beyond justice, social virtues such as charity (i.e., love and benevolence), generosity, and even liberality, as far as those in control are concerned, are necessary to create the bonds of fellowship for which narrow justice is a necessary but not a sufficient cause. Then if all these social virtues actively flourish—among shareholders, controllers, management, administration, workers, union, and all concerned—social justice in the wide sense has come to fulfillment. The overall institution and its subinstitutions will be operated according to just law, regulation, and order. Idyllic and even incredible, but this is indeed the meaning of social justice understood as a Christian ideal.

Finally, many modern writers identify social justice with distributive,[20] meaning by this justice in distribution. But this makes no sense. Just distribution calls for a fair wage and benefits, followed by equitable taxation and return or availability of public goods, so that it requires the operation of commutative and distributive justice (in the sense I have given the latter), plus social justice to regulate the operation of institutions. A justly functioning economy surely needs criteria to govern institutions and the cooperation of individuals and groups from their side. But if ''social justice'' has already been appropriated for just distribution, to what shall recourse be had to judge the general working of institutions? Everybody who has a sense of wrong in not finding suitable work or is aggrieved by the way in which government or employers or other institutions treat him complains of social injustice, by which he does not at all mean wrongful distribution. The identification of social justice with just distribution is perhaps partly due to the overhang of individualism, inclining some to think justice is exclusively a matter of individual satisfaction, neglecting the social side of receiving and contributing.

* * *

The above account of economic principles flowing from Christian thought is obviously selective. My procedure has been to comment on a few fundamental institutions of the private enterprise economy and analyze the impact of justice, pointing to some of its ramifications. If between principles and applications there remains a world of intermediate criteria and applications to be explored, the foundations and the methodology of the crossover are my preoccupation. Further, that an apologia for private enterprise is not at all my aim should be evident from numerous qualifications made concerning the exercise of economic freedoms. Indeed, it is perfectly true that the institutions in question may be so badly constituted and operated that government may be obliged in the interests of the common good to curtail them through nationalization, controlled wages and salaries, a measure of overall planning, and the like. Yet however necessary their correction, Christian social thought normally issues in a case for economic freedom and private property along with such consequences as private enterprise, the market, and competition. The existence of minimally equitable distribution is usually the most important consideration justifying intervention, since it is so radical a requirement for individual and social welfare.

Chapter 5

ALTERNATIVE ROUTES

Thus far Part 2 has presented some centrally important social and economic principles relating to the economic "order"—those given only suggest the more complete account necessary—primarily using neo-scholastic or natural law thinking. Without question this must be backed by Scripture and the teaching church and does not stand as independent thought of some sort.[1] My reasons for preferring this approach, as said, are that it permits a more systematic outline of socioeconomic principles, crosses over more surely to applications, and leads on more easily to a critique of economic science.

Such an approach, however, is often not welcome to Protestant thinkers, mainstream and evangelical, and is toned down by some modern Catholic writers. Many of the former are accustomed to proceed directly from the Word of God, relying on the inspiration of grace, and have somewhat neglected (it is hard to generalize) the formation of the sort of systematic moral theology (cf. Preston, 1981, chapter 12) encouraged by the Catholic practice of confessing sin. Then, since about Vatican II many Catholic social thinkers have shown some preference for direct scriptural guidance and drawn on more diverse theological sources. Liberation theology is a prominent outgrowth. Hence there is advantage in my complementing the previous chapter with a discussion of deriving economic principles directly from Scripture and newer Catholic approaches, to exemplify what may be accomplished.

SCRIPTURE AS SOURCE

1

Disregarding scholarly problems of content and arrangements of what Christians call the Old Testament, the Jewish scriptural writings are arranged by *The Jerusalem Bible*[2] into five sections indicative of their content: the Pentateuch or five initial books of the Jewish people and their Law; the historical books, numbering fifteen; the seven books grouped together under the title of Wisdom; and the eighteen prophets. These books are a history of the Jewish people from the period of Abraham (about 2000 B.C.) down to the time of Christ and, the story of Rome excepted, the fullest account we have of the rise and decline of an ancient people. The Wisdom books and prophets summarize Jewish spirituality, and the Psalms celebrate it, while looking forward to the Messiah who will deliver Israel from its enemies and bring it to final mastery in virtue of God's promise.

If one reads the Bible with what would seem to its authors a strange purpose, some economics properly speaking can be found chiefly in the books of the Law setting out the Covenant between God and His people, along with much detailed regulation of Jewish life. It is not what we now call economic analysis, but it has great interest and importance as a reflection of a religious code passing directly to social and economic life without the barriers of specialization and compartmentalization that characterize present attitudes. Chapter 20 of the book of Exodus states the Ten Commandments and gives various economic regulations (relating to slaves, injuries, just transactions, et cetera). While mostly concerned with priestly life, chapter 25 of Leviticus deals with sales of property, loans, and prescriptions for estimating values. In Deuteronomy the commandments are repeated (chapter 11), followed by the deuteronomic code (chapters 12–30); social and religious prescriptions predominate, with what is economic present more by implicit than explicit reference. Then in Proverbs (e.g. chapter 6:11) and Ecclesiasticus (e.g., chapter 4) one encounters many sayings connected with riches, poverty, loans, and power; while Isaiah (chapter 61) and Zephaniah contain much-quoted passages on Yahweh's preference for the poor and oppressed.

What matters most respecting things economic in the Old Testament is a perspective of the upright life as essentially religious, with the service of God and fellowmen integral parts of it (cf. Psalm 112). Socioeconomic thought is inseparable from God-oriented thought and life; keeping the economic and religious in separate compartments is inconceivable. In this respect, as in many others, Christianity built on Jewish foundations. Of course, in the case of both Judaism and Christianity, distortions arose, such as the split between religion and ordinary life, outward conformity but inward corruption, and the use of religion to justify oppressive behavior toward others. I am pointing to the highest ideals of the Old Testament, even if there was a darker side to the life and aspirations of Israel in the context of the times.

2

Coming to the New Testament, clearly the teaching of Jesus is first and foremost religious and not a plan of social and economic reform. In our own day it has become frequent to refer to Christ as a social reformer, with some justification if one focuses on implications drawn from his words—for example, his attitude toward women, giving to God and to Caesar what is due each, the value of the individual in the eyes of God—but it is incorrect to use Jesus' teachings primarily for such purpose (though opinions differ). They are primarily a doctrine of redemption and salvation and of the coming of the Kingdom in the hearts of men and women. A certain indifference toward material things is insistent, with many commands given to avoid accumulation and assist those in need. What the New Testament has to say regarding economics is to be found not so much in specific statements by way of direction or prohibition, but rather in its general condemnation of materialism and self-indulgence and in its call to service, obedience to the Will of God, and care for the needs of one's fellowmen, who are brothers and sisters and equally children of God.

What specifically can one find in the way of an economic message in the Gospel stories? There is little explicit reference in John, who wrote a deep meditation on the significance of the coming of Christ (there are even no strictures on the rich), so that we may confine attention to the synoptics. Well-known directives are: Man does not live by bread alone, renounce the world, obey the commandments, be generous in lending and giving, forgive evil, you cannot serve God and mammon, do not fret over the needs of this life, avoid covetousness and laying up of riches,

85

and give alms. If there is a passage with at least some sustained economic reference, the Sermon on the Mount (Matthew 5) points to a set of values that differ fundamentally from the thrust of economic liberalism. The Beatitudes seek to replace materialism by spiritual values and call for a very different perspective on human life from that posed by continual economic progress and enrichment.

The Acts of the Apostles contains several vignettes of early communities practicing the sort of communism later characteristic of religious orders (Acts 4: 32). The letters of Saint Paul give important injunctions for economic behavior: government officials are God's officers (!), pay taxes and avoid debt (Romans 13); the worker deserves his pay (1 Timothy 5: 18); let slaves be obedient, let all work hard for God's sake, and all are equal before God (Ephesians 6); let idlers not eat if they will not work (2 Thessalonians 3: 10); and the love of money is the root of all evil (1 Timothy 6: 10). Plainly, certain of Saint Paul's directions relate to the context of his times (acceptance of the condition of slavery, for instance, repeated in 1 Peter 2; and notoriously the status of women, 1 Corinthians 11: 1–16).

<h1 style="text-align:center">3</h1>

To summarize at the most general level, one obtains three things from the Bible bearing on economic life and thought: (a) An overarching Judeo-Christian explanation of the nature and purpose of life: God created the world, man chooses to serve God and goodness or to seek himself and destruction, work is imposed on mankind, and God saves His people through time (where Jews and Christians differ on the modalities of this)—in fact, He has entered into a covenant. (b) Numerous injunctions for economic behavior, individual and social, within the context of righteous, God-fearing living. (c) Some prescriptions bearing directly on economic institutions particularly drawn from the outline of the Jewish Law in Leviticus and Deuteronomy and relating immediately to the primitive economy of Israel. For instance, one may derive implications for the legitimacy and desirability of private property (Numbers 27: 5-11; Leviticus 25: 23–34), the specification of some economic rights to fair wages and prices (Luke 10:7; Ecclesiasticus 27: 1–3), the social benefits of property (Acts 4: 34–53), and even a measure of redistribution (Deuteronomy 24: 19–21), but not so far as to impose equality (Ecclesiasticus 33: 10–13).

Clearly faithful performance of the life-style urged by biblical injunctions would mold the established patterns of activity we call economic institutions. It does not follow, as emphasized (introductory remarks to chapter 4), that similar economic systems will arise in Christian societies, since the history and evolution of peoples plus the deviance of sin play their part; but a similar code and spirit will inform them beyond the differences of time and place. Then, given the idealistic nature—uncompromising and extreme ("Be perfect as your heavenly Father is perfect," Matthew 5: 48)—of Christian ideals, alongside the corruption of social institutions that readily sets in, a constant aspect of scriptural injunctions is judgment and recommendations for reform of actual economies. These will be in general terms, so that the role of intermediate criteria or middle axioms enters, plus the guidance of economic science.

4

To move to a sensitive area, after acknowledging the importance of Scripture for all Christian socioeconomic thought, two difficulties arise from direct reliance on it (as insufficiently supported by theological reasoning and church teachings), namely, differences in interpretation and the crossover to applications. As for the first, clearly differences may arise concerning interpretations of Scripture to suggest desirable economic institutions. Authors such as Griffiths (1982), Vickers (1982), North (1973, chapter 18), and Pemberton and Finn (1985) instance how biblical references can be used to derive such principles, whether institutional or operational (notably, individual ownership of property and need to share its benefits; necessity and key role of work; care for the poor and oppressed; fair prices and wages; harm of excessive riches and power). A surprising, or perhaps not so surprising, similiarity is found along with divergences. Yet in addition to such a list, one may be embarrassed by another that could be compiled—acceptance of slavery (Leviticus 25: 44–46; Deuteronomy 15: 12–17), subordinate status of women throughout the Old Testament, provisions of the Jubilee year ending all debts (Leviticus 25), framing of economic measures for the benefit of Israelites (Deuteronomy 20: 10–20), the economic power of the priesthood (Leviticus 27), and no food for those who will not work (2 Thessalonians 3: 10). Of course, the latter may all be given a satisfying interpretation; but critics may not unreasonably say that the authors in question have further criteria governing their preferred selection, where church tradition and the present evolution of societies suggest themselves.

My conclusion, which respects the different convictions of others, is that excessive or overly literal reliance on Scripture for socioeconomic principles contains its hazards.[3] It is true that such writers do display a great deal of surefootedness in discerning economic guidelines, since prayerful aid is a normal action of the Spirit. One may hear quite remarkable expositions of the Beatitudes (Matthew 5: 1–10) as injunctions for economic life, stressing condemnation of riches and power and an option for the poor and oppressed. Yet one does better to stick with the sort of ordered intellectual approach exemplified by the natural law or neo-scholastic tradition, itself growing out of a theology inspired by Scripture and shaped by the teaching church, while linked with natural ethics and underpinned by philosophical discipline. It is in essence a middle way between too personal an inspiration from Scripture and too intellectual an approach. Further, many overtly proceeding from biblical sources (for instance, the *Pastoral Letter* on the U.S. economy discussed in section 9) are in fact relying a good deal on church teaching and a reasoned consideration of the themes they perceive need developing.

5

The second acknowledged difficulty (cf. Preston, 1981, chapter 5) of proceeding directly from the Bible to the modern economy is the crossover from moral injunctions for conduct to the complex institutions that actually shape so much of what we do. Let me give some examples of how the natural law approach, complemented by Scripture, proves to be more efficient. From the Bible we obtain directions concerning the need to pay and receive a fair wage: The laborer is worthy of his hire (as above), and this is complemented by many exhortations to justice in all dealings (Leviticus 19: 11; Isaiah 56: 1) and by praise for work (Ecclesiastes 3: 22). But in the modern economy a just wage would involve consideration of, at least, precise amount, fringe benefits, social estimation of occupation, responsibility and seniority, job security, efficiency of work, absence of discrimination, family wage, condition of business, work conditions, and role of union-management negotiations (cf. chapter 6, sections 1–5). Then, since just wage is a factor price, a good deal of the general state and working of the economy must be taken into account, including adjustments for inflation, impact of taxation, and distribution

88

of public goods. It is, in consequence, a good deal more practical to confront such questions within a systematic framework of socioeconomic principles than to advance simply with Scriptural injunctions to the intricate detail of the modern economy.

Or, as regards care for the poor and oppressed, many biblical passages affirm the case for social use of property, the duty of the well off to assist them, and the regard the ruler should have for their welfare (Jeremiah 22: 15–16 and 23: 5–6). But in modern society we have to consider the role of unemployment insurance, welfare systems, pensions, marital support, many forms of discrimination, and special provisions in various legislation having reference to the poor. Again there is a large middle area requiring a systematic traverse. As a third example, there is the much debated role of government in the mixed economy: there is little to be quoted from Scripture beyond the most general concepts of the ruler helping provide for and oversee the welfare of the community. How this is to be translated into the role of the state in influencing the allocation of resources, redistributing income and wealth, and stabilizing prices, employment, foreign exchange, et cetera, places extraordinary demands on directives concerned primarily with individual behavior. They remain a foundational part of a Christian solution, but we also need a well-elaborated approach to the setup and working of private and public institutions.

Thus my case for preferring a primarily reasoned approach to the principles necessary to mold and reform economic institutions, underpinned by Scripture and the teaching church. Biblical citations arouse conscience, but what we must then do in the economy requires information and analysis.

RECENT CATHOLIC APPROACHES

6

However fundamental the statement of economic principles given in chapter 4, it may well strike the reader as somehow out of touch with a world of rapid change, media headlines, and television opinion swapping—which is the first reason to convert an account of rights, institutions, and justice into something more attention-grabbing. There is a better reason: Millions of people today suffer from hunger, disease, and severe deprivation as the broad result of the population explosion, rapid development, migration to cities, extreme inequalities of property owning, and general economic inefficiencies. Consequently Christian economic thought has faced the need to bring its thinking and statements to bear urgently and relevantly on the extraordinary scale and intensity of hardship in so many countries.

For about one hundred years (from roughly 1860, beginning with von Ketteler's work, until 1960 or the pre–Vatican II period), Catholic apologists generally had recourse to neo-scholastic thought, with its medieval origins, and centered on Aquinas. The many forays of Maritain (see Bibliography) into social and political questions are typical of this style. But discontent with medieval-based philosophy grew in the post–World War II period, given its constant reference to a far-off era, its isolation from contemporary philosophy, and its constraining definitions and categories. Scholastic thought is a vast edifice where part interlocks with part and complex modifications have been made over the centuries. Hence Christian social thinkers turned increasingly to recent and contemporary philosophy. A further source arose even abruptly around 1970, drawing on Latin American experience, Marxist currents, and also (if questionably at times) papal and episcopal documents. Thus in may episcopal texts, some Vatican documents[4] and much nonofficial writing one encounters such transformed statements of principles, both basic and reaching out to applications, as preferential option for the poor, priority of labor over capital, rights of native peoples, ecological balance, need for forms of planning, the case for "socialization," self-reliant and humanizing development, different forms of solidarity, et cetera. These have been accompanied by pressing statements of concern for the plight of modern man, generous recognition of the advances and contributions to welfare of modern science, expression of readiness to do whatever the church can to alleviate suffering, and increased appeal to Scripture and to considerations of general humanity.

Prevalent themes are that many Western economies are now so organized as to favor the powerful few and to exploit the poor and marginalized. Freedoms are abused by those in effective command and do not really exist for the masses, and in underdeveloped countries military force is frequently used to shore up corrupt regimes.[5] Meanwhile, communist and Marxist countries, despite their faults, have the welfare of all as their first premise and do in many instances implement minimum standards. Hence loud criticism has been voiced by some Christians of

90

private enterprise, capitalism, the market system, transnational corporations, and the like. This is often accompanied by statements that the quest for social justice is now a full part of the church's mission in the modern world and that every committed Christian must play his role, whether by active participation, prayer, monetary contribution, or mere solidarity of heart and mind. The importance of prophetic statements and discerning the signs of the times is stressed. The older style of Catholic social thought was more concerned with harmonizing existing society and bringing peace to structures founded on private property and enterprise, workers grouped in their unions, stable family life, and benevolent government. Instead, social thought should be dynamic, and evolution through conflict is the route to altered institutions and structures, which will continually evolve (cf. Baum, 1982, 1984).

7

While many of these newer themes deserve closer examination, let me at least address the widely invoked "preferential option for the poor." Not unsurprisingly, a special concern for the poor and suffering emerged in many official and nonofficial statements of Catholic thought from its nineteenth-century origins, given frequent expression of this in the Old and New Testaments (e.g., Isaiah 49: 13; Zephaniah 3: 19; Matthew 25: 31–46). But something different appeared about 1970, due doubtless to the extraordinary contrasts of material well-being of which we are now so conscious. Initially the church began to speak of the need to identify with the poor of less developed countries (*Mater et Magistra*, paragraphs 68, 157–159) and to reexamine its privileged status in some of them. Vatican II gave further attention to this, and some (limited) emphasis appears in *Gaudium et Spes* (part 2, chapter 3). Much more followed in *Populorum Progressio* (See note 4). But it was in Latin American countries, to their credit, that concern for the poor became intense, receiving striking expression in the Medellin documents.[6] "Solidarity with the poor" and "option for the poor" were commonly heard phrases, so that the church and the Christian conscience of many became preoccupied with their implications. The concept of "conscientization" (my version of *conscientizacion*)—the awakening and stirring of conscience for their plight—was adopted from Latin American thinking.

Analysis of this preferential option for the poor proves no easy matter. The Medellin statement distinguishes three sorts of poverty: material, spiritual (meaning detachment from material things and total dependence on God), and voluntary commitment to material poverty, so as to identify with the masses of the poor and seek spiritual liberty.[7] But leaving the deep questions thus raised and taking simply the consequent need to improve the material lot of the poor, is it an addition to the traditional statement of socioeconomic principles, or is it only a singling out in a new guise? Is it truly filling a gap, or is it a variation of an old theme? Clearly, from the outline of economic rights given in chapter 4 and the discussion of distributive and social justices (chapter 4, sections 12–13), we have a statement of principles covering much that would follow from an option for the poor. In the economic order, all are entitled to the material requirements of physical and mental health, and society has the duty of ensuring them through the operation and management of the economy. Further, the older approach is superior, in that it leads on surely to further elaboration and links up with a well-developed body of thought (open to stimulation and evolution, of course). One cannot help noticing that the "preferential option for the poor," which occurs as a striking phrase in so many episcopal statements and individual writings, is typically left hanging and followed by no obvious development, apart from emphasis on the need for radical reforms and perhaps resorting to the planned economy.[8]

Yet even if this option for the poor could be contained within older statements, it is the sort of anguished and timely rephrasing we need to jog consciences, in the way television clips of starving people go miles beyond the prose of reports. It does forcefully remind us of the demand of social justice and charity (I retain this noble word) to improve the welfare of the marginalized. Further, improving the material lot of the poor is an authentic inspiration from the Old and New Testaments;[9] clearly we have something additional to what natural socioeconomic principles have to say. The *preferential* side of aiding the poor goes beyond what we may discern by natural reason and reflects prophetic utterance in the Old Testament and later revelation by Jesus. This said, the welfare of all, and not just the poor, is God's plan (cf. Vatican *Instruction on Christian Freedom and Liberation*, 1986, paragraph 68). Also, ill-judged attempts to help the poor in preferential ways can in fact lead to considerble harm; and our painful history, even in advanced countries, tells us that the large numbers of poor and marginalized will always reemerge. (As usual, Jesus was right; [Matthew 26:11].)

There is also a theological question whether the kind of social doctrine represented by option for the poor should be at the centre of the Christian message of evangelization and salvation. Should social reform be the *central* Christian message or instead an accompaniment of it? My conviction is that principles of socioeconomic life can never be the central message of Christianity, but that option for the poor appears an essential addition to it at this stage of history. The central Gospel message (some dissenters apart) remains repentance, redemption, and salvation first and foremost from the dominion of evil, with salvation from material calamity in second place (cf. Luke 12: 4–6). Nevertheless, love for others is an indispensable accompaniment to the love of God; and given misery in so many parts of the present world, where the word of God is inhibited from coming to fruition, relief from abject poverty is a necessary accompaniment to the properly spiritual message. At this stage of evolution of the world and the church, it has become correct to make social teaching a part, subordinate but essential nonetheless, of the main message of redemption and salvation. So many millions live in subhuman conditions that it cannot for many reasons proclaim a merely spiritual message without alluding to their radical material needs.

A last remark on a large topic is that option for the poor is a good illustration of how a Christian approach can go far beyond the merely humanistic. A caring society may indeed take many steps to assist the marginalized: there may be resolute efforts to help the poor escape from the poverty trap (caused by reduction of aid as income rises); there may be a vast educational and structural undertaking to help the marginalized take some charge of their own affairs, to improve their self-image and assert personal dignity. But state agencies are unable to furnish the love and esteem for the person essential to give the marginalized a sense of true personal dignity. Monsieur Vincent, the French apostle of the poor, was accustomed to say, "What matters more than the bread you give the poor is the love with which you give it." For they need to experience that love that is the life of God, and the suffering Christ seen in them by his followers is the way.

8

Liberation theology has become a prominent area in Catholic social thought since about the mid-1960s. More correctly, one should speak of "theologies," since protagonists differ somewhat in their analysis and presentation.[10] All Christian theology has its liberating aspect: Jesus frees his followers from the dominion of sin and holds out that perfect freedom that lies in accepting the Will of the Father. Whether spiritual, psychic, bodily, or material oppression be in question, in Christ one finds the means to rise above it. People can be reconciled and problems dissolved. But liberation theology can be taken beyond this to become an ideology, harnessing the spiritual to the service of the material and proposing marxist-style thought and action. It revives the same sort of temptations affecting the American social gospel movement (White and Hopkins, 1976) of an earlier time.

One protagonist defines theology as a "critical reflection on historical praxis" and faith as "liberation praxis."[11] The present economic environment—its institutions, laws, customary operation—thus appears as an evolutionary process dictating the nature and practical outcome of our response to religion. Perceived injustices point to their just correction, and this perception shapes theological reflection, producing even a new "hermeneutic" (interpretation) of Christianity today. A fundamental theme is that theology issues in a doctrine of social reform. Just as Moses of old followed God to lead his people from the land of enslavement, so with Jesus as their leader Christians today must lead their brothers and sisters to the promised land of material as well as spiritual welfare. Some liberationists even speculate on new "theologies" of necessary violence and revolution.

Hence liberation theology risks becoming an ideology or a set of ideas reaching toward a particular economic and political system (in effect introducing a false god in place of the Eternal One of the Judeo-Christian heritage). Marxist themes of alienation, class war, the necessity of violent conflict, and socialist transformation are readily adopted, leading to the planned economy and authoritarian state. Worse, some link Christian belief, action, and the very nature of redemption to this quest for social and economic reform, so that the whole is, so to speak, baptized and sanctified. Quite apart from this subversion of Christianity, an obvious danger taught by enough history is that recourse to authoritarian solutions will be destructive of Christianity itself. Marxists may use Christian dissent but will turn to eliminate religion once in power. Not unsurprisingly, a Vatican "instruction" duly appeared to condemn Marxist elements in the theology of liberation, especially the notion of praxis leading to valid theological truth, and to reaffirm a more traditional Christian approach to poverty and its material correction.[12]

94

Yet any discussion of liberation theology should not omit recognition of its positive side. Quite apart from its intrinsic interest and possibly fruitful addition to theology (where opinions differ), associated with it in a practical way has been a large popular movement of grass roots communities, prayer groups, and a revivified Christianity in many areas of Latin America. Also, it has given world-wide publicity to the conditions in which millions live, jolting the consciences of Christians and all persons of goodwill, presenting Christianity in a much more concerned and caring aspect than its frequent former acceptance of the status quo did. The dangers of mingling the spiritual and material messages remain, however, and Latin American Catholics have been divided into conservative reformers and liberal activists who debate needed reforms in distribution and possession of economic power.

But setting aside the controversy associated with liberation theology, what has it held out that is substantially different in relation to the sketch of social and economic rights contained in chapters 3 and 4? Is it merely repeating these same ideas setting out from an apparently different (and perhaps dubious) approach, or is it holding out new principles and intermediate criteria? In one sense we have nothing different: If the newer style of principles is emphasized—option for the poor, solidarity, priority of labor over capital, et cetera—at bottom it is still a question of the fundamental economic rights of all, fair wages, correction of excessive maldistribution, plus a controversial interpretation of the dividing line between the private and social aspects of property and of the role of government in redistributing control over the means of production. Yet there is also something distinct: Gigantic injustices have called forth a different version of traditional principles and recipe for their application than in more democratic societies having already a long history of economic and social reform, which will perhaps prove explosive.

9

Given extreme maldistribution, high unemployment, and even subhuman living conditions in many countries, not unsurprisingly, a number of statements have appeared from church groups in recent years to demonstrate their concern and propose Christian solutions. The procedure followed in the most impressive and best formulated of these, the *Pastoral Letter* on the U.S. economy,[13] is worth some attention. The statement is conceived along a classic approach: Identify leading problems, recall

Christian teaching and its norms for social life; derive judgments and recommendations by drawing together norms, specialized knowledge, and advice of those engaged; and conclude with an exhortation to all persons of goodwill. Evidently such a document is dominated by immediate concerns, and naturally the *Pastoral* is colored by wide reference to the ideals, institutions, and experience of the American people.

What are the outstanding problems of the U.S. economy today? Unemployment, poverty, job insecurity, farming distress, materialism, meaningfulness of work, and domestic link-ups with world poverty—these engage the Christian conscience (rather than the federal deficit, actual and potential inflation, interest and exchange rates, and explanatory theories, which preoccupy economists). The "Christian vision of economic life" (chapter 2) yields criteria for judgment and action: Men and women are made in the image of God, deriving therefrom their personal dignity and rights. The Old and New Testaments are cited to show how God wants His people to live, the preferential option for the poor being a particularly important message. This lengthy appeal to Scripture is complemented by a "long tradition of theological and philosophical reflection," which is in fact heavily relied on in approaching the modern economy (even if, wisely no doubt, in a document seeking general appeal, there is no reference to the natural law and neo-scholasticism).

This Christian vocation suggests ethical norms for economic life: Social living is built on love for and solidarity with all; commutative, distributive, and social justices offer basic criteria; and the marginalized and powerless are entitled to minimal benefit and participation in economic life. All this can be restated as an elaboration of human rights, where those of the poor and vulnerable are of the highest priority. Labor unions, owners and managers, governments, and other groups and institutions must cooperate in mutual respect to seek a common good requiring due shares, rights, and participation for all in the life of the nation. What an economy does for and to people, and how they participate are the criteria of a truly human and Christian perspective.

The second section of the *Pastoral* (chapter 3) deals with selected policy issues. The church is not wedded to any economic system or program, and four topics are singled out relating moral values and economic issues (if final recommendations and decisions must be left to lawmakers, economists, and other specialists): (1) Full employment is the foundation of a just economy, and after reviewing familiar problems, the bishops plunge resolutely into recommendations, notably a call for cooperation along public and private sector groups to overcome unemployment. (2) Poverty, affecting notably minorities (including blacks), single parents, and children, is a scandal in so wealthy a country. There is a presumption in justice in favour of minimum levels of well-being and against extreme inequalities of income and wealth. One key point is that the poor should participate in programs designed to assist them, setting aside paternalism. (3) The agricultural crisis mainly concerns moderate-sized farms lying between agribusiness and part-time operations, and the *Pastoral* speaks out for the maintenance of adequate income. The remaining concern (4) is the U.S. and the world economy: The former is not showing the leadership and contributions its stature warrants in the North-South dialogue, trade problems, and reducing expenditure on armaments.

10

Probably the central issue aroused by the *Pastoral* is whether the ills perceived in the U.S. economy should be cured by advancing toward more central control and direction or instead by placing more reliance on individual initiatives and freedom.[14] The first way makes for more regulation, civil servants, outlays, and taxes, along with forms of planning, the second instead to less control and government and financial intervention. The prudential side obscures matters. One set of protagonists see a need for central policies and coordination: the poor and unemployed are there in their millions, and existing aids are grossly inadequate. The other responds that controls feed on themselves, inefficiencies and abuses grow, and the marginalized are not in fact helped. But it is significant that the *Pastoral* does not call simply for government to correct unemployment problems, but also addresses the private sector and labor unions, urging local, regional and national initiatives to find job-creating strategies. Also it emphasizes that responsibility for relieving the poor falls on all, and the marginalized should participate in planning relief programs. The appeal made for a "new American experiment: partnership for the public good" (chapter 4) is in some respects the most striking novelty in the document. Cooperation within and between firms and regions, partnership in development of national policies and common action at the international level—all this reflects the communitylike character of Christian social thought, in opposition to the "rational," self-interested calculation of individualism.

97

To address planning more generally, its advocacy to solve the problems of unemployment along with other welfare concerns is increasingly encountered in modern Catholic social thought, official sources no less than, say, liberation theology. John Paul II's *Laborem Exercens* (1981, paragraph 18) speaks of "rational overall planning" as the mode of solution to present unemployment problems. A similar recommendation was made in *Populorum Progressio* (Paul VI, 1967, paragraph 33): ". . . individual initiatives alone and the mere free play of competition could never assure successful development. . . . It pertains to the public authorities to choose, even to lay down the objectives to be pursued, the ends to be achieved, and the means for attaining these. . . ."

Several qualifications should be put in place respecting advocacy of state planning by church leaders: The role of subsidiary bodies has always been stressed; there are many forms of overall planning, ranging from corrections of private enterprise, to provision for minimum welfare for all, to French *dirigisme,* and on to the wholly planned economy of the Soviet sort; fruitful state planning in a free society supposes a measure or cooperation that enterprises and unions usually are not prepared to give; and governments mix political and military objectives with their economic aims. Further, whatever the form of planning advocated, this is really an intermediate recommendation lying between the overall responsibility of government for the common good and the practical question of how to go about achieving it. Still, Catholic social reformers have often shown a mistaken predilection for governmental direction as the central element in planning, whereas governments and their departments consist of fallible people of little experience and capacity in enterprise and risk taking, who readily cover up their mistakes with financial and legal power.

Hence John Paul II's call for planning to solve full employment problems should be interpreted in something other than the sense of controlling, bureaucratic planning, and certainly "one-sided centralisation" is rejected in paragraph 18 of *Laborem Exercens.* The style of this pope's encyclicals frequently requires one to take the general sense of what he is saying, rather than literal interpretations, as in the case of the more precisely composed statements of previous pontiffs. Similarly, the type of planning suggested in the U.S. *Pastoral* is best interpreted as a "rational coordination," calling for as much local and regional initiative as possible. Orthodox economics has heard many similar appeals (e.g., Musgrave, 1977).

11

For my purpose the most interesting question raised by the growing number of church statements (Catholic and Protestant) on ethico-economic questions, where the *Pastoral* summarized above is the most striking example, is the methodology they exhibit in attempting to cross over from principles to applications. If we might visualize this as a space taken up by increasing specification, the role of the church at the most general level—say the Vatican, a national church, the World Council of Churches—is presumably to issue declarations at a high level of generality. Then the local church will interpret them for specific situations, which it knows and can qualify appropriately.[15] A nice question remains, however, as to whether the church as such should attempt detail at any level, since it then enters the prudential domain of ad hoc judgments and recommendations and will inevitably become embroiled in controversy. Many assert that it is better listened to and more effective when it sticks to proclaiming principles for political and economic life, avoiding the specifics of policy. Yet others insist that church leaders must dirty their hands with detail if they do not wish to remain uninvolved.

A crucial issue is the collaboration necessary between economic science and the increasingly detailed recommendations derived from socioeconomic principles. As the latter reach more closely toward applications, what kind of validity can they have without the support of economic analysis? Can socioeconomic thought compel us to accept that the solution of poverty and unemployment calls for a "rational coordination," a muted form of central planning, in apparent neglect of what economic science and experience may have to say on planning? May socioeconomic thought hold that firms and even sections of industry are "best" run by all immediately concerned, implying heavy worker participation, in defiance of what economists may urge respecting efficiency and national and international competition?

Practical people may simply conclude that they meet in a gray area where politicians and committees thrive, but the academic issue is the degree to which an autonomous economic science may intervene to correct social ethics.[16] May the latter reach out only so far, and must it then appeal to economics to analyze its recommendations, controlling options? While we will return to the "autonomy" of economic science later (chapter 7, section 6; chapter 8, section 7), my position is that it is finally the servant of ethics and advisor for its applications. Admittedly practical judgments may force one socioeconomic principle to be suspended in favor of another (say, justifying nationalization of enterprise for the common good), but it would be strange if ethical recommendations for economic life were systematically declared so impractical that analysis of the "facts" must dominate the thrust of moral principles.

There are subtler objections to applications of Christian economic principles (Waterman, 1985). Since economic science regularly cooperates in arriving at policy recommendations, and if these can be derived from non-Christian principles, are there properly identifiable Christian applications (i.e., secondary norms and measures)? Some brief replies are: (i) Certain ethical principles are already broad policies (e.g., the right to work and the common use or stewardship aspect of property imply policies of full employment and redistribution). (ii) But Christian recommendations respecting the economy normally become contingent as they reach toward secondary norms and detailed measures (is full employment compatible with 4 or 7 percent unemployment in this country and these circumstances?), so that the latter are guideposts and constraints, rather than fixed. (iii) Must general principles and following criteria be derivable from only Christian premises to be identified as consequent (humanists, for instance, may assert a right to work and social obligations to provide it)? Here the effort at taxonomy becomes trivial, since principles and norms prominently associated with any philosophy may often be derivable from another (may Christians alone admit to an obligation to love their neighbor?). What is ultimately Christian in norms and reflected action, if it comes down to this, turns on the internals of informing Spirit and grace that confer their authenticating character,[17] rather than externals.

Beyond distinctions and classifications, what matters is the obligation that may devolve on believers to heed injunctions of their leaders. When, say, bishops urge secondary norms, even applied measures, to improve redistribution of incomes and property, must their flock be obedient, or may they escape through appeal to different practical judgments, expert or not? In this hazy area, it seems one must conclude to some general obligation to take serious notice of judgments on factual situations, less so recommendations for reform, of spiritual leaders for whose guidance the community prays continually (and whose opinions are, we hope, assisted by wise advice and expert analysis). While social obligations to act are much less certain than individual responses to conscience, presumably at some point injustice is so blatant as to require some sinking of differences on the path to correction.

Chapter 6

WAGES AND INFLATION

Socio-ethical principles and economic theory[1] are usually two ships that pass in the night, each conscious of the other but separate worlds. Lengthy interdisciplinary work is essential to bring about an effective meeting, since one needs to become steeped in the thought habits proper to each. However, not to attempt to bring the economics and ethics closely to bear on one another is a gross omission, so that the purpose of this chapter is to illustrate how Christian thought can modify what conventional economic analysis has to say, taking wages and inflation as examples. From a wealth of topics one central institution and one vital policy question have been chosen, which may be discussed in a sufficient if limited way.

JUST WAGE

Wages are only part of the wider topic of income distribution, where payment flows reflect reward for work (wages, salaries, commissions, et cetera) or returns from property (rent, interest, profits), though there are also prizes, gifts, and other nonearned income. Income received represents, in the first instance, the fruit of work and property utilization, which is then modified by taxation (notably income, sales, and excise taxes) and the return of public goods (such as "free" education, medical care, and social assistance). Over time, this modified flow of income, which we spend, save, or donate, along with what we inherit or acquire by gift, chance, or even illegally, builds up personal wealth. In what follows we are concerned only with the immediate question of fair wages, the "functional" payment to labor as a factor of production, not the wider matter of equitable income distribution.

If my aim is to marry the economics and ethics of wage determi-

101

nation, let me stress tirelessly that there is no "Christian theory" specifying the just amounts of wages, interest, and other income. Instead, ethical principles grounded in religious belief link up with intermediate criteria applying to the economic institutions in question and their working. It is then up to individuals to translate such guides into applications, taking account of available data and technical analysis, and seeking the compromises between ideals and reality typical of this imperfect world. The liberty, conscience, and responsibility of all must be respected ordinarily, along with the diverging views they give rise to.

1

The theory of wages found in economic texts is part of the marginal productivity theory of income distribution. This assumes each factor makes an identifiable contribution to some productive process; and the relation between this and supply cost of the factor or its desired reward determines the quantity hired and actual price. What is fundamentally a market theory of wage determination is easily conveyed in a simple diagram: If we suppose that units of factor A are hired one by one, while all other factors are given, the amount of product each factor gives rise to may at first rise, but will eventually decline step by step. (Intuition and some experience are the basis of the assertion.) For example, if we suppose a given factory set up to produce, with machinery, materials, management, et cetera, in place, the hiring of workers one by one will eventually result in diminishing returns per worker. The latter times the price at which the additional product is sold yields the declining marginal revenue product curve (ab), which is in effect the demand curve for labor.

On the other side, labor is presumed to supply itself at a price that induces work: it may be unchanging or it may rise steadily (cd), reflecting the need to attract labor from other occupations or induce longer hours. The meeting of demand and supply at E produces wages OP_o and quantity OQ_o. Many refinements can be added: The wage must bear income tax, the cost of various benefits may be split between employer and employee (modifying the demand and supply sides), workers may engage in "job search" costs before accepting employment, et cetera. The most important is the role of unions, which control the offer price of employees.

While there is a good deal more to be said about this theory of wages, this is the essence found in texts. The microanalysis makes it the centerpiece of its discussion of distribution, and the macro treatment (of

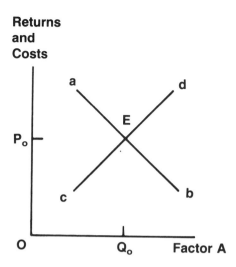

Returns and Costs

(y-axis: Returns and Costs; points labeled a, d at top, E at center, P_o on y-axis, c, b at lower portions; x-axis: Factor A with Q_o marked, origin O)

wages as a whole) uses it to account centrally for the volume of employment generated (especially in monetarist discussions). Firms demand labor (of all kinds) according to what it contributes to saleable products (which is the strong side of the theory), and workers are supposed to weigh their returns against the pain-cost of labor and leisure time lost (which is the weaker side). Some recent versions have employers and employees behave according to their rational expectation of real (price-deflated) wages (e.g., Parkin, 1982, chapter 24).

Sticking to the chief issue, most economists would regard the marginal productivity theory as conveying an important truth (with which I agree) about wage and employment determination, at least in market situations. Whether the wage can be identified with the worth of the marginal product is, in most cases, the awkward point.[2] Despite qualifications, broadly our industrial and commercial experience in economies marked by private enterprise is that factors are paid what they are worth. This is so, despite the unfortunate circular demand side of the theory, where the contribution of factors A, B, C, D (say employees, machinery, materials, management) is determined by varying one while holding the others constant, each in turn. In practice workers naturally object to the idea that the given shares of capital, management, et cetera, set limits to their own contribution, so that the quarrel over wages is really one over relative shares. This troublesome aspect of the theory does not render it useless, since in many situations the controllers of capital can impose their requirements—they have power, as institutionalists, say (chapter 8, section 10)—if capital is not to be withdrawn and the enterprise fail.

103

Turning to ethical principles, commutative justice requires that equivalents be rendered in price contracts, and certainly everybody believes a fair wage is due, no matter how the matter is put; but disagreement over measuring the value of human labor is more agonizing than in the case of things. The basic Christian position is that labor cannot be separated from the dignity and welfare of the person, so that an amount consonant with decent minimal living standards must always be paid.[3] It is not possible to view the matter as merely a market transaction, where supply and demand determine any outcome, however low. As a virtue, exchange justice obliges the employer to respect his obligation, as it also requires the employee to render the work agreed on. Today the wage in question must be taken to include fringe benefits, normally partly contributed to by the employee and partly paid for by the employer, who may shift his share forward or backward. Such indirect costs are often a large proportion of the wage package. Further, in modern conditions it is necessary to relate the adequacy of the wage, at least at low levels, to taxation payable and public goods returnable. The latter belong to the domain of distributive justice (see chapter 4, section 12) but their relevance to a just wage cannot be left out of sight.

What shall one say of evident differences in the worth of labor, so that a doctor is paid more than a teacher and the latter more than an unskilled worker (bearing in mind that professional associations and unions influence this social valuation)? A simpler form of the same difficulty is that workers at the same job may perform differently. The general response to such problems is that commutative justice, following universal experience, does not simply place all human labor on an equal level and call for an equal wage. Instead, the different kinds create a sort of scale,[4] which is basically set by evolving social estimation, the services of doctors being much more highly valued, for example, than when Molière made fun of them. Or piece rates may be justified in certain types of work. Further, in adjusting the relative standing of labor over time, the market is only reflecting the freedom of individuals to alter their choice of goods. There are many other considerations, such as responsibility and seniority, which usually enjoy recognition. Then justice is also opposed to discrimination on the basis of race, color, religion, sex, et cetera (all important issues I cannot take up), even if many situations may counsel an evolutionary approach to equality.

If the above emphasize primarily employers' obligations, some considerations should be added respecting the supply side: First, labor contracted for must be rendered efficiently with no holdbacks and cheating. Second, organized and unorganized labor should not demand excessive wages, since society in general may be harmed by resultant inflation and unemployment. The usual difficulties are institutional in that labor-management bargaining proceeds on an individual union basis, not economy-wide, so that jealousy and leap-frogging lead to spiralling wage costs. Third, individuals have an obligation to offer their work for reasonable remuneration, not abusing unemployment assistance. Some account must also be taken of the state of the enterprise: Wages cannot ordinarily be pushed to the point of causing harm to its viability, since the welfare of others is damaged, though neither should wages be held down to save a failing business that should be dissolved, implying a tenuous but workable distinction.

Yet if the initially clear impact of commutative justice seems to disappear beneath the above and other considerations, our universal intuition still comes through that a fair day's work—of professional, unskilled, skilled, unionized, and nonunionized workers, even of legislators who can set their own remuneration—demands a fair day's pay. Commutative justice remains the bulwark, like the right to private property, despite difficulties of implementation.

3

One long-standing issue is the family wage.[5] If commutative justice requires that the wage assure everybody a minimum standard of living, does this include dependents, so that a family wage is always in question? An excellent case can be made. In the modern economy, the means of production are controlled by the relative few, since destructive competition and economies of scale have eliminated more equal and more widespread ownership. The vast majority of workers, largely urbanized owing to the mechanization and commercialization of farming, are dependent on a wage. Since all but a few will marry and have dependents, remuneration must provide for a normal family. The case for a family wage emerges strongly in principle, even if some arbitrary decisions must be made for practice on the size and range of the "family" (limited, say, to spouse and two children)

But this excellent idea runs into considerable difficulties. Presumably a similar job should pay a similar wage to all, but families are of different sizes and sorts, and the attempt to pay such a wage to all could prove inflationary, cause marked capital-labor adjustments, and push some businesses into bankruptcy. The upshot is that the family wage must be sought by roundabout methods, such as tax concessions, direct and indirect supplements for children, health benefits, et cetera. Some conclude the very notion should be jettisoned: Let the single person's wage be the requirement of commutative justice, with concessions and supplements added for each household situation. This said, from a socioeconomic point of view the family wage remains the ideal, even if social conditions require the cooperation of distributive and social justices to achieve it in practice.

4

The third stage of just wage is application of the sorts of criteria sketched. The process is obvious enough and played out annually in hundreds of negotiating sessions in the advanced, basically free economy. We begin with the general principle, pass to intermediate guides such as decent minima of living and nature of the work, and end in the pages (sometimes hundreds) of labor-management agreements. In each bargaining situation there have come to exist a large number of issues that must be settled, often in an adversarial context. The procedures entail all the human phenomena of committees, strategies, maneuvers, confrontations, compromises, intervention of arbitrators, et cetera. Determining the just wage is, moreover, not simply a static thing; over time, inflation, productivity improvement, altered standing of industries and classes of labour, et cetera, lead to a constant process of adjustment. What may be just price in any situation only leads to ongoing determination as circumstances change, resolved more or less successfully today and tomorrow.

At this stage of wage determination, social ethics is obviously prominent, as well as the positive facts of supply, demand, and pertinent government regulations. The employee is deeply concerned with how justly he is being treated and the employer cannot avoid this as a matter of conscience, even if their relative assessments be far apart. Yet the usual puzzle is whether tortuous formal bargaining plus many simpler ways of reaching agreement still leave intact the possibility of knowing

106

just remuneration. Given so apparently hazardous a translation into practice, does a useful degree of determinacy attach to the moral principles? Surely yes, since this complex process is essentially no different from that attending the application of other principles and virtues. "Love your neighbor" is a command we understand quite well, which must be translated into the myriad details of living, not simply as an emotion but in actions. Correspondingly, the principles and criteria of a just wage can be validly applied, even though the lines blur, mistakes arise, and opinions will differ (cf. chapter 4, sections 11–12). The beginner's error is to think just wage and price require for practice some sort of divine determination of value.[6]

5

There is another aspect of just wage that requires notice, namely the social justice of the common good. Given the overall state of the economy—its structures, operation, and general well-being—and the labor force seeking employment, it may be the case that a too high level of wages stands in the way of sufficient employment. Certainly the point has been advanced repeatedly to help explain the present persistent high level of unemployment in Europe, Canada, the United States, and elsewhere. Such an assertion raises complex issues, to say the least, and would call for a discussion of modern composition of labor forces (containing more youth and women notably), changing concepts of full employment (compare the 3 percent suggested by Beveridge in 1944, the 7 percent hazarded for Canada in the 1980s, and the "natural" rate of the monetarists), the extraordinary mobility of capital in the modern world, and a good deal more. Leaving that aside, if the overall level of labor remuneration is necessarily connected with the general health of the economy and if too high wages and benefits in Western countries are one factor making for excessive unemployment, social justice requires that demands be restrained. Equally employers have the social obligation of making available as much employment as possible, so that the diversion of so much investment funds to takeover bids in the 1980s is plainly unjust.

The conclusion is that positive inquiries into wage determination and ethical criteria need one another, to analyze both what the "facts" are and what they ought to be. Any theory of wage setting always has values

107

embedded in it, explicitly or implicitly. Despite denials, the marginal productivity theory of income determination implies that prices determined in factor markets are inevitable and right and part of the overall micro and macro equilibria[7] envisaged. But obviously we do not think mere market determination of wages is always right, since the freedoms involved are often abused. Employers take advantage of weaknesses on the supply side to pay wages below decent minima. Workers abuse the strength conferred by a union to exact excessive wages, the effect of which is generalized across the industry to create inflation. Or professionals limit the supply of entrants to enjoy semimonopoly benefits.

But if a merely positive or factual theory of wage setting is incomplete and misleading, it is always my position that economic theories should wherever possible be utilized as part of crossing over from ethical principles to applications. The marginal productivity theory does generalize the lessons of experience and remind us of the force of the market, so that it has its qualified importance. Like all positive theory, it must not become a straightjacket and is certainly not a source of final criteria. One must particularly be on one's guard to attribute theory too much significance merely because its "scientific" precision makes it seem far above the muddy process by which ethical principles are translated into practice. The upshot of this linking of ethics with demand and supply economics is that the positive economics of wage determination is transformed into the social economics of it (cf. chapter 10), where values are identified and discussed as part of market forces.

INFLATION

6

Let me begin this second application by recapitulating how Christian thought relates to economic policy. Christianity is a religion that on its intellectual side issues in a theology, itself underpinned by a structure of concepts and thought. Drawing on the natural law (roughly, injunctions for conduct discernible in a "right" interpretation of life) and on revelation, it passes from ethics and moral theology to a set of broad principles for the economic order, which must be led through middle criteria to applications, where economic science and experience collaborate. It is also my position that economic science needs revision respecting its positive character and methodology, as discussed in chapters 7 and 8, so that it is not some independent arbiter of socioeconomic thought.

As for the authority attaching to a Christian approach to economic policy, clearly it declines from principles to applications. While moral precepts are always binding, any Christian may certainly err in the prudential order and, if economist as well, be caught up in the hazards of practical advice. There is also a useful distinction between judgments on existing institutions and facts and recommendations for reform. Often it can be seen with sufficient consensus that situations contravene economic justice (say, the level of unemployment or inequality in distribution), but the path of reform is harder to discern. Further, the Christian will always bear in mind that there is an Adversary working to turn intended good into harm.

The thrust of the following discussion is to illustrate how ethical concepts may be applied to a policy preoccupation and to point to the inadequacy of conventional treatments that slide over the moral side of behaviour and institutions. How could such an omission do other than lead to incorrect understanding and faulty recommendations?

7

In the early 1980s, high inbuilt inflation became a frightening problem for many Western societies (even if the middle of the decade has seen some relief), undermining not merely the efficiency of the economy but the moral strength of participants as well. A widespread belief arose that the recommendations of economists amounted to moving the furniture about while deeper causes remained untouched. Let me outline how socio-ethical factors are neglected as an essential part of the causes and cure for inflation by noting the failure of present policies, pointing to the quarrel over distribution, asking how basic corrections may be set in motion, and attributing lack of confronting the moral side of inflation to the mechanistic nature of economic analysis. To some extent the material has to be addressed to readers familiar with economic discussions of inflation. While everybody experiences it, its causes—like all price formation—ramify into every level of the economic process with complex feedback and interaction, so that analysis cannot be simple.[8]

Let me begin by summarizing the approaches to correcting inflation associated with neo-Keynesianism, monetarism, expectations analysis, and income policies—in brief, the furniture that gets moved about. Neo-Keynesian remedies for inflation (a heritage from J. M. Keynes, d. 1946) consist in increasing strategic taxes, lowering public outlays, and focussing more on interest rates than the money supply to influence spending decisions and choice of assets held. Probably a fixed exchange rate fits the package better, to avoid the need for monetary action to defend some flexible rate. But, runs the criticism, governments never find the courage for decisive action, lags upset fiscal devices, a familiarized economy anticipates maneuvers, the shifting Phillips' curve[9] shows the uncertainty of fiscal interventions, and fixed exchange rates are too rigid. If the general accusation is that those in command fail to use the levers properly and those who follow disregard the signals, be it noted these are moral issues not simply to be shuffled off as features of an unsatisfactory Keynesian era (roughly 1950 to 1975).

Monetarists, on the other hand, urge that the rate of increase in some defined money supply be lowered, since theory and fact show a strong link with national product growth and inflation.[10] Constrict the growth of money, and allow interest and the exchange rate to find their own levels. But monetarist policies have their own problems: Is growth in the money supply cause or effect of national product growth; is the relation between the two sufficiently stable; is there a predictable link between monetary base (bank reserves and cash) and money supply; can any concept of the money supply be surely manipulated given the array of convertible liquid assets? There are political problems also: Will a government give up its policy-setting prerogatives in favour of controlled change in the money supply, refraining from large deficits and central bank borrowing and allowing interest and the exchange rate to find their own levels? The worst is the underlying philosophy: End interventionism, allow the new "natural" economy to regulate itself, and the outcome will be greater welfare than what we presently seek in wrong-headed ways. But how the new laissez-faire economics is supposed to work against the background of faltering values in society is a question that monetarists pass over as "not the concern of economists."

Theoretical explanations of inflation have been given some lift by the advent of 'rational expectations'[11], by which economists generally understand conformity between some behavioral reaction or anticipated outcome and the predictions of valid, tested theory. The assumptions of the latter correspond to the conditions of mathematical expectations, conferring probabilistic certainty on projected outcomes. Expectations theory has been particularly used to undermine neo-Keynesianism and shore up monetarism: Workers, investors, entrepreneurs have all learned (we are told) to calculate in real terms, discounting nominal prices by the expected rate of inflation, knowing that some real (price-deflated) situation will only restore itself. Accordingly they use steadily improving information to interpret and offset fiscal and monetary maneuvers, so that the latter lose the shock they need for effectiveness. Since the guessing game that may develop is harmful, a preannounced and stubbornly maintained rate of change in the money supply is the best tactic. All of which tends to reinforce the birth of a new classical economics (Klamer, 1984). But after its novelty, rational expectations merely has you recasting macro-economic theory in a new dress, along with the implication that how you will "rationally" behave (cf. chapter 8, section 4) is how you *ought* to behave. Its response to inflation and policy still leaves out the moral dimension and only repeats in a new-old guise the notion of individuals maximizing their advantage plus the invisible hand for social benefit.

There remain incomes policies. Given a certain breakdown in conventional weapons and near-panic respecting rate of change in wages and prices, a democracy can be forced to accept voluntary or involuntary guidelines that interrupt the normal adjustments of the market economy. By now the lessons of many incomes policies have been learned. Overall we know that they draw government into neglecting monetary and fiscal discipline while controls are in place and that a free and disillusioned society is unwilling to accept them at more than some decent interval. The medicine has only temporary effect, and it is soon back to old habits.

If conventional policies are ineffectual, plainly the search is on for other explanations and corrections. Supply-side economics holds that inflation should be attacked by improving labor mobility and education, investment incentives, energy use, entrepreneurial abilities, et cetera. In a recent version of it, improvement of savings and investment (get those taxes down!) will generate an enhanced quantity of goods and services to offset the excess demand side on which we have concentrated too much. Or, leaving the economic arena, one may turn to "sociological" or "political economy" causes of inflations: Consumers are blind to the signals of higher import prices, unions are hell-bent on catch-ups, politics bedevil economic decisions, et cetera. But while not neglecting helpful insights regarding such factors (cf. D. Bell, in Hirsch and Goldthorpe, 1978), present pessimism respecting inflation is really to be traced to a more fundamental level, namely, a belief that without moral change in the behavior of participants no corrective policies for grave inflation are going to work within the framework of a free society.

8

To bring out the moral dimension, let me focus by way of example on distributional issues in the prices-wages adjustment process. Lack of concern for community welfare is the point at which we continually fail.

It is simple fact, experiential and statistical, that prices will (neglecting subsidies and controls) rise in proportion to the rise in cost/remuneration of factors of production, less any increase in their productivity and less also any increase in relative share of income. To take labor, percent increase in product price must equal percent increase in labor costs (= increase in wages less any increase in labor productivity) less percent increase in distribution accruing to labor. Further, the rise in nominal prices, again in percent or proportional terms, must be the sum of increases in factor rewards, weighted by the relative share of each in total income distributed. This identity is (cf. McKee, 1973; Denison, 1979, pp. 7 and 17), of course, a statement of causes in the sense of a statistical summation of contributions to higher prices, with causality, properly speaking, lying beyond. But the familiar point is that shifts in distribution, among labor groups and between labor and property income, are necessarily an element determining the rate of inflation.

An example will assist. Let us assume a union asks a large firm for a 20 percent increase in remuneration (wages plus fringe benefits). The cost of living index has risen by 10 percent over the past year, productivity is estimated to be rising by 2 percent per annum on the average, and "catch-up" respecting other labor groups is sought at 3 percent, so that the union asks for 20 percent overall in anticipation that 15–16 percent may be the final result. Labor-management bargaining arrives, say, at the latter, regarding which two key points emerge. First, management may have no overriding incentive to resist a large wage and benefit increase, since it knows competitors and other firms will make the same concessions. With some impunity, it will proceed to increase prices by the percent increase granted wages, less rising labor productivity, but doubtless guarding the share of property income. Why should management oppose this process when its own remuneration will rise proportionally and shareholders require only to be kept reasonably content? Second, other unions and firms then go through a similar process, the former possessed by the justice of catch-up claims and the second accepting the inevitability and fairness of according its own what has already been granted others. Supposedly it is then up to government to ensure that aggregate demand rises sufficiently, through increased public and private outlays and expansion of the money supply, to float off the increase in costs and prices.

9

Obviously the process sketched gives rise to many moral issues concerning its results for individual firms and unions and more general inflationary consequences. Let me draw out just two matters—the focus of bargainers on individual welfare and the quarrel over relative distribution.

The type of bargaining carried on between firm and union has frequently been analyzed: Instead of the simplistic notion of a buyer purchasing labor services according to their marginal productivity (see section 1), there is a large seller-buyer standoff, with agreement reached after lengthy strategy and wearing tactics. Something close to the entire gamut of human emotions and tactics is involved, where the two parties go at each other with no real concern for the welfare of society and sheer exhaustion aids settlement. Then this kind of local maximizing behavior is supposed to issue in more efficient and improved welfare of the whole. Evidently a certain naïveté underlies this supposition, for it can be true only if the parts obey laws or a moral system that brings about good functioning and order. Whatever may have been Adam Smith's precise view,[12] there is no necessary reason why mere maximization of efficiency or cooperation between parts will lead to sure benefit of the whole economy. Hence neither management nor labor can escape an obligation to take into account the wider impact of its actions; if particular settlements do not reflect justice in its wide as well as its narrow sense, the outcome for society may precisely be spiralling inflation.

Next, individual union-firm bargaining, with its emphasis on catch-up respecting comparable sectors of the economy, readily turns into a quarrel over relative distribution. As one union obtains the gains insisted on to offset inflation and falling behind, others are drawn into the same process. A merry-go-round ensues where time erodes temporary benefits, since improving productivity or cheapening imports can alone bring lasting real gains. Such externalities to the bargaining process clearly have their moral dimension, raising issues of social justice no less than harm from contaminaton of air and water. Can it be unreasonable to hold that bargaining should consciously take into account how excessive settlements result in theft from others through inflation?

International distribution may enter no less than national. Consider the common claim in the later 1970s that wages and salaries in Canada (as elsewhere) had to rise in step with the cost of living, when everybody knew that a prime cause of inflation was the rising cost of imported oil and its consequences. While the actions of OPEC countries had their vulnerable side, world consumption of oil products had to be slowed and a marked standard-of-living imbalance between North America and the countries concerned required some correction. In such a situation, Canadians had to accept a slower rate of wage increase than the rise in the consumer price index to allow the change in international distribution to proceed. Not an easy point to get over, but the moral obligation to acquiesce is clear even if the extent of the correction and its allocation must encounter the usual debate and compromise.

Labor-management bargaining in North America (and elsewhere) has long been marred by insufficient concern for community welfare. We have in our legal and institutional arrangements cultivated an adversary mentality where nobody is obliged to make allowances for effects on the community. It is curious to contrast union-management attitudes of the West with a number of Far Eastern nations, which appear to rely on Confucian thought to extend the discipline and loyalty of the family to the economy and society. Then Japanese labor-management relations are often characterized by a traditional search for consensus and harmony in decision making. Ideally, communism sees all men as brothers, so that the work of everybody cooperates in furnishing the needs of all. Evidently Christian thought, too, essentially implies a doctrine of solidarism[13] in labor-management bargaining, in each instance and extending to the whole economy and beyond national boundaries.

10

What remedies may be sought for disregard of community welfare in the price-wage adjustment process and for neglect of the moral-behavioral

114

dimension in the causes and correction of inflation (cf. Hirsch, 1976, chapter 10)? Let me touch on two points: Plainly, if one group of participants limits its wage or dividend demands, while others do not, the marginal cost for restrainers rises intolerably. The second matter is the need to get inside participants to change heart and mind, since lasting compliance can scarcely be secured without this.

Three solutions for the first problem may be instanced, presuming we rule out an incomes policy. One would modify the bargaining process by building in tax or other incentives (say, a loss of subsidies) so that if firms grant more than some guideline increase in wage and benefits, they incur penalties (presumably it would be unthinkable to attach penalties to unions.) The point of such tax incentive programs (Weintraub, 1971) is to leave the bargaining process intact while influencing participants and avoiding direct wage and price controls. Many difficulties arise concerning the mobility of penalized capital, alleged passing forward to consumers of corporate taxation, et cetera. How successful programs of this type may prove is difficult to say, since no country has tried them on any scale and unions have made little response to hints of lowered taxation as reward for restraint.[14] But such schemes still leave the doctrine of individualistic advantage in place and fail to tackle the issue of changed attitudes and concern for the community.

A second approach is arbitration. This admits the bargaining process cannot solve wage-setting problems, either in the interests of the parties themselves or the community, and hands the task over to outside tribunals. One is then into proposals for an arbitration court, with Australia a familiar example, or judgmental tribunals of some kind (cf. Meade, 1978, p. 433). Considerable problems exist regarding their operation and objectives. It is one thing to turn to such tribunals on an isolated basis, as governments often do, but another to set them up permanently. Initial wage negotiations may become futile. Further, were they permanent, a different structure for labor unions or wider groupings for bargaining purposes may become necessary, since a backlog of cases can cause such a system to collapse. There are many reasons why wage tribunals could prove cumbersome and perhaps self-defeating, yet they have the advantage of getting the settlement of firm-union differences into a community perspective. It is easiest to see why union leaders do not want them, since their factional leadership is undermined.

A third suggestion is to turn from fragmented bargaining to negotiations between larger union and industrial groupings. It could be a question of combining unions dealing with a single enterprise or grouping enterprises with larger union organizations, even if geographical divisions would be necessary in countries like Canada and the U.S. The point is to lessen present obstructionism based on historical and locational forces, along with the secondary fallout from picketing, boycotts, et cetera. While a number of countries have made considerable progress along these lines (Sweden, West Germany, Austria, and Japan), one wonders how long it will take the more individualistic Anglo-Saxon countries to evolve toward communitywide negotiations.

11

But, looking beyond technical and structural improvements, no improved system of labor-management relations will better the outcome for inflation unless everybody has the will to bring this about. As important as good institutional arrangements are, what counts is a readiness to make them work. Governments respond to this need by calling for ''responsible and enlightened'' behavior: The need for authority, threats, stick and carrot will diminish as all acquire better community awareness and perceive their true interest. The art of politics, the worldly-wise say, is to harness the strength of individual self-interest for community purposes and well-being.

One familiar song is more education: Let us inform, reason with, and persuade all participants, so that rational and humane solutions can be found to social problems. But the evidence of the massive post–World War II educational effort, especially in North America, is that the absence of an inner moral code leads only to heightened and more destructive egotism, to the shadow of community without its substance. The problem is to change the heart, not merely the mind, and an education bereft of recourse to fundamental values has no way of doing that. We have lived through a curious era in which secularized schools and universities have sought to pass on a vast array of information while holding that moral values must be left for individuals to find themselves, or home or church to inculcate as they are able and see fit. But rational humanism is of little use as a source of individual and community values without religious faith to underpin them. Finally, the ability to love others as oneself, which is the essence of social awareness and concern, is divine so that the self-interest required to overcome problems like inflation[15] has to be sought in the motives usually provided by religion or possibly genuine socialism of some sort.

Price formation ramifies into all levels and facets of the economy, so that inflation is the result of price-setting behavior at every stage of the production and marketing process. Hence a purely positive analysis of it is a truncated exercise and the correctional process will be that much harder without moral cooperation. Economists have with much truth been accused of constructing mechanistic models to analyze and recommend respecting inflation, growth, the business cycle, competition and monopoly, et cetera. Our actual world is instead one where politicians screw up economic measures for partisan advantage, firms and unions flaunt signals and lock into some passionate struggle over who will win, people in general are more muddle-headed than rational anticipators, we seek or manufacture the information needed as much after we act as before, and the issue of world redistribution instanced by OPEC opportunism or the gigantic borrowings of the less developed countries is steadily more urgent. Model-like explanations of inflation and corrections for it have only limited relevance, since they do not reflect to a useful extent extraordinarily varying human behavior. One may respond that more sophisticated models, as in the case of meteorology, would do the work more adequately, but moral reactions keep questioning the assumptions that precede any system of quantitative relations.

But the most relevant question for my purpose is, just what difference does a Christian approach make to correcting inflation, as well to just wage determination? We return to the theme touched on at the conclusion of the previous chapter: In what ways does Christian policy differ from that derived from, say, humanistic premises? Really two matters arise here—the passage from principles to applications (the externals) and the motivation and guiding spirit. As for the first, principles give rise to subsidiary criteria or guideposts: A just wage requires minima for decent living, family welfare, concern for the common good, and other criteria sketched; correction of inflation requires a readiness to cooperate with government measures and to limit individual advantage for community welfare. There remain the details of wage agreements and debate on appropriate antiinflation measures and requisite cooperation throughout the economy, where economic analysis and experience contribute. Final applications actually may differ little from those that could be arrived at from different premises, though subordination of individual advantage and proper self-realization in community welfare do appear distinctively Christian. Yet what is preeminently so is the transcendant spirit that informs Christian action. A radical reaction exists to individualism and mere self-interest. Plainly, humanistic values may conform more or less to these ideals; what they cannot supply is the motivation and grace stimulating Christians toward ideal conduct (always provided they use the essential means).

Part 3

ECONOMIC SCIENCE AND THE CHRISTIAN MIND

INTRODUCTORY REMARKS

Parts 1 and 2 sought to outline integral Christian thinking and the principles of social and economic life consonant with it. We come now to economic science, where my aim is to point to the deep rift that has developed with regard to certain of its basic premises and methods. Christian economists have long been obliged to adopt compartmentalized thinking. However important personal religious beliefs and practice, in undertaking economic enquiry and communication they kept such premises out of sight and worked within a restricted range of reference acceptable to colleagues of different backgrounds. While this proved a more or less tolerable procedure over say the last fifty years of sustained positivism, we have reached breaking point. The dissolution of values is such that, for Christians at least, glossing over these compromises is counterproductive.

There has been a great deal of writing in the 1970–80s on the crisis confronting modern economics (cf. Introduction, section 2). For many it is centrally the breakdown in macro theory, where we no longer have any widely accepted analysis and policy for the correction of stagflation.

At its simplest the problem is that Keynesian analysis of deficient demand, plus supply side adjustments, leads to no satisfactory way of improving employment without leaving inflation unchecked; moreover, government deficits rule out the massive stimulation that might be attempted. Monetarist policies have achieved some success in curbing inflation, but at the cost of severe recession (1980–81); and their theoretical advocacy has included acceptance of a supposed natural rate of unemployment and a new (laissez-faire) classicism. Others are discontented with modern economics for the reason that it has no effective way of coming to grips with many contemporary social issues (cf. Mishan, 1969). A terrifying armaments race and nuclear destruction menace the human race, but economics is busy with preoccupations irrelevant to them. We give microscopic attention to monetary theory while unemployment seems insoluble; we analyze the 'economic' aspects of trade and capital flows while millions die from hunger. When the economist does focus on social problems, it is usually from a utilitarian perspective (e.g. E. Mill, 1978, on the environment), so that too much escapes his narrow calculus of advantage.

A Christian will see the present crisis of economic science as reaching to a much deeper level. Formerly a broadly accepted social philosophy and structure of values were in place in the West, so that an essentially positive economics (along with other social sciences) could pursue its narrow inquiries with some justification and impunity, anticipating that its specialized results would be modified by prevailing values. But over the 1960–80s it has become apparent that the background itself is fast dissolving, so that the social sciences have no sure way of linking up with an underlying framework and direction of society. Materialism, urbanization, secularized universities, loss of faith in the Judeo-Christian tradition, and multiplication of value systems—these and other factors have created confusion of belief. In this setting conventional economics may intrigue the mind with specialised analyses, but how do these relate to wherever society is heading into the twenty first century?

The conclusion of many (institutionalists, social economists, Marxists, and others) is that it is now essential to incorporate values explicitly as part of economic science, not just of political economy. (See chapter 8, sections 9–10, and chapter 10.) My specific interest is in the virtual impossibility that has developed of harmonizing Christian principles at this urgent time with important areas of mainstream economics. Hence two chapters will discuss its general philosophy or mind-set and then its methods of inquiry, both of which block off the entry of Christian thought. A following chapter on welfare economics and the place of government in the market economy will illustrate these differences, and a concluding chapter on social economics set out a plan of synthesis.

It should be emphasized that my quarrel is not immediately with the vast mass of hopefully accurate, factual knowledge. As in other social inquiry, there is an accumulation of studies that stand in their own right as correct enough descriptions of data, institutions, and their working. Of course, even apparently straightforward material on, say, banking should contain normative material, since discussions of lending and interest always skirt moral aspects. Or factual work can be wrongly directed through lack of guidance by a correct philosophy, especially where policy recommendations are concerned. A large proportion of economists' research, for which society pays, goes into deriving dubious results concerning socially insignificant issues, where the pages of academic journals offer many illustrations. Hence some integration of positive inquiry with values should lessen the misdirected lines of investigation that so easily develop.

Chapter 7

THE SETTING OF ECONOMIC SCIENCE

What university economics is about, how successful a discipline it may be, and how it should be changed for the better have long been the subject of debate, good-humoured and acrimonious. Criticizing economics and economists is a game as old as the science itself, and everybody has a favorite joke. While some familiar criticisms will be repeated, my interest is the clash that has developed between a Christian approach to economic life and knowledge and conventional economic science, making some suggestions for its removal. Only a selective critique is intended, so that just two points are raised in this chapter—the subject matter and aim of economics and the background it normally assumes (i.e., liberal individualism).

One matter meriting repetition (cf. Introduction, section 4) is that nowhere has a definition been given of the 'Christian mind' to which reference is constantly made. If my clear meaning is a projection of critical and judgmental attitudes reflecting basic Christian doctrines, as lived by and molding believers, to go further, spelling out principles and consequences carefully, would render my work confessional and polemical. One drawback is an inability to derive tightly formulated criticisms of economic science and its setting, and a reliance on persuasion and illustration. Despite this lack of a more systematic approach, however, it is not difficult to conclude that the presently widely accepted object and purpose of economic science do not accord with Christian thinking and that the framework of liberal individualism is equally foreign to it.

1

Economics is considered to begin with the work of the French physiocrats (who favoured the rule of nature) about 1760 and Adam Smith's *Wealth of Nations* (1776). Dominated by English writing until perhaps World War II and after that by American, economics is now an international discipline, like other social sciences. Leaving aside its history and status today for discussion elsewhere, let me pass straight to my concern of whether economic science can be properly divorced from values, first general and then specifically religious. Some years ago, Keynes (1924, 1933; essay on Marshall) wrote perceptively of how religious values and influences were dropped generally from economic analysis and writing in the latter nineteenth century. Open attacks may have been few, but the silence of secularism took over. With its diversity of racial and religious backgrounds, the United States reached its own version of neutrality a bit later, but even more affirmatively.

If we ask what modern economic science is centrally concerned with, one reply is that it is "the science of what economists do"[1] (and the same must be true of many disciplines). Professors will teach and train students accordingly, and textbooks—usually written with an eye to the market—will reflect a certain consensus on some field and its content. After this quasi-definition, most economists appear to think their discipline studies human behavior in what is conventionally marked off as the economy in a positive or factual/nonethical way (cf. chapter 2, section 9, and chapter 8, section 6), and that it is concerned with the issues of efficient production, equitable distribution, and stable growth before the preeminent facts of scarcity, inequality, and economic fluctuations. But whether the social sciences may be successfully pursued as strictly positive inquiry is in fact a long-standing dispute and central to my alleged clash with the Christian mind, so that the matter must be outlined carefully. Let us divide the definition of economic inquiry into *what* is studied and *with what aim*.

2

The question of what may be the subject matter of economics has received three main answers. The earliest (Say, 1803) was simply to classify the functions of the economy into such leading categories as production, distribution, exchange, and consumption. The drawback is that you are merely affirming that the subject of economic study is the economy, while offering one description of what is entailed. Also, such classifications are inevitably imprecise: Production might include any kind of making, so that one may lessen, but not eliminate, this hazard by marking off as economic what is ordinarily marketed or subject to the "measuring rod of money" (Pigou's phrase, 1932, p. 11). Yet one cannot finally provide better than a descriptive definition of the subject matter of economics, since alternatives are no clearer.

The second statement, associated with Marshall (1920, p. 1), shifts the emphasis to man: "Economics is a study of mankind in the ordinary business of life; it examines that part of individual and social action which is most closely connected with the attainment and with the use of the material requisites of wellbeing." He added that economics did not exclude the study of wealth (the original purpose of economic inquiry) but went on to become part of the study of man. The drawback of this reference to the attainment of well-being, increasingly for many, was that it made betterment (at least with respect to "poverty and ignorance," pp. 3–4) part of the aim of economic inquiry. Whether economics should in fact be concerned with welfare, a proposition regarded as part of the Marshall and Pigou heritage, became greatly questioned. Christian thought, however, must obviously welcome the emphasis on man and welfare.

A third statement was popularized by Robbins (1935). Scarcity is the preeminent fact confronting us, and *the* economic problem is limited means in relation to the competing ends for which they may be utilized. But this attempt to mark off its subject matter must fail, since scarcity of means occurs in many activities not obviously regarded as economic. To use Robbins's definition, we must resort to the tautology that economics studies the scarcity of means commonly considered economic. Another difficulty is the distinction between ends and means, where the intention is to restrict values to the former. The ethician would be concerned with the choice of ends and the economist with the disposition of means. While not unhelpful, the distinction involves deception, since one cannot so neatly separate phenomena. (A wage may be means or end according to the situation analyzed.) In any event, economic means—workers, entrepreneurs, management, capital, property—are very much connected with human behavior, so that the attempt to handle them in a value-free way breaks down.

3

Turning to the formal purpose of economic inquiry, one longstanding answer was to advise[2] the sovereign or a country on the best means of amassing wealth. Many tracts preceded A. Smith's recipe based on natural liberty, and this broad aim of political economy is still very much alive (if not the recipe), more so in underdeveloped countries seeking to improve national product and capital as quickly as possible. The older countries, however, became preoccupied with internal distribution as the nineteenth century wore on, so that by the end of World War I the advancement of welfare had added itself to mere creation of wealth. In Pigou's celebrated statement of the problem (1932), welfare would be advanced by a larger amount of national dividend (meaning net income or product), its improved distribution, and the equalization of marginal social product in all uses of factors (implying their best allocation to production, while allowing for costs falling outside private accounting; cf. chapter 9, section 1, and note 2).

How Marshall and Pigou thought economic science could be used to advance human welfare is still worth careful note. They had economic welfare first in mind; not that this could really be separated from its wider reality, but it was a large part of the latter and the economist's obvious concern. Economics would contribute to human betterment, first material and then general, through scientific analysis and recommendations, where values would enter at appropriate points to check and guide objective findings. But then the difficulties surge: Preoccupation with scientific economics grows to the point of crowding out or minimizing the intended link-up with values, when in fact the latter affect the foundation and direction of economic inquiries, and today there is no longer a framework of accepted values to give the sort of correction Marshall and Pigou could take for granted.

A third approach is to deny any purpose, at least that of an ethical or normative kind. The only aim of economic science is to analyze and comprehend the "facts," elucidating causes and testing theories. If anybody wishes to use this information as politician, moralist, et cetera, this lies beyond what the economist is competent to do. Thus Pareto announced at the beginning of his *Manual* (1906) that his object was merely to know and to understand, not to recommend. Building on such attitudes, Weber suggested (1917; Shils and Finch, 1949) the distinction between means and ends, which Robbins (1935) elaborated for economics and textbook writers entrenched.

Now it is one thing to deny ethical purpose to economic inquiry and another to deny *any* purpose, since this makes social science decidedly unattractive and flies in the face of two centuries' belief and practice by

126

economists. Accordingly Robbins made the search for efficiency the immediate outcome for economic analysis, naturally enough, since economizing is an obvious sense of the word *economic*. But efficiency only introduces the values of minimization of cost or maximization of output (cf. chapter 8, section 5). Denial of purpose is, in fact, a fiction that textbooks pursue in their opening pages or methodologists affirm in their corner. In practice—in classrooms, corridors, and studies of policy—the economist speedily forgets that piece of rubbish, making purpose part of economic discourse. Sociologists and psychologists are no different.

4

Should individual and social values be an integral part of the inquiries of economic science?[3] There are two basic arguments for leaving them out and treating it as an objective examination of factual data: firstly, values always repose on some system of ethical and/or theological belief,[4] and what is of faith is undemonstrable according to conventional methods of logical analysis and experiment. In that sense they cannot be scientifically established. Granted one may take another view of what is scientific knowledge, but present conventions massively interpret it as what can be established (or falsified) by logic and experimental proof. Second, introducing values into scientific inquiry generates confusion and lack of communicability, since there are so many different premises of thought among intellectuals. Hence to remain fully comprehensible and capable of sure progress, economic science should be left value-free.

But there are powerful objections to this position, rendered painfully clear by fifty years of economic positivism. Values are like air, impregnating behavior and forcing their way back in as you try to eliminate them; if indeed you succeed, you are no longer discussing truly human behavior. Thus positive economics does not succeed in eschewing values, but only substitutes new ones where mere maximization and equilibrium are the silliest. Strive as you will to treat these as mere devices to give direction and term to reasoning, inevitably they become "good" in the absence of values properly speaking. Further, those who purportedly leave aside ethics in fact infuse their own value systems into their work,[5] since their influence is irresistible. The codes of secular humanism, scientific positivism, and individualism are evident in the work of so many economists, who for one reason or another leave the Judeo-Christian tradition aside. Economists would do a great deal better to make their value premises explicit (cf. Myrdal, in Blaug, 1980a, p. 139), becoming more conscious of how their work is molded by them and the direction of their thought.

Walras thought he could solve the divorce between economics and values with a threefold approach: *Pure* economics would consist in scientific analysis of phenomena; *applied* economics would be concerned with industry, trade, banking, et cetera, extending to policy; and *social* economics would be concerned with distribution and social justice. The not unsurprising outcome was that he worked intensively on his *Elements d'économie politique pure* (first edition 1874, last 1926; see Lessons 3–4 for the division), initially somewhat on the second, but almost not at all on the third. Dividing up economics in the way suggested had the best of intentions, but the outcome was to neglect ethical and even applied work in favour of a fascinating but largely irrelevant Platonic world.

5

What position should Christian thought adopt on the subject matter and aim of economic inquiry? The answer is to combine some summarizing description of the economy with human behavior as the centerpiece, while adding welfare as purpose. Thus economics would be the science that studies human activity in production, exchange, distribution and consumption—or any equivalent classification—with the aim of improving individual and social welfare, first material and then rounded. Such a concept is close to Marshall's statement, though it goes beyond study of the "facts" to introduce ethical values from the beginning, not merely as a correction after "science" has finished its work. Also, the definition suggested is not far removed from the economics practiced by the bulk of the profession, since welfare (if only material) does emerge consistently as the main concern; but the frank introduction of ethical values from the beginning and their intended harmonization (by believers) with Christian thought would bring important differences.

This suggestion would give economic science moral purpose, rejecting a purely factual type of inquiry, but stops short of attempting to confer a specifically Christian character on it. The first step is justifiable in that economic behavior is always moral (leaving aside indifferent acts—say, paying employees by cash or by check)—interest rates are set by conscious decision, not as chemical reactions—so that supposedly factual studies only deceive by leaving out an essential aspect. But I do not go on to assert that the welfare aims of economic science should extend to Christian principles of individual and social life, since this would give a special character to a social science manifestly concerned with pluralist societies and engaged in by specialists of many backgrounds. It is enough that economics and economists incorporate the ethical thrust of inquiries and that humanists, Christian, Moslems, et cetera, further modify this as may be required to suit their perspective. For example, in the early 1980s banks made massive loans to underdeveloped countries at floating rates of interest, so that as deposit rates rose, the interest burden rose also. Economic analysis would, in my approach, examine not merely the factual situation, but also the welfare implications of banking stability and hardship in the countries concerned. Then a further, specifically Christian piece of analysis might be that part of the interest charges relates to an "unproductive" transfer of capital for consumption purposes, so that payment of it has reduced economic justification. (Notice that such analysis remains distinct from political or social economy, itself concerned with policy recommendations; cf. chapter 10, section 3.)

Evidently I have equivocated respecting this introduction of values. If it is true that economic science inevitably raises them and that recommendations for welfare should be part of its definitional aims, ideally a Christian approach would impose its own premises. Indeed, were a specifically Christian analysis or solution being proposed for an appropriate audience, this would be legitimate. For instance, it could be affirmed that work should wherever possible have a humanizing character and that mere maximization of output should be sacrificed wherever possible to obtain it. On the other hand, given the necessity of linking up with non-Christian, pluralistic societies and an economics profession reflecting them, a prudential case imposes itself for halting at insistence on the introduction and specification of values (this at least, since otherwise Christian principles cannot even connect up with economic analysis), and not normally introducing some exclusive version.

6

The issue being skirted in these reflections is obviously that of the autonomy of economic science. Would not the insertion of values as guidelines for inquiry analysis, judgment and recommendations limit freedom of inquiry and assessment, the more so if values were related at some stage to theological premises?

To respond, the autonomy of scientific inquiry presumably turns on two basic matters: What is the distinct field or aspect of reality under consideration, and with what purpose is the investigation being conducted; and what methods are being employed to arrive at truthful findings? Restricting myself to the first issue (the second is taken up in chapter 8, section 7), insofar as definition of its field is concerned, any social science is simply concerned with aspects of reality or phenomena that enough like-minded specialists agree to mark off for consideration. But sciences studying human behavior run into the problem of values immediately and directly; they may wish to eliminate moral purpose, and validly in some areas (how the sense of smell works or how bond yields are calculated); but in the area of properly human decisions, a purely factual approach is misleading in that it will always erect quasi-values. The case is different for the physical and physiological sciences, which may in principle successfully mark off a value-free field of inquiry—say, the nature of electricity or the nervous system—even if neglect of the moral implications for individual and social life will generate problems eventually.

Hence economists may certainly declare that the study of scarcity or economic resources, or choice about their use, or simply the economy, et cetera, is the proper subject of their inquiries. But the definitions of subject matter and purpose given, the *what* and *with what aim* usually encountered, are deficient both in themselves and certainly from a Christian perspective. Notably, scarcity is *the* economic problem, many texts pronounce, meaning that the latter would not exist without it. But, taken in an absolute and overall sense, the resources of the world are not scarce at all. Of course, there are regions into which too many people crowd or that lack sufficient water or good land. But the earth as a whole has never lacked and does not prospectively lack resources in the broad sense, and history shows steady adaptation and creativity as we solve apparent shortages with new discoveries or inventions, as man is meant to do. Alternatively, if one takes scarcity in the relative sense of shortage of means in relation to competing wants, to declare this to be the economic problem is merely to say the necessity of economizing is imposed on us. The Christian can accept this but interprets it according to Genesis (3: 17–19): After an original fall from grace—some cataclysmic event that introduced potentiality for evil and living in disharmony with God—the human race became compelled to work hard to earn the means of livelihood and comfort,[6] and this entails choice of means. In this case, the economic problem is the need to manage work well in relation to our needs and welfare (where economizing is only one aspect), and economic science studies this behavior.

If scarcity fails, will choice do? Is it compelling to say that economic science is concerned with analyzing the process of decision making by individuals and societies on the use of resources? After some advantages, the drawback remains that the evaluation of decisions inevitably arises, so that either you accept moral welfare to be the aim of economic inquiry or you stop short with the quasi-values of efficiency, maximization, et cetera. Can it be useful to stop at mere analysis of decision making as a strategy or game of some kind (cf. chapter 9, section 9) and do analysts stop there anywhere? Their premises (knowledge of options, freedom, aim, et cetera) are already the elements of a social philosophy. Again, analysis of choice, which still requires to be specified as economic to properly concern economists, is only part of the wider problem of economic behavior and the completest sense of welfare.

In sum, the bases commonly offered for the autonomy of economic science will not stand and are certainly deficient from a Christian point of view. We may agree to leave values aside, but then the subject matter and aim of economic science make little sense.

7

If a Christian approach would make values and welfare part of the premises of economic science, let us turn to the role of social philosophy as shaping the latter. Clearly, any social science must in its elaboration reflect or imply some philosophy in the broad sense of a systematic interpretation of human life. From its eighteenth-century origins, Western economics has in fact been closely allied with liberal individualism, with the growing secularization of society converting originally Christian values into those of a nonreligious humanism. This is most obvious in its micro division, where individual choices, values, and behavior are concentrated on, less so in the area covered by social welfare programs. Before this, Christian thought must have a mixed reaction, welcoming the importance placed on individuals and their freedom of action, but rejecting the excesses that downplay obligations to others and communal welfare.

Liberal individualism is a familiar set of ideas, though not easily pinned down in its origins or a systematic statement (cf. Keynes, 1927). Individualism is often traced to the Protestant Reformers who (leaving nuances aside) taught an individual interpretation of Scripture, justification by personal faith, and the nonessential ministry of priest and church between individual and God. Despite their continued insistence on charity and good works, care for others, and a unified church, growing divisions in fact split up the reality of community and handed it over to the nation. Today individualism is a multiple product of the original emphasis placed by Christianity on the worth of the person and taken over by humanism, the exaggeration of this at the expense of the rights of others and the community, political liberties won with the decline of monarchy and its replacement by pluralistic democracy, and a certain economic independence obtained through prosperity and growth. It is hard to be an individualist without the fact or prospect of economic independence.

Historically liberalism grew as the fruit of the eighteenth-century enlightenment and rationalism, emancipation from the rule of monarchy and landed classes, and the entrenching of rights in law and constitutions. J. S. Mill's *On Liberty* (1859) is a classic statement: Individual liberty of thought, discussion, and action should be limited by society only where significant harm to others results (p. 15); the (admirable) precepts of Christ, to be distinguished from those of Christians and Christianity, need supplementing by other value systems (pp. 62–63); but egotistic indifference to the well-being of others is not at all intended (p. 93). Utility is "the ultimate appeal on all ethical questions," in the largest sense of progressive well-being (p. 16). While Mill's high-mindedness is evident throughout, his entire argument rests on intuitions of goodness, welfare, and the value of liberty. The parallel with religious faith is startling.

Liberalism today is a wider thing, reflecting such influences as worldwide insistence on personal freedoms and rights, individualism in economic and social affairs, ethical relativism, economic prosperity and growth showing the advantages of the system of natural liberty, the failures of authoritarian regimes and controlled economies, and the presumed guidance exercised by education and humanistic values. National and racial temperaments clearly play some part in accepting and modifying it, with (for example) Latin peoples easily rejecting compromises in favour of nonliberal solutions. But while much more can be said on the present character of liberalism, what matters for my purpose is its historical and continued strong influence on economic science. Modern leading spokesmen have been Ropke, von Mises, von Hayek, and Friedman,[7] all reacting against socialist controls and planning in favor of the free market.

To mention a few examples of its long shadow in mainstream economics, the goal of consumer behavior is taken to be maximization of utility or satisfaction, on the basis of personal preferences accepted unquestioningly; in a series of dubious pieces of analysis, such as the economics of marriage, entertainment, democracy, sport, or whatever, individuals act to maximize their utility; the firm seeks to maximize profit, with law alone dictating any social concern; it is normal for unions to be concerned exclusively with egotistic benefit for their members; and central planning and state interventions are automatically questioned in favor of the market. One can indeed give instances where the economics is modified by social considerations, say measures promoting more equality in distribution, but the usual optic is still how to maximize the outcome for individuals, substituting this for community welfare.

Criticism of this traditional approach flourishes in contemporary economic writing. For instance, Boland (1982, chapter 2) argues that neo-classical economics (meaning centrally microeconomic theory) is built on the presumption of "methodological individualism"; i.e., economic institutions and explanations of their working are assumed to reduce to the decisions of individuals, where the only given premises are their psychological states or preferences, and where theoretical results depend for their validity only on conventionally accepted criteria, rather than successful inductive proofs (cf. chapter 8, section 6). Or Simon (1983, p. 75) justly points out that the decision-making monads of individualism obviously influence and are influenced by others. Yet the radical problems lie at a level neither cares to address: Not merely does positive economic analysis disregard the ethical qualifications that must be attached to any exercise of liberty, but it fails to introduce the concept of community (i.e., a communion properly speaking, not a mere grouping of individuals) to counterbalance that of the individual. To resolve the tension arising between liberty and libertarianism, one must focus not merely on the rights of the individuals, but as well on the mutual obligations consequent on living in the communion of the family and the wider groupings that correspond to society. Rights to work, to a livelihood, to education, et cetera, imply the obligation of others to provide these things, according to social arrangements put in place for this purpose.

The point is well illustrated by Pareto's concept of a social optimum (see chapter 9, section 2), where a group of individuals supposedly obtains some maximum position when no further improvement for any one of them can be made without harming somebody else (while ruling out interpersonal comparisons to permit the weighing of gain against loss). Pareto reached this proposition by treating everybody's utility as a function strictly of his own preferences, the group for him being only a *collection* of individuals. But if instead society is taken to be a *communion* with initial mutual rights and obligations, if everybody is necessarily his brother's keeper, the optimum in question loses any meaning. Pareto got around the problem himself by declaring community to be a sociological concept, which merely defined away the flaw in his economics.[8]

8

Various reactions have appeared to the liberal individualism prevalent in economics, the more interesting being the attempt of micro theory itself to escape from the clash of its exaggerated individualism with general humanitarianism and the social currents of the welfare state. To refer to a technical example, the introduction of altruism may be commented on by referring to two articles by Gary Becker. In the first (1974), he seeks to incorporate a general treatment of interactions into the theory of consumer demand by making the utility function of A depend, *inter alia,* on the characteristics (R) of other persons that affect his own performance and welfare. By assuming that A is prepared to spend some of his income on modifying R, Becker can maximize A's utility, subject to a budget constraint of outlays on own goods bought and on influencing R. Such an approach to social interactions is a setup for the usual rigorous analysis consisting in maximizing a few functions via the indifference apparatus, and Becker proceeds to apply this ''scientific'' technique to the family, charity, et cetera. In a later article (1976), inspired by socio-biological studies of the importance of altruism for survival, he presents a more general view of the altruistic person (h) and the egotist (i). The former is willing to give his wealth to i up to the point where increments to it convey the same utility to both h and i. Meanwhile, i, also governed by maximization of his own income, has an incentive to act as if he were an altruist, since certain actions benefitting h will also benefit himself. The conclusion is that, whether motivated by altruism or egotism, voluntary transfers can make all better off, to the limits of their own utility calculations.

In comment, one might simply reject Becker's key premise, which would reduce one of the noblest human motives to a more cunning sort of egotism, and one might quip (cf. Hirshleifer, 1979) that this theorem will not work unless the altruist has the last word and thus control over the lowest kind of egotist. Or one might smile at the nonoperational character of Becker's argument, which could only be applied in a loose and dubious way to the family and other examples given. From my viewpoint, the chief objection is that the technique in question, which is characteristic of the positive-rationalist approach, compresses the richness of altruism into a few skeletal functions for the purpose of the usual maximization exercises. The qualitative fullness of what might be called benevolence or love for others is pushed through the all-purpose machine for the sake of rigorous analysis, like similar studies of the "economics" of marriage or sport. Then this highly specialized view (which may have elements of truth for certain supposed altruists) is taken in a reductionist way to be the substance of such relations. The narrowly positive analysis becomes the economic interpretation and, by default, a substitute for wider discussion of the values that underlie the topic in question. The bad manners of eating with one's fingers or selection of a marriage partner are reduced to calculation of competing utilities!

9

It is time to summarize the approach of the Christian mind to the aim and orientation of economic science.

Clearly there cannot be a specifically Christian version of the physical sciences or, say, mathematics, since their subject matter permits full autonomy, even if it remains true that as a total way of life, religion will influence the interpretation and direction of all inquiry. Consequently one may properly speak of the independence of such sciences, while seeking their harmonization and integration with Christian truth. But respecting the behavioral sciences, insofar as they focus on the moral side of decision making, things are not so straightforward. Economic analysis, to take that case, necessarily encounters values, so that it is possible to conceive of a specifically Christian version of it—as of relevant parts of sociology and behavioral psychology. Of course there is no specifically Christian version of why the exchange rate depreciated by 10 percent or why the real wage rose 5 percent last year, insofar as effects are simply ascribed to causes. But economic analysis does not stop at data and connections, but infuses judgments and recommendations into its work. In this way, the *possibility* arises of a specifically Christian economics. This said, given the fact of a pluralistic profession investigating pluralistic economies, Christian thought will advisedly respect the qualified autonomy of an economic science constituted on the kind of basis with which it can harmonize, namely, one acknowledging appropriate moral values. There can be only limited merit in going further to contemplate a special version of economic analysis for a limited audience.

Then, if Christian thought is critical of liberal individualism and its consequences for economic analysis, what different setting would it provide for the latter? Clearly the alternative social philosophy it holds out strikes a middle road between liberalism and libertarianism, equally individualism and socialism, set by its concept of freedom reflecting religious values and its doctrine of social relations. The individual and liberty are of the greatest importance, but community and an ethical interpretation of liberty modify their exaggerations; conversely, submission of the individual to the whole and denial of freedom in favor of planned control are equally wrong.

Many consequences suggest themselves for pieces of economic theory: For instance, consumer behavior would be studied for its relation to individual and social welfare (cf. McKee, 1984b), understood in ethical as well as material and utilitarian senses; the firm would be an enterprise concerned with maximizing not only gain but also the welfare of employees and consumers of its products; inflation would be studied not merely as the effect of a sort of physical misalignment of aggregate demand and supply, the money supply, the labor market, et cetera, but also as the result of decision making that sets advantage for self over costs to others; human work would be seen as an essential part of individual and social welfare, rather than simply in its productive role; and so on. I am not merely suggesting that values be taken into account at the stage of recommendations for policy (political economy to some) but advocating that their role be part of analysis itself. The effects of inflation and unemployment have moral-behavioral causes as well as the factual ones talked about.

136

Chapter 8

METHODS OF ANALYSIS

This chapter focuses on methodological and epistemological aspects of modern economic science, approaching it from a Christian viewpoint and setting aside compartmentalized thinking. To a large extent they effectively block off the sort of links and even an openness to Christian thought that are desirable. Much of the criticism will be familiar stuff to those dissatisfied with the relevance of current economic theorizing, but not specifically interested in the ethical rationale that is my concern. Naturally, I wish to go further than internal dissatisfaction and emphasize a Christian reaction. Methodology and epistemology—the methods of inquiry in any science and the kind of knowledge generated[1]—are not pleasant topics, but they go to the heart of what is taught and supposedly known in modern economics and what it signifies for human well-being.

1

If the Christian mind is normally appreciative of the applied data and analysis of economic science, as regards theory (systematic statements of cause and effect) it is more sympathetic to a middle way between too rarified abstraction and mere generalized description of institutions (cf. sections 8 and 10). This epistemological point is quite fundamental, both since it is necessary to be aware of the kind of knowledge proposed and since it bears on the appropriate use to be made of mathematics as technique.

Does economic reality consist only of particular events, or may one perceive also a world of metaphysical entities in the manner of pure economics, abstractions that are truer realities than what we immediately experience? Without plunging into the deep waters of what may be reality, while the detailed and real are what we immediately experience (not excluding the nonmaterial and spiritual from the real), we also have an irresistible tendency to generalize and even to conceive of the existence of nonmaterial entities at a second remove. All science has a deep urge to pass from primary observations to generalizations, and the laws it formulates are taken to be its more important and fascinating part. The process of arriving at them presents itself in some such idealized way as: observation of phenomena, induction and deduction suggesting some generalization, verification through continued observation and comparison, and then formal statement of the result, using exact assumptions and deduction to lead to the conclusion (which is the program of positivism, cf. section 6 and chapter 3, section 9).

As often remarked, however, laws in the various sciences are not usually found this way at all, coming rather from intuition before being verified later or modified by experiment. No matter; my point is the role and importance of abstraction and idealized reasoning in economics, one outcome of which was to conceive of a world of pure economics, a tendency common for about sixty years after the work of Walras (say, 1880–1940) and perhaps an aftermath to the search for natural laws of distribution, production, and value in the first part of the nineteenth century. In Walras's famous example (1874; cf. Pokorny, 1978) the entire consumption stage of the economy was conceived as coming into a gigantic, stable equilibrium as individual preferences, prices, and quantities arranged themselves over successive rounds of exchange to fit a maximization condition. Naturally, the premises determined the outcome. Still today academic journals present articles belonging to the realm of pure economics, in the sense that they are cerebral exercises in a world of arbitrary concepts, having (as far as most can see) no significance whatever for real experience.

At the beginning of his *Economics of Welfare* (1932, pp. 6–7), Pigou rejected both pure and merely descriptive economics in favor of one adapted to form the basis of an art. Many economists would today join him in objecting to their science being given over to excessive abstraction too remote from potential or even feasible applications. Christian thought is sympathetic to this position, since an economics too given over to Platonism[2] moves around in an endless space of ideas, remote from the concerns of welfare. Rather than conceiving of economic realities (interest, rent, capital, et cetera) as reflecting pure entities, Christian thought—like Marxist and perhaps all thought grounded primarily in values—is more comfortable with "moderate realism" (a phrase taken to characterize the approach of Aristotle to reality). The immediately real we experience (material and nonmaterial) is what exists, it gives rise to universal ideas and generalizations that we manipulate in reasoning, and it remains the landing place to which we return. Moderate realism signifies a middle ground between too abstract and too descriptive an economics. We guard against taking off into a realm of speculative thought that has no need or desire to be checked by the experience of daily life. The upshot is that Christian thought (quite apart from where individual Christians may be led in their work) has little sympathy for excessively abstract economic speculation and must regard many writings as merely Platonic exercises.[3] Economics should not indulge in the sort of intellectual creation that may be pursued legitimately in pure mathematics.[4]

2

The use of mathematics in economics has a good deal to be said in its favor, but strong criticism has always been heard. It is a language, all agree, that translates economic concepts into symbols free of word associations, permits the logical reasoning that is of the essence of mathematics, and substitutes conciseness and precision for literary argumentation. Also, various sectors of the economy present themselves like systems of interdependent variables, where outcomes depend on complex interactions, so that calculus and the simultaneous equations quickly solved by electronic methods appear apt techniques. Granted there is some appropriate place for mathematics, then let me comment on difficulties and abuses associated with modelling and the dominance of quantitative reasoning over qualitative.

In seeking to generalize and predict, economic science has become addicted to modeling, meaning the practice of representing economic situations in mathematical propositions, ranging from the simplest ideas, say the dependency of quantity bought on price, to complex representations of the economy, say input-output and macro forecasting systems. It is not sufficiently appreciated that all mathematical conceptualizations are ideal and never more than approximate representations of what is represented.[5] This approximation is intensified by the extraordinary number of variables in economic situations and their being generally subject to behavioral as well as physical influences. While the tentative nature of economic theories is generally recognized, nevertheless the mathematical ideal of exact premises, rigorous reasoning, and precise conclusions easily enthralls economists (the disease is not confined to them), so that any connection with the real world can become remote and not even matter. One enters into a realm of invented concepts, which can be imagined a sort of Platonic reality if you stay immersed in it. A host of examples could be given—for instance, much of the content of graduate courses in microeconomics, to judge from widely used texts and examples of examination papers.[6]

Now, my concern is not so much to repeat widespread criticism of mathematical modeling in economics, but rather to emphasize from the perspective of Christian thought the blocking out of values and ethical considerations that occurs. Models necessarily begin with exact premises and proceed through rigorous reasoning to precise conclusions, at which stage one may be invited to introduce value judgments to modify them. But the difficulty is that ethical considerations are not simply coats of paint you apply to a finished edifice to alter its appearance to your taste. Instead they affect the premises and reasoning of economic behavior from the inside, so that the conclusions emerge rather differently. Mathematical modeling results in a kind of armor plating that simply cannot admit values, since they do not fit into the quantitative logic that is the essence of it.

The reader may inspect, for example, the chapters on consumer behavior and the theory of the firm in such classics as Samuelson's *Foundations of Economic Analysis* (1947, chapters 4 and 5) or Henderson and Quandt's *Microeconomic Theory* (1958, chapters 2 and 3). Values enter implicitly into the initial setting of consumer preferences and key assumptions governing the firm's activity and in both cases respecting rationality, maximization, and the place of equilibrium. But the methodology of the reasoning is such that any explicit entry of ethical questions is impossible, since the formal logic does not permit it. The initial premises dictate the route and the conclusions. Probably, too, understanding the mathematics will be so demanding for most people that the work of reflecting on the significance and the ethics of what has been argued will never be undertaken. What is not discussed does not matter, at least within what is called economics.

3

This blocking out of ethics connects up with the second major difficulty with mathematical modeling, namely, its overemphasis on the quantitative at the expense of the qualitative. From the period of its infatuation during the latter nineteenth century with the physical sciences, economics has made the quantitative its first preoccupation, since this permits exact knowledge and apparent scientific achievement, before the loose, descriptive treatment that alone seems possible of what is qualitative. To some extent, of course, the latter can be converted into quantitative knowledge: Subjective sensations translate themselves into physical phenomena (used notoriously by lie-detector machines), consumer sentiment has long been given quantitative assessment, and quality of life studies often reduce it to statistical categories. But there is a limit to this kind of conversion, and the danger of reductionism exists.

Since contrasting the two tends to disappear into an unclear consideration of how well the quantitative may be made to represent the qualitative, directly and indirectly, it is better to reflect on the limited picture of economic reality that emerges when quantitative modeling leaves out the social context. Suppose a hundred persons at a plant put in a day's work with all of its events and exchanges. From all this an economic model extracts a calculation of what factors have been used for given output, focusing on costs and efficiency. Essential information, indeed, but the social and ethical sides are systematically excluded, since conventional methodology is not fashioned to take them into account. They are presumed to belong to sociology, industrial psychology, social ethics, et cetera, and what economics has to say links up with them only after its analysis is concluded. This is the result not only of the intention to exclude values, but also of the technique of conventional economics. Christian thought, however, will harmonize more readily with a less rigorous social economics ready to go beyond a merely quantitative approach to take account of how this shades into wider considerations. Are the hundred people in the plant aggressive individualists concerned with personal gain, or instead are they a community seeking one another's good, cooperating with goodwill and respecting authority? Do they pilfer and slack off on the job? Such things matter, as all admit, but mathematical models are ill-adapted to catch this side of the productive process (cf. Leibenstein, 1980, chapter 3).

Turning to a more formal example of how mathematical modeling disregards the qualitative and ethical, in *A Treatise on the Family* (1981) Gary Becker presents a narrow economic framework for analyzing the many aspects of family life. He assumes that individuals maximize their utility from known preferences and that all behavior is coordinated by explicit and implicit markets (p. ix). The traditional theory of consumer behavior (chapter 1) is taken as the model of a single-person household, where the individual proceeds to maximize his position by purchasing commodities (i.e., children, health, whatever, in addition to goods as such) subject to the constraints of time and income. Their prices are their costs of production (p. 8). Marriage raises the division of labor in the household—how much time should each partner devote to the market and household sectors?—and the choice and quantity and quality of partners to maximize preferred commodities. Becker goes on to the demand for children, their opportunities, altruism in the family, nonhuman families (animals and insects, also, are taken to maximize), divorce, and other matters.

The essential themes are the efficiency of choice and maximization of (untouchable) personal preferences, both subject to various constraints, where the technique is mathematical. Such procedures are their own proof: Men and women are shown to act as Becker assumes they act (pp. 62 and 113 for example); efficient marriage markets behave as the author has reasoned (p.66). Clearly a wall is gliding between economics and ethics, since many aspects of family life—where large and small moral choices continually arise—are analyzed as positive-economic and quantitative. Take more specifically the example of pp. 7–8, where Becker asks us to treat time and goods as inputs into the production of "commodities," meaning children, esteem, health, altruism, envy, pleasures, and whatever else is "consumed" by a family. A utility function may be written: $U = (Z_1 \ldots Z_m)$, meaning that utility depends systematically on all commodities. Many do not have market prices since they are not purchased, but we may imagine them to have shadow (or "as if" market) prices equal to their cost of production, meaning the goods and time spent on producing all the Zs. Then one may maximize the function in question subject to the full income constraint of allocating all time to the market sector.

If these are premises, evidently the qualitative disappears in the quantitative, and a bizarre analysis purports to explain the central phenomena of marriage and family behavior. The chief objection from my point of view is that Christian ethics cannot even get at the reasoning along its route, since mathematical premises and the chain of deduction exclude it from the beginning.

A notorious aspect of economic theorizing on behavior is the supposition that individuals behave rationally, but the limited interpretation used excludes any explicitly ethical sense and thus any effective participation of Christian thinking. *Rational* is equated with *logical,* reflecting consistent and maximizing choices. Given an initial assumption that an individual ranks his preferences in an ordered way, consistency of choice implies transitivity (if A is preferred to B and B to C, A will always be preferred to C, and so on for n goods, all other considerations remaining unchanged). Since it is normal to prefer more to less, maximization is the term. Again it will be noticed that we are heading into mathematical-type reasoning, with exact premises, definitions, and conclusions. The complexity of actual behavior is drastically simplified, so that a scientific mold can be given thought. Geometric diagrams and functions loom, and much of the point of the definitional language is to facilitate their use. A whole stable of terms make their appearance—weak, strong, robust, exacting, less demanding, vigorous, rigorous, scientific, precise, et cetera —to color the reasoning and premises.[7]

Next, attempt to avoid it as one may, rational adds to itself the note of reasonable, normal, justifiable, or acceptable, with their ethical overtones. Were there in place a generally acknowledged and understood morality such as the Christian code, there would be less danger of such confusion, but the situation of fading Christian ethics and its replacement by a vague humanism renders the equation rational = normal = ethical of dubious meaning. Generally economists insist that rationality should not have normative overtones, but the sheer weight of discourse, omitting the specifically ethical, overwhelms the qualifications. On page 1 of his text the microeconomist may define rationality in an ethical neutral way, but by page 20 his conclusions on consumer behavior have equated it with what is normal and right.

The Christian concept differs in important respects, as surely does any more philosophical approach. After simply meaning pertaining to reason (thinking is a rational operation), rational implies the right use of reason and its criteria. In a traditionally Christian way of putting the matter, what are the norms of ''right reason''? When is the intelligence in its understanding and judging role being so exercised that its procedures and conclusions may be termed reasonable in this sense? The reply is straightforward: The rational is what accords with God's plan for right living or the natural law so interpreted. When we perceive, understand, discern, and choose in accordance with the purpose of human life, in small things and great, we are being rational.[8] Conversely, when we turn aside from God's law, our choice and behavior are irrational. In equating rational with *consistent* and *logical,* economic science has taken one aspect of how reason functions and appropriated the whole to it. Instead, rational includes a great deal more, where consistency and logicality are only part. This evidently clears up the temptation to equate consistent = rational with what is morally correct = rational. Preferences that are known, ranked, and consistently chosen may be wrong and irrational from a moral point of view: The criminal, insane or pervert may behave logically according to the microeconomic theory of choice, but irrationally by wider canons.

Clearly the sense of rational proposed and that customary in economic theory can be reconciled, though care is necessary. The individual consumer or investor is in one sense the arbiter of his own preferences, but, if a Christian, must mold them according to a code of objective morality. Within such wider guidelines, consistency and logicality fall into place as normal operative (but not exclusive) characteristics of what is reasonable. The fault of economic science has been to seize on a part of what is rational behavior—almost a technical part, one might say—and to blow it up out of all proportion, given the aim of achieving mathematical-type precision for the sake of too narrow a concept of science.

To comment on a well-known technical example of how misuse of the concept of rational behavior creates a supposedly insoluble problem, a prominent issue in choice theory is whether a group of individuals can arrive consistently at some collective decision in which their individual preferences may acquiesce or at least are respected. Arrow's general possibility theorem argues that four apparently reasonable conditions reflecting rationality and individual sovereignty do not rule out a noncontradictory outcome, a result over which students are often invited to mull.[9]

What is of interest here is Arrow's interpretation of human rationality as coterminous with deductive logic and his insistence on the need to proceed rigorously from individual preferences to social choice. His mistake is that while all that is logical is contained in what is rational, the reverse is not true: Rational means according to reason, and the first rule of reason is to think and act in accordance with human nature. In the tradition of Christian thought, propositions are known either by simple perception of basic truths, or by ratiocination or reasoning proper, or by

144

the light of connaturality (formed virtue, cf. chapter 2, section 5). Normal or natural behavior is the standard by which we judge the procedures and goals of knowing and choosing, so that economic criteria such as consistency and logicality or maximization are only partial in their scope. This is not to say that inconsistent or contradictory choices are rational, but that the fullness of well-ordered human behavior is the standard. Rationality is not an priori concept chosen by the mind, and getting surely from premises to conclusions is not reducible to only logical deduction or the necessity for it.[10]

5

Turning next to the issue of maximization, *economic* has always had the two senses of "related to the economy" and "economizing," with the latter leading to efficiency and maximization as leading aims of analysis. Along another route, rational behavior is commonly interpreted to imply choice of more over less—on the part of consumers, labor, investors, entrepreneurs, et cetera—so that *maximization* is again the term. Minimization of costs or disadvantages is the correlative. A surprising amount of technical attention can be given the formal conditions for maximization in mathematical economics. Problems are cast in the form of interdependent variables, so that calculus techniques may be used to define the direction (negative or positive) of change and first and second order conditions for maxima, subject to one or more constraints.

Leaving aside the mathematics as sufficiently commented on, Christian thought will readily accept the aim of efficiency but be reserved on the degree and kind of maximization. In most environments, efficiency is entirely necessary for the survival and success of businesses and farms, to feed the billions that inhabit the earth, and to run nonprofit (including church) undertakings properly. True, there are extraordinary people who cast efficiency aside to offer hardships to the Lord; a Francis of Assisi often so behaved, if we may accept the shadowy accounts of his life, and so encouraged his followers. But these are exceptions, not the rule. One qualification that Christian thought does surely bring is the belief that wider values have some impact on how factors may be combined in more efficiency at the cost of people found redundant; or the electronics input, such a rule omits too much. Many business mergers result in more efficiency at the cost of people found redundant; or the electronics revolution underway is displacing thousands too quickly.

In one sense, maximization can always be defended. If immediately overstressed in terms of output and profit, the aims may be extended to include welfare, social benefit, moderation in behavior, or whatever. The mathematical techniques are so general that any set of variables may be maximized subject to any set of constraints (presuming noncontradiction, et cetera). Heroic sanctity is a path toward a maximum, no less than the operation of an oil refinery or a conglomerate. More relevantly, economic maximization is commonly taken to concern personal satisfaction, output, profit, and investment returns, with moral values and the more refined and humane side of life systematically excluded; in which case it is easily at odds with Christian virtue and thought. One has only to recall the terrifying strictures of Jesus on the excessive pursuit of riches. Much later, some of his followers proceeded to identify Christian living with the sort of sober, industrious work that leads to wealth accumulation. A certain detachment from worldly success and the demands of charitable giving may have been held out as ideals, but overemphasis on industriousness steadily allowed wealth accumulation to poison Christian society. The United States is the classic example of where such puritanism may lead.

Accordingly, maximization of a narrow group of positive economic objectives cannot be reconciled ordinarily with Christian thought as a goal for personal and group conduct. Instead it requires to be corrected by a sense of moderation and wider criteria. Taken in this way, objection ceases at some point. The obvious difficulty for practice is that those who moderate their search for gain may succumb to the unprincipled few whose only curb is the limits to legal compulsion. Those who want to stay in some business or type of employment have no option but to run as hard as the pack, at which point presumably the answer (beyond law) is the creation of institutions to exercize restraint for the common good and of an different social climate (weak now in the West but not unknown, say, in conformist Japan).

As for the practical outcome for economic analysis, it is hard to see any good substitute for the goal of maximization (though one may well contrast the more meaningful concept of maximization through time with the timeless concept of it associated with calculus). From a technical point of view, the study of behavior needs some terminal point toward which even the simplest of models depicting reality will lead. What seems to be required is a readiness to qualify it, with insistence, so that narrow maximization is recognised as such and always framed with reference to rounded individual and social welfare. The mathematical models conventionally used prove nothing about economic behavior, but merely represent the assumptions and propositions enunciated. Verification is another matter and, in the nature of the case, is often difficult or impossible.[11] Even the most elaborate presentations are usually reducible to concepts of maximization subject to constraints.

6

Let us turn next to more general methodological criticism. While this is a long-standing phenomenon as in other social sciences, the last twenty-five years have seen intense debates over the validity of the positive program of research and neo-classical formalizations, partly growing out of conflict over macroeconomic theory and partly feeding on endemic surges of interest in methodology, perhaps connected with deceptions in the search for laws in physical science. Only two points connected with my aims need be brought out, namely, the dependence of methodology on conventional acceptance and the role of faith in seeking sure economic knowledge.

The positive approach (cf. chapter 2, section 9) to economic science is approximately this: Examine economic phenomena; form a hypothesis connecting effects with causes; test it; and engage in a back and forth process of reformulation and verification until satisfactory generalizations are reached. Much could be added, but this is the essence. Then there is considerable merit in stating correct results rigorously: Pose appropriate assumptions, deduce conclusions exactly, and utilize mathematics for a concise, logical statement. The theories of consumer and firm behavior are simple examples, encountered in some form in elementary texts. While there is much to be said for this procedure, and it resembles what the physical sciences do (with the powerful adjunct of laboratory experiment), there are inevitable difficulties.

In practice, satisfactory proof is rarely possible for economic theories. (a) Inductive proofs are always flawed (cf. Boland, 1982, chapter 1)—we can never test a proposition exhaustively, and the future is uncertain. (Will the sun rise twenty years from now?) Whether you seek to verify or falsify makes no difference; the data could vary next week. (b) Econometric verification—implying the use of regression analysis to

147

confirm single or simultaneous equations—has a modest record of success, to say the least. Continually modifying the model to fit the data has generated deep scepticism, and if forecasting be taken as the primary confirmation of theory, econometric work has proved of limited value. One critic (Lucas, 1975) has argued that the structures of models should be continuously adapted to reflect expectations as altered by events and policy changes, which raises extraordinary technical problems. (c) Then in the nature of the case, no sort of proof is possible for some economic theorizing—for instance, the perfectly competitive firm. On the basis of assumptions never found in the real world—a firm so small as not to be able to affect market price and selling a product identical to that of similar firms—cost and revenue conditions plus an assumption of maximizing gain lead to ideal production and gain. But perfectly competitive firms exist nowhere, so that key propositions can never be verified (cf. chapter 4, section 11). Finally, (d) in economics one must contend with kaleidoscopic data: Social habits, tastes, mental states, social institutions, et cetera, all change, so that even shortly spaced periods present situations where old proofs are no longer applicable.

While there are numerous other problems connected with the methodology of current economic science—the attempt to found theory on individuals as monads, heavy reliance on given psychological states, the problems of putting behavior into the context of evolution over time, linking up micro with macro theory, et cetera—enough has been said to point to two conclusions. First, the methodology and epistemology of any science (i.e., methods for seeking truth and the concept of truthful knowledge about its subject matter) mainly depend for their acceptability on the consensus of an investigating "club" (cf. Boland, 1982, Part 3). They are presumably subjected to critical examination by the latter and by philosophers of social science, but at any time sufficient agreement on criteria is the basis on which findings are evaluated. "All theories of [scientific] knowledge proceed from the question of what is knowledge, and how can it be obtained" (Feyerabend, 1975, p. 212); and clearly it is the case that economic theories reflect assumptions, reasoning, and conclusions that depend on conventional acceptance. Scientific, rigorous economics and its verification and falsification are what enough economists agree to treat as such.

Clearly some form of faith underlies willingness to acquiesce in the consensus and its evolution over time (assuming mere advantage is not the motive). If inductionism can never construct a finally satisfactory proof, in economics more so than in physical science, and if logic necessarily begins with assumptions and never concludes in the complexity of reality—"its chain of conclusions hangs loose at both ends, both the point from which the proof should start, and the points at which it should arrive are beyond its reach" (Newman, 1874, chapter 8, section i)—then belief must enter to underpin mere theorizing. While this merely repeats a point made in an earlier chapter (chapter 2, section 3), emphasized by M. Polanyi (1958), it is useful to insist that economists' work reposes on faith no less than that of other social scientists. Naturally, it is a Christian view that faith extending to the theological domain must underlie that on a human level, since regressing from the latter leads to it. I can place contingent trust in knowledge[12] associated with physical and social sciences, provided I finally believe in the existence of absolute knowledge and truth (another name for God). Without this transcendent link, however, one must rely on even more blind belief than Christians are often accused of having.

7

This discussion brings us back to the question of the autonomy of economic science, which may be taken (as said in chapter 7, section 6) to depend partly on defining some aspect of reality for consideration and partly on the methods of investigation and standards of truthful knowledge agreed on by specialists. If these things repose on an evolving consensus—economics is, in a deep sense, the science of what economists do and believe they know—then Christian thought may very legitimately dissent from the aim and methods of conventionally accepted inquiry and reject criticism of its own ethically based recommendations. Indeed, any radical approach to economic life and behavior can treat the claims of economics to independence based on its scientific method only in a qualified sense. It is perfectly possible, of course, to acquiesce in methods currently in use and leave debate to internal methodological discussions, accepting the twists and turn agreed on by the profession. However, setting aside compartmentalization of thought requires the Christian mind to call rather for substantial modification of current methods (along the lines suggested in previous sections).

Take, for instance, a recommendation frequent in Catholic social writing that more state intervention is necessary to help correct excessive unemployment. To this economics may offer at least two criticisms: the dubious history of fiscal interventions and (my concern here) an assertion

149

that a "natural" rate of unemployment will persist despite them, given that the supply of and demand for labor reflect the real (price-deflated) forces of the market (see Lipsey et al., 1985, pp. 688 and 722). Yet each stage of the latter argument and the verifications attempted merely depend for their acceptability on professional conventions. Nobody has defined and demonstrated convincingly what the natural rate of unemployment may be for any country. Indeed, not a few instances of using scientific economics to criticize unorthodox recommendations amount to saying that received thinking rejects them. Basing the case for the autonomy of economic inquiry founded on a special methodology and epistemology simply invokes some ruling consensus.

These remarks do not belittle the techniques in question nor the fund of experience and history drawn on. Invariably ethically based recommendations for economic reform, especially at their applied stage, will call for the collaboration of economists and for modifications in the light of criticism. Every area of the modern economy demands specialized understanding. This said, "scientific" economics is heavily influenced by assumptions and techniques that have a certain arbitrary character reflecting a conventional approach to economic behavior, so that it cannot claim some sort of rigorous independence or objectivity with respect to the judgments and recommendations of Christian thought. The independence in question reflects a preferred interpretation of the evidence and methodology—not to be taken lightly, but hardly graven in stone.

<h1 style="text-align:center">8</h1>

After methodological criticism within orthodox economics as such, a number of quite basic shifts in the orientation of economic science have been proposed almost from its eighteenth-century origins. The more important have been the historical, Marxist-radical, and institutionalist, though others include a Christian reaction in the early part of the nineteenth century and a variety of attempted socialist corrections. Let me make a few comments on the first three from a Christian viewpoint, while leaving the case of social economics for my conclusion.

If the historical school proved a passing though lengthy phenomenon, it did leave a widespread legacy of dissent from neo-classical economics and advocacy of a wider social and cultural approach to analysis and policy, the influence of which is still felt. Located mainly though not exclusively in Germany, this prominent nineteenth-century group extended its influence well into the present century among some English and American writers (see J. Bell, 1967, chapter 14). Essentially, it criticized the observation-deduction methods used by Ricardo and Mill in their search for natural economic laws and held that study of the development of institutions and events over time was the valid way to derive generalizations (cf. Schumpeter, 1954, p. 807). Economic institutions and phenomena were inseparable from a total social and cultural context, and many historical economists ostensibly embraced the cause of social reform and progress, usually from a conservative standpoint. While their voluminous and often extraordinary studies of economic history made their work influential, little in the way of laws and precise analysis ever emerged. A bitter *Methodenstreit* of the 1870–80s pitted advocates of mathematical and abstract methods against those preferring historical and literary procedures.

Christian thought must have some sympathy with the approach and emphases of the historical school. Attention to the evolution of institutions, the wider cultural context, the place of social ethics, and the attack on excessively abstract and deductive analysis strike responsive chords. Yet qualifications remain: the historical school over-reacted against a priori theory in favour of evolutionary study, whereas Christian thought has readily proceeded from the deductive implications of its view of man and society. Rights, role of community, freedom, private property, and other topics developed earlier (see chapter 3 and 4) are supported partly on such grounds as common experience and consensus, but partly also by deduction from the truths of faith. This spills over into sympathy for the kind and degree of deductive economics that Christian thought can accommodate.

Also, Christian thinking retains strong reservations respecting the kind of Hegelian thinking that, in some historical writers, regarded social institutions as in part the result of an inner deterministic evolution. The organic version of the state implied is not the same as that ordinarily associated with Christian thought. (See chapter 3, section 4). The free exercise of choices, acceptance or rejection of divine grace and guidance, and the deviations of evil lead Christian analysis to regard social and economic change as subject to contingent, not deterministic, outcomes.

9

Marxist thought is impossible to categorize. The master composed a mixture of philosophy, sociology, and economic analysis that is as brilliant and captivating as it is confusing and repelling, and his work has been followed by a century of attempts to clarify and revise his ideas. To mention at least some central elements, society supposedly evolves in a dialectical process of continued conflict and synthesis where the material and economic dominate the formation of institutions; the capitalistic system systematically exploits workers, causing alienation and the class struggle; and eventually its contradictions will burst the structures of oppression, and an ideal socialist order will emerge where purified men and women live in harmony. The economic analysis of Marxism centers on the labor theory of value and its relation to profits and prices, the contradictions of capitalism (exploitation of workers, falling rate of profit, successive crises), the critique of classical (and later neo-classical) economics, and an elaboration of the planned economy run on scientific and cooperative lines (by latter-day socialist and communist writers.)

An obvious feature of Marxist socioeconomic thought (Marx, particularly, and most disciples) for Christian social thinking is the extraordinary likeness to what it has to say in criticizing the abuses of capitalism, rejecting liberal individualism, and proclaiming the true nature of economic life and the virtues of work. The similarities belong to a large middle area, offering judgments and recommendations in general terms respecting the abuses of the economic order, but excluding foundations in social philosophy and particular solutions. Also, the place of faith, insight, and conviction are common to each. Then there are the differences: Marxism rejects religion and its regimes try to stamp it out as an enemy of communist society, and there is at root a very different philosophy of man and reality. Subtler clashes concern aspects of Marxist doctrine that seem close to Christian thought but are in fact remote, such as the necessity of continual class struggle, violence for the sake of purification, and discovery of right principles through praxis.

The methodology of Marxist economic thought is sui generis, since its concepts and methods of analysis are bound up with sociological and philosophical strains.[13] A Hegelian vision of essences, transposed into the material (the Feuerbach modification), is at the root of it: Inner dynamic and conflicting forces are present in social and economic phenomena, resulting in continual change and sure progress. Observation, analysis, deduction, and application to practice all have their place in perceiving and furthering this process. With this, Christian thought both sympathizes but parts company: reasoning from philosophical (plus the-

152

ological) premises to social principles and on to economic analysis and applications is equally its procedure, but not the strange agglutination of all three that characterizes Marxism. Its principles retain their absolutist form and do not emerge relatively from evolving economic relations, even if their translation into practice rightly reflects the influences of time and place. Then Marxist thought comports a strong faith that simply sweeps aside those parts of economic science that do not or cannot be made to conform. Tests, verification, and prediction are finally unimportant, since they deal with mere appearances, not the underlying reality and its direction. The Christian approach, too, rejects aspects of economics as the consequence of premises that relate to religious faith, but it also respects the integrity of all science and whatever sure truth it reveals, seeking to integrate it.

10

The institutional school of the United States, the leaders of which were Veblen, Commons, and Mitchell, equally reacted against excesses of the deductive-abstract methods of the neo-classicals to concentrate on the formation and operation of institutions in a legal environment. Though the group scarcely survived the post–World War II rise of macroeconomics and the teaching prominence given neo-classical analysis, by the 1960s neo-institutionalism had gathered strength. The characteristics of what is often now referred to as evolutionary economics have been summarized this way (Klein, 1978): What we do in any economy is greatly fashioned by its institutions; the economy is a sociopolitical and cultural entity; values are to be taken in a wide sense; equally productivity and efficiency are not to be interpreted in a narrow, mechanical way; institutions are part of an evolutionary process; markets are judged by the norms of the economy, not vice versa; concentrations of economic power determine the outcome of modern political economy; and progress toward a just and humane society, rather than mere growth, should be the goal of the economy.

As a practical matter, neo-institutionalism issues in systematic criticism of mainstream economics, especially neo-classical and its methods of analysis, and in programs of reform for economic institutions, notably wherever concentrations of power are perceived. It rejects excessively abstract and deductive techniques of analysis, which conceive of economic entities as belonging to some universalist world, albeit found in different patterns of time and place. Instead it emphasises close, descriptive attention to evolving institutions and their legal and customary framework and constant change. It is not hostile to mathematical analysis as such, but certainly to its excesses that obscure the institutional side of economics. Reforming suggestions are mostly directed at the excessive power of large corporations, unions, and misused government policies and regulations. Vested interests are to be broken up, to allow the economy to evolve toward more humane and widely beneficial objectives. While Christian thought has some sympathy with all this, as remarked, it also guards some appropriate place for deductive thought in social science.

The central weakness of neo-institutionalism—or its strength, as some protagonists see the matter—is the philosophy of instrumental values. Pragmatism, an American philosophy associated chiefly with Peirce, James, and Dewey,[14] holds that the reality of phenomena are circumscribed for the individual by the practical effects he perceives. In the ethical domain the moral worth of an action turns on its practical aims and consequences in achieving some end. Termed instrumentalist by Dewey, such a normative philosophy implies that moral knowledge is bounded by experience, values are only instruments for solving particular problems, and their worth turns on their usefulness as solution. Such an approach rejects the divine criteria of conduct invoked by Christianity and other religions, indeed any source of absolute values. Ayres became the major channel[15] by which instrumental value theory passed into economics and influenced many neo-institutionalists today.

If pragmatism and instrumentalism present less problems for those prepared to accept relativist, situational ethics, it does considerably embarrass those committed to the Christian religion. Consequently there have been many assertions (cf. Hill, 1978, pp. 319–20) of the compatibility of the latter with the former, plus disputes. My suggestion for reconciliation is to posit Christian principles as the foundation of values and to accommodate pragmatic and instrumentalist thinking as part of the middle criteria and applied stages. For example, the value of human labor is a universal, objective, and inviolate principle, founded on the dignity of the person; in this time and place its renumeration requires specified conditions and reforms that we may define instrumentally, using intermediate criteria deriving from first principles but guided by practical situations and expert knowledge. Admittedly such an approach cuts the heart out of a purely relative approach to social ethics, but just as obviously Christian thought cannot acquiesce in pure pragmatism and instrumentalism. Neo-institutionalists understand this perfectly well.

11

In this chapter I have suggested that a Christian approach to economic science, using integrative and not compartmentalized thinking, will strike a balance between excessive abstraction and excessive absorption in the real. It will reject both a Platonic conception of economic reality as comprising pure entities and a Marxian concept, which remains embodied in the material and concrete. Mathematical modeling is accepted but treated with reserve since it is readily blocks out values and reduces economics to a narrow perspective, cutting off the social and cultural context. Then Christian thought does not accept what is commonly proposed as rationality in economic theory, since it places consistent and logical behavior within a wider context of criteria growing out of an ethical system. Equally maximization and efficiency as the goals of economic activity are values to be sanctioned but modified. Such a position on the methods and epistemology of economics partly sympathizes with the criticisms of historical, Marxist, and institutionalist thought, but partly distances itself from them. Christian thought also notes that current economic analysis and research depend for their acceptability on consensus of the investigators and that a degree of faith is unavoidable.

A recent interesting fad in subjecting economic discourse to critical analysis, bringing out the arbitrariness of method, is to observe the nature of the rhetoric employed (for instance, McCloskey, 1983). By what process of logic, proof, language, even art does some writer or speaker seek to persuade the reigning consensus of the truth of what he is arguing? What conventions and artifices are employed to shift opinions and reactions in his favor? Obviously this interesting question concerns every book, article, and discussion. While enlightening, the unsatisfactory side of analyzing rhetoric is that one easily avoids the need to conclude on the methods of argumentation by halting at a discussion of techniques and offering readers the stone of taxonomy. How the game is played and classifying devices obscure whether anything really matters.

Stepping around digressions on rhetoric and pointing again to the central issue, Christian misgivings on economic method turn chiefly on the question of values and links with the wider social, cultural, and religious context. In suggesting modifications, a Christian approach strikes a middle way between excesses. On the one hand, it is attentive to the history and development of institutions, accepting their inductive implications but without rejecting deduction from social principles and human behavior. On the other it accepts the necessity for abstraction that is the stuff of science, along with the helpfulness of modeling, but rejects formalistic excesses that quit reality for a world of creations of the mind, overplaying logic in formulating a science of human behavior.[16] All this entails a cost and a gain. Economic theory would find its pretended rigor curbed, and courses in mathematical economics would spend as much time reflecting on epistemology and the limitations of what is taught as on actual theorems conveyed. Frustrating but salutory. The modifications of which I speak would introduce a certain looseness and even woolliness, foreign to the present character of economic science and probably antithetical to a majority of practitioners. The gain is a wider perspective close to actual economic practice and much more valid from an ethical point of view.

Chapter 9

WELFARE ECONOMICS AND GOVERNMENT

After the general criticism of the setting and methodology of economic science of chapters 7 and 8, let me pass to two extended illustrations of the weaknesses emphasized. The first is hardly fair, since theoretical welfare economics is a well-scarred battlefield, with probably a majority of economists not taking it seriously. The second, the role of government in the market economy, is also a vulnerable area. My aim is to point to a certain incompatibility of the conventional discussion of each with Christian thought and to indicate the sort of revision required if they are (possibly) to be brought into harmony. If some of the following material is technical for general readers, this sort of discussion is required for its credibility with economists.

WELFARE ECONOMICS

Welfare economics is not the same thing as the economics of the welfare state, even if there is a connection. The former is a specialized attempt within positive economic science to define situations of greater welfare for consumers, producers, and the economy as a whole; the second denotes the public programs of improved education, health, and social security, et cetera, that were adopted for social and political reasons little connected with economic theory. The interest given welfare economics has been sporadic. Probably it has heightened in recent years, at least among devotees, owing to our debates on social justice, interest in cost-benefit analysis, and an ongoing need to find some foundation in social science or philosophy for welfare measures, at a time when ethics has been not welcome in positivistic thinking. Let me sketch the history

157

of welfare economics, explain the concept of the Pareto optimum, present the main propositions,[1] and give the reaction of Christian thought.

1

The pursuit of welfare has been associated with economic thinking from its earliest recorded examples—Deuteronomy, some Greek philosophers, medieval and mercantilistic writers—but theoretical welfare economics, which really identified itself as a specialized topic in the 1930s, may be traced only to about 1900. Marshall (*Principles,* 1920, p. 1) thought the objective, scientific study of economic phenomena would contribute first to material and then to rounded welfare. The central device he used was consumer surplus. Supposing a consumer to buy some good in units, he would experience diminishing utility from successive units and be prepared to give only a lower price for each. (Thus he might buy one shirt at a sale for thirty dollars, two for twenty-five dollars each, and three at twenty-two dollars each.) Hence the purchases of the consumer ordinarily gave him a surplus of utility, hypothesizing that he would have paid more for the first than for later units. It follows that any modifications to the economy that lowered prices—more efficiency, better competition, less trade protection, et cetera—would all increase the amount of consumer surplus, with this serving as an objective proof of more welfare. While this neat device in fact raises complex problems that are still debated, let us pass over that side of things.

In his *Economics of Welfare* (1932, p. 57) Pigou switched from consumer surplus to the size and distribution of the national dividend as a measure of improvement in welfare. Economic science must be concerned with quantitative relations (pp. 8–9), and economic welfare could be marked off as that part of social welfare that may be brought "into relation with the measuring rod of money" (p. 11). We can be reasonably sure that economic welfare so measured increases as the size of the national dividend increases and its distribution changes in favor of the poor (since more urgent wants can be satisfied). Further, and taking into account the distinction between social and private product (monopoly, for instance, causes them to diverge; today we add pollution), the national dividend will be maximized where some use of resources causes the values of marginal social net product ("net" allows for all costs, including the maintenance of capital) to be equalized.[2] Thus a case enters for more efficiency, less monopoly, subsidizing declining cost industries, et cetera.

Pigou's treatment of his central themes contains a number of subtle qualifications and is still worth reading (including his lengthy discussion of fair wages).

The approach of Marshall and Pigou and their followers is usually termed the old welfare economics. First, it took utility to be measurable in a cardinal sense; that is, after some qualifications[3] the amount of satisfaction experienced from purchasing and consuming a good was roughly measured by the amount of money one was prepared to pay for it. Second, utility analysis maximized consumer welfare where the last dollar spent on various goods brought in the same extra amount of utility. Third, interpersonal comparisons of utility were made freely, even if more often implicitly than explicitly. Thus tax modifications of income assumed one could compare its marginal worth for different individuals, or proposals to lessen tariffs assumed that benefit to some outweighed harm to others. Fourth, while increases in welfare were linked simplistically with increases in utility and consumer surplus, welfare in a wider sense was understood to be in the background.

The new welfare economics, with which the names of Hicks (1939b) and Samuelson (1947) are particularly associated, is marked by the reverse of some of these characteristics. First, cardinal utility was resolutely rejected in favor of ordinal (one merely ranked one's preferences as opposed to giving them an absolute value), on the grounds that the former could never be precisely measurable. Second, since interpersonal comparisons admitted by the older welfare economics involve value judgments, which are undemonstrable, the new strictly avoided them. The unrealism of such a step in relation to political decisions and ordinary behavior cost it dearly in terms of acceptability. Third, the new welfare economics was marked by rigorous insistence on the value-free character of economic science. Hence the conclusions of analysis could only be about the relative efficiency of different states, with their desirability depending on personal values. Fourth, a new indifference technique (fathered by Edgeworth and developed by Pareto about 1885–1905, familiar to most who have had a course in elementary economics) steadily replaced the older utility method. Hicks's essential position was that one could achieve the same results with the new technique as the old, while avoiding inconveniences and adding improvements.

Regarding its main propositions, welfare economics is concerned with the attainment of a superior state of welfare by initially the individual and then the group. In the tradition of liberal individualism, the first is defined as the individual having more of what he wants. This is rendered precise by supposing he has a given income and tastes, is faced by a set of commodities with known prices, chooses consistently, and prefers more to less. The optimum is where he has attained his most preferred position, subject to income and other constraints. While this is straight-forward enough, given the assumptions made and the attitudes of indi-vidualism, the group case gives problems. Taking individualism strictly, the group can only be a collection of individuals and their good a mere summation. If changes occur, the good of the group surely improves only if at least one person is better off while nobody else is worse off (re-member, we may not compare gains and losses of welfare); and the maximum must be where no further change can be made without benefit to one individual necessarily causing harm to somebody else. Pareto advanced this proposition in his *Manual* of 1906 (1966, vol. 7, p. 354), though it was Hicks (1939b) who initiated the prominence given the Pareto optimum.

Clearly, this conception of the group welfare is embarrassing, since it makes society into an atomistic collection of individuals concerned exclusively with his or her own good and since economic policy invariably benefits some at the expense of others. All tax measures do that. Con-sequently a variety of compensation devices have been explored to take care of the problem of benefit to one individual leading to harm to another; for example, a change might be acceptable if it conferred such benefits that those harmed could be compensated for less. But all such schemes are conceptual propositions, unverifiable in any factual way; the ruling out of interpersonal comparisons (but cf. Sen, 1982, chapter 12) remains the rock on which they founder.

To the uninitiated, the concept of the Pareto optimum must seem quite insubstantial: Defining the peak of group welfare as where the good of any one member cannot be improved without necessarily harming that of another is indeed a remote idea. But the next step is to link that proposition with reasoning that, though still Platonic, points to optimal situations in the consumer market, production, and their combination (Bator, 1957). While these demonstrations are too technical to be usefully reproduced here, their elaboration in texts[4] is a pretty thing; as far as theory goes, the results are quite correct in that the premises adopted lead to them.

<h1 style="text-align:center">3</h1>

Merely from the point of view of positive economics, quite apart from Christian thought, there are many difficulties[5] with an elaboration of the Pareto best for the consuming and producing economy. Yet the most important problem concerns the possible application of welfare economics to practice. At least the old version seemed to make the rough compromises with reality that rendered application possible: Money prices and incomes measured utility in an approximate manner and interpersonal comparisons were freely used, so that redistribution through taxation and public goods and other measures permitted one to conclude to social improvements. But the new welfare economics seemed to rule out the possibility of practical reference: The indifference apparatus could hardly be linked in any practical way to consumer or firm behavior (the murky theme of revealed preference[6] scarcely improved matters), interpersonal comparisons were ruled out, and the Pareto optimum was quite unknowable in any practical way, not to speak of the overall best.

It was with some relief, then, that many proceeded to claim modern cost-benefit analysis (which has received marked attention over the last fifteen years in theoretical economics, in addition to its longer role in business applications) represented ''welfare economics in action'' (Mishan, 1976, pp. 58–59; Winch, 1971, chapter 9). The central idea is to evaluate all the costs and benefits of some investment proposal and, according to certain rules, establish which set outweighs the other. The technique is applicable to public as well as private projects, with the former taking in more indirect aspects and probably justifiable at a lower rate of return over a longer period. It is widely though far from exclusively used in private enterprise, where ''animal spirits'' (a phrase of J. M. Keynes) add themselves to a variety of motivations for investment and conquest.

At all events, does cost-benefit analysis shore up theoretical welfare economics properly speaking? Not at all. It does help draw out the practical side of measuring burdens and benefits for some maximum outcome over time and can be applied to any individual situation (even Hamlet's great problem) as well as to private and public investment. Yet it places an objective monetary value on all considerations introduced (as opposed to restricting itself to subjective preferences), freely uses interpersonal comparisons (public costs financed by taxation necessarily do this in relation to prospective benefits), and is not made the slightest use of—can this even be conceivable?—to set some Pareto optimal outcome. Cynics say that cost-benefit analysis can be used to justify or condemn any investment project; you merely rearrange the data and calculations to get a preferred outcome.

4

From the point of Christian thought, the prime question is whether the substance of welfare economics can be rescued and reshaped so as to be brought into some sort of harmony. On this, three negative comments initially.

'Good,' 'preferences,' 'welfare' and similar concepts are used in positive economics in a personal sense unconnected with any code of objective morality. Define *good* as what the consumer wants and *welfare* as more of it, treat choices as purely a matter of personal decision, and you are on a collision course with Christian thought. A variant affirms that whether or not individual and social conduct should conform to some objective moral code, this involves a later correction of choices initially treated in a positive, individualistic way. The difficulty is that what is systematically bypassed and omitted becomes unimportant and drops out of sight.

A second objection to Pareto-type reasoning is that it uses a narrow concept of rationality (see chapter 8, section 4) to which I have objected repeatedly. The individual is supposed to have an ordered set of preferences that he knows and acts upon consistently, and given the motor principle of self-interest, maximization is the best or most efficient outcome. The analysis of the group is similar in principle, though the consequences of individual behavior for others and compensation for harm pose special problems. The techniques of strict logic and mathematics are generally employed, so that the results convey an aura of scientific work before one confronts the numerous problems. Namely, the conclusions follow from the premises put in place and seem untestable, which is a strange procedure from the point of positivism. Then the logic and

162

mathematics have to be calculating or manipulating something—utility, preferences, advantage—and however colorless that something is made, it has to resemble some concept of the good to have significance, but the method of inquiry used is incapable of getting at the good in any meaningful sense.

Third, premises of the Pareto optimum are antisocial and irreconcilable with the *ad alterum* characteristic of the Christian message. The notion of good is again the root of the problem: Define it as essentially egotistic, and the good of society can only mean the goods of a collection of individuals. There is no real union and no common good as such. But in Christian thought society is a community of other-directed persons (see chapter 3, section 3), and there is a common good in addition to self-interests. Despite individual freedom to opt out, the people composing the tribe, the kingdom, the nation, today's global village—whatever the concretization in time and circumstances—are a communion for common goals and mutual assistance. The Pareto optimum, however, remains an essentially individualistic piece of reasoning, supposedly restricted to the economy and certainly out of touch with society properly speaking (cf. chapter 7, note 8).

5

More generally, if my desire is for an economic science revised from the standpoint of a validly underpinning social philosophy, could one set aside individualism, omission of values, and the rest and in some manner fit the material of welfare economics into place in the areas of middle criteria and applications? Unfortunately, such an enterprise seems to offer little hope of any success, certainly for a Christian approach to welfare.

The concept of individual and social well-being that harmonizes with Christian thought could be expressed in various ways. One summarization is the practice and flourishing of the virtues, since welfare is first a state of the spirit or soul. A certain material welfare, at least the minima necessary for decent individual and social living, is the obvious accompaniment. In this the New Testament version advanced on that of the Old Testament, where the latter—in the evolutionary phase of Judeo-Christian thinking—made a certain worldly prosperity the reflection and reward of righteous living. Christianity, however, clarified the principles of resurrection and life after death and placed on its adherents the duty of

163

imitating the Master. Consequently redemptive suffering, of limitless dimension and supererogatory at some point, is an inescapable component of true welfare lying beyond and above prosperity in an ordinary human sense.

Consequently, various nuances modify a Christian concept of economic welfare. Let it be granted that all members of society have certain rights: to work, living standards, distributive justice in taxation and public goods, conditions of work, and all the rest. Valid conceptions of individual and social well-being emerge. People who are hungry, badly housed, and treated unjustly in many ways are likely to be handicapped spiritually. Christian thought still raises the perspective of a welfare that transcends what is materially and even spiritually comfortable. "He that saves his life shall lose it" is the divine injunction, so that the notion of consumers getting more and then most of what they prefer, the dangers of material gratification, and the merit of self-denial and subordination of the immediate to the transcendental cannot be taken lightly.

As for the technical apparatus of welfare economics, it is difficult to see how much of it can usefully be preserved. Certain parts could possibly be adapted to reflect different welfare premises; for instance, setting ethical criteria in place to guide preferences, one might then reason to some maximum position using either indifference or utility techniques. But the devices of indifference analysis are so remote from real situations and so deformed by merely quantitative emphasis that they do not appear to correspond with the "moderate realism" (cf. chapter 8, section 1) that fits with Christian thought. This at least with respect to consumer behavior and the optimal allocation of production factors to firms; possibly they have some useful purpose in relation to other applications (international trade and the rest). Then putting together the consumption and production sectors to arrive at some overall optimal situation has no practical or theoretical importance, since the theory is so flawed and the results cannot be related to practice.

Despite all the objections one can bring to it, for want of something better the Pareto optimum seems to lead a charmed life. One prominent writer (Netzer, 1974, p. 27) has found it a "Copernican landmark" in economic thinking; another has tried repeatedly to establish a link between it and social justice (Worland, 1981, p. 283; 1967).[7] Some think cost-benefit analysis is an applied road heading in its general direction. Others have tried to render social what is a piece of recalcitrant individualism by including the welfare of others in individual welfare functions. Despite all this, the Pareto optimum is a concept irreconcilable with any truly social economics: It reflects extreme individualism, eschews values of any objective sort, and cannot be connected up with community. It is hard to avoid the conclusion that a Christian approach to welfare economics can only leave aside the Pareto optimum as unsalvageable. Probably this verdict also applies to the whole of theoretical welfare economics.

ROLE OF GOVERNMENT

My second illustration of the inability of mainstream economics to deal with a matter going far beyond its individualistic-rationalist premises is the place and role of government in a basically free economy. Economic theory typically seeks to restrict the entry of government and, by implication, justify it, on the basis of market failure. This is coupled with an analysis of how public choice decides the shape of public intervention within a presumed framework of social contact. A Christian approach to government, however, requires a social philosophy in place to specify its general role and functions, whereupon the themes of market failure, subsidiarity, collective choice, and social contract can be used as one moves on to the detail of what government shall actually do in a basically free economy. All this proves a particularly good illustration of how one might integrate Christian thought with a segment of prevailing analysis.

6

The enormous growth of government in most Western countries in the present century has occurred in roughly four stages: two world wars, where for a variety of reasons it extended its share and control of the economy, without a corresponding retreat at the close of hostilities; the 1930s, when private enterprise required special help and welfare programs were extended; and the 1950–60s, when in the wave of prosperity generally experienced governments embarked on extensive spending on education, health, pension, and other welfare programs.

In modern economic writing, the role of government in the advanced and basically free society is analyzed around four main topics. (a) ''Market failure'' is typically used to mark off the area of public intervention. Theoretically, private enterprise might produce and distribute needed goods and services, presumptively in the most efficient manner, but it breaks down in areas classified as allocation of resources to production, distribution, and stabilization. In the first, the ''free rider'' problem[8] shows clearly that a market system cannot efficiently price and allocate certain goods and services to their users. (b) But market failure only introduces the role of government, since applied decisions must decide when private enterprise fails and the mode of intervention. Voters have to agree where and how private provisions of goods and services should be supplemented by tax-financed sources, and their representatives should reflect their wishes. The contribution of economists to the democratic process of committees, negotiations, and the rest has long been known as the theory of collective choice (now renamed public choice). (c) Beyond market failure and collective choice there has to be some explicit or implicit philosophy into which any approach to government fits, and typically we are offered a version of social contract. Modern society is taken to be a grouping of free individuals, each with his own preferences, and whether or not it is a natural institution, the bottom line is that individuals negotiate democratically to arrive at a workable constitution.[9] The latter provides a framework of law and government within which all go about their business with a maximum of freedom. If you delve for the values underlying this view of society, you are into the familiar currents of liberal individualism, logical positivism, and scientific humanism. (d) Then, after this kind of analysis, numerous investigations have tried to clarify what has in fact led to the great expansion of the public sector. Wagner's law, income elasticity of demand for public goods and services, the displacement hypothesis of Peacock, the relative productivity theory of Baumol and others, the ironies of Parkinson, and the soberer theory of bureaus have all[10] sought to explain the swelling monster. As unmanageable as much of this material is,[11] it impresses on us that theories of market failure and collective choice can scarcely reduce all to order with simplistic rules to decide what government shall do.

After this initial look at the terrain, let me link this mainstream account of the place of government with Christian thought, using the same four topics in a different order. How may a values-oriented refashioning of economic science use these themes?

7

In the body of thought to which I subscribe (cf. chapter 3, section 4), government is taken to be a natural part of an organic concept of society, which is not a mere collection of individuals who choose to agree or not on the need for government. Instead the way we are made leads us to congregate together and acquiesce in the natural role of government, though its practical modalities vary. Its essential purpose is to promote the common good of society, which consists partly in the welfare of individuals and partly in their integration into the good of the whole (again a bodylike idea). Evidently, government must protect some appropriate place for a horizontal and vertical diversity of economic institutions, since personal freedom and rights require respect and assistance. Further, it possesses authority, which consists not merely in the power of coercion but more important in the right to obtain the cooperation of those whom it serves.

Given such a philosophy, there is no difficulty in fitting social contract in, since one has only to turn to the old view of an explicit or implicit social pact between rulers and ruled (Charles and Maclaren, 1982, p. 191; Gough, 1957). As medievalists saw the matter more readily than us, all authority was from God, earthly government was an analogue of divine government, its practical modalities were decided by human arrangements, and the natural law was the guide of rulers and ruled. With the present pluralistic character of society, one cannot expect many to acquiesce in such a theological underpinning of social contract, but treating it as a purely human agreement, having no foundation in some standard of absolute values, is no less an inadequate basis for government.[12] If you begin and end with the liberal view that a group of individuals, each with his own values, freely contracts to determine every aspect of the constitution and rules for society, you are into ethical relativism (cf. Buchanan, 1975, p. 164) and self-destructive forms of liberalism.

8

Beginning as a search for solution to the social welfare function, the theory of collective choice has grown into an important field for economists and others. The essential question is how a group of self-centered individuals, each seeking to maximize personal choices, may arrive at collective decisions that are a best outcome. Its chief themes are perhaps these: (i) the prisoners' dilemma (below) and similar "maximin" exercises (you maximize some irreducible minimum of benefit) illustrate that individuals will better their lot if they agree on some code of behavior, rather than each pursuing his advantage in isolation; (ii) while unanimity is strictly necessary for a Pareto optimum outcome (2 above), since everybody must accept the nonharmfulness of steps leading to it, in practice we must settle for some majority rule determined by its costs and benefits; (iii) in a democracy we elect representatives to a governing body, so that we need a way of relating their actions to the wishes of voters; (iv) parties form both at the individual and representative level, so that the behavior of coalitions requires analysis; and (v) subsidiary topics include the Arrow impossibility theorem (see chapter 8, section 4), log rolling, information seeking and costs, et cetera. "Public choice" has become, at least in the United States, a favored name for the field, being the title of a learned society and its journal and suggesting that the theory of collective choice should address itself primarily to how government arrives at its decisions and responds to voter preferences.

If Christian thought is to use and incorporate as much as possible of this material, it will begin by changing certain ground rules. Notably, (i) it is essential to begin with objective social values, drawn from a fundamental ethics and not based merely on agreements among contracting individuals. The latter will assist in spelling out intermediate criteria and implementation, but both stages must reflect the values in question. (ii) Self-interest must be amended in a radical way to include the good of others, not merely in the form of superegotism termed altruism. (See chapter 7, section 8). My own good, which I rightly and naturally pursue, includes disinterestedly the welfare of others (because this is the only valid way love works) and is thus furthered beyond any degree possible through mere self-interest. (iii) It follows that the Pareto optimum, the concept of a best where nobody's egotistic good is harmed as that of others rises, is to be discarded as a goal for collective decisions. (iv) As for methodology, a Christian approach cannot acquiesce in exclusive or central reliance on strictly logical reasoning from amoral assumptions, with its usual quantitative garb and perversions of group decision making.

If such provisos call for radical modifications to the theory of public choice, just as evidently they are necessary for the latter to make useful contributions for the real world. If you take as your basic postulate that "man is an egotistic, rational utility maximizer,"[13] such a definition leads easily (and is so intended) into quantitative, strictly logical reasoning, with its portrayal of social decisions as mechanical deductions. Values are ostensibly left at the doorway but in fact become identified with normal, efficient, maximizing behavior and equilibrium outcomes. The mental fascination of all this, its pseudo-scientific air, and its demonstrations have been dissected many times, but they are like a drug that the addicted cannot put aside. Christian thought, on the contrary, would alter the method and content of such reasoning, rejecting its formalism and taking into account cultural and psychosocial influences, error-laden information and expectations, and also moral evil, all normal features of decision making.

To take one instance of the sort of revision in mind, the prisoners' dilemma assumes two accomplices suspected of some crime and held in isolation have each an incentive to confess and turn state's evidence against each other, so that a maximin solution emerges (i.e., the logic of the situation forces each to choose a lower outcome than that possible if they are able to cooperate with each other).[14] The problem can be extended to various trading and behavioral situations in economic life, and Rawls's choosing "behind a veil of ignorance"[15] is a close cousin. The significance of such games, narrowly, is that disloyalty may be more advantageous than cooperation and, more broadly, that better maximin solutions depend on better rules being in place for self-interest. For some addicts such rules appear (to judge from their silence) a *substitute* for ethics; the latter may be preferable, but are not likely to be agreed on by our present pluralistic society and in any event cannot be scientifically established. Others (Rapoport, 1961, p. xiii) see the study of "conflict behaviour" as a *supplement* to ethics, sharpening our perceptions of how people define intermediate goals and decisions in relation to their ultimate values. In either case, almost total silence descends regarding any ethics of right and wrong and the fascination of quantitative reasoning largely overwhelms conclusions for actual behavior.

Maximin games and strategies have to be underpinned by objective values, since without them one cannot impute any sense to the goodness of choices beyond the purely subjective. Smaller or larger outcomes are only that; whether they are ever desirable is the prior question. Then if the good of each individual is redefined to include that of others, sought in a supererogatory way (the Christian ideal), individual choices become posed differently from the behavior of two criminals so often used as a model for decision making. (Supposing one took the decision making of Francis of Assisi instead!) Introduce not only an ethics but a saving array of virtues as well—say justice and the charity, compassion, and mercy that go beyond it—and it becomes much more possible to accept maximin studies as contributing to a better understanding of conflict resolution. Undoubtedly strategies, coalitions, persuasion, information, mixed outcomes, et cetera, are part of political and economic behavior, with ethics operative but too little acknowledged, so that we can gain from analysis of how egoists behave before reconsidering it in a wider context.

9

Market failure is both a factual and a normative way of marking off the actual and potential role for government in a free economy. More precisely, it concerns public goods and services that cannot be allocated exclusively to buyers and priced accordingly. Its looser interpretation includes merit goods[16] (such as education), correction of certain externalities and destructive competition, and redistribution and stabilization policies. Modern urbanization has clearly extended the area of market failure, mulitiplying externalities and intensifying the need to provide welfare. There is also the historical inability of private enterprise to finance large public works projects, owing to lack of capital and excessive risk. Market failure proves to be a wide net, where many social and political factors add themselves to the intellectually teasing problem of defining the pure public good (Head and Bird, 1972, chapter 1).

Market breakdown can be harmonized with a Christian approach by treating it as a way of getting from general principles to their applications. If one views the crossover as a process of introducing intermediate criteria to arrive at detailed decisions, market failure helps show when and where government should intervene in the economy. Further, my approach to government stressed the principle of subsidiarity (see chapter 3, section 4), which holds that a more highly placed institution or part of society should respect the working of a lower, where market failure is a helpful guide for its interpretation.

If market failure is finally no more than a loose way of marking off the proper area of government intervention, clearly wider economic and social considerations help pin it down. Determining the category of merit goods, as also the tolerable limits of externalities, calls for considerations going beyond narrow maximizing criteria. Like M. Jourdain, who discovered he had been speaking prose all his life, those who press beyond initial analysis of market failure to applied studies (Borcherding, 1977) are quickly into the material and focus of social economics (cf. chapter 10). Solving the limits of government contributions to education and health care by cost-benefit exercises alone is impossible. Narrow economic reasoning may have popularized the concept, but market failure does not suffice to handle the domain into which it leads.

10

Turning to applied studies that have tried to account for the remarkable growth of government outlays in advanced mixed economies, Wagner's law of expanding state functions as society becomes richer is long-standing but posed at too general a level to throw much light on the actual process. Its positive counterpart, telling us the demand for public services expands faster than national income, is a definitional tautology, while the displacement hypothesis (government absorbs private enterprises and activities as the aftermath of, say, war disruptions) is helpful only for one-shot explanations. So, after the productivity thesis of Baumol (note 10), which does throw light on distributive pressures driving up public service costs, the most interesting attempt to explain expanding government is the so-called theory of bureaus.

Maintaining that bureaucrats are motivated by self-interest, Downs (1966) takes as his central hypothesis that officials seek a complex set of goals "rationally" (more is better) and that the social functions of an organization strongly influence its internal structure and behavior. His book is a taxonomic survey of the setting up, functioning and characteristics of bureaus. He posits five types of officials, all utility maximizers of self-interest with some admixture of altruism (pp. 83, 88), and has little to say on why government bureaus expand (chapter 21). As Niskanen (1971, p. 8) justly remarks, Downs focuses on managerial behaviour within bureaus, stopping short of developing the consequences of maximizing behavior on budgets and output performance. Niskanen's own thesis is that entrepreneurial bureaucrats try to maximize their operations by extracting the largest budget possible from their political masters. Drawing extensively on the theory of the firm for maximization and efficiency reasoning, his remedies for excessive and inefficient government operations consist in giving incentives to bureaucrats to economize their operations, returning some of the latter to private enterprise, and improving the political review process. If Niskanen's book is a stimulating analysis of bureaucratic growth and how to curb it, its drawbacks are heavy reliance on the theory of the firm, since so much of what government does cannot be quantified and put to market tests, and its absence of adequate normative standards.

Such applied studies seeking to throw light on what may be called the inner process of the growth of government departments (the final stage of the application of principles, in my approach) are usually marked by omission of the role of a social ethics, since the positive work in question does not know how or does not dare to incorporate it. Niskanen is reduced to accepting, "in the absence of a more appealing alternative, the standard Pareto criterion for what ought to be done" (p. 190), which amounts to saying he has no normative standard, since such a criterion is of no practical use whatever. Without a frank introduction and elaboration of values, applied studies of the growth of government have no guide to evaluate their findings and recommendations. Assume the principles of Christian thought, however, and theories of the growth of bureaus become underpinned for their judgments on unnecessary government expansion and regulation and given direction and goals.

* * *

A purely economic theory of the place and role of government in the economy may fairly be styled reductionist thinking. (See chapter 2, section 4.) What government actually does and what it should be doing in the economy (as in the political and social divisions) is a reflection of many considerations—philosophical, historical, evolutionary, "natural," contingent, et cetera. From a positive point of view, involving efficiency and maximization of output as main guides, one may do much to infer and delineate the area of legitimate intervention in the mixed economy. But reducing this role *wholly* to a question of market failure is absurd, since one has introduced a preconceived framework of thought and criteria deriving from a narrow concept of economic life and left aside centuries of discussion on the origins and nature of the state.

To analyze public choice of the modalities of government intervention as quantitative reasoning aimed at maximum advantage for the group is equally reductionism. There is again the same curious desire on the part of protagonists to delimit the process by which a group of people reach collective decisions to logical constructions of some sort. But if individual decision making results from a mixture of logic, persuasion, chance, intuition, cussedness, et cetera, so does that of the group. After the event, of course, one can make up patterns of logic to explain what happened, and the analysis may be pretty enough; the test is surely whether one can predict decisions, and there have been no spectacular achievements from public choice theorists. Further, ethical motives are conveniently omitted or downplayed in the interests of scientific, communicable knowledge. Supposing group decision making is only a logical reflection of unquestioned individual preferences is far from all that needs to be taken into account in analyzing public choice. Ethics continually bursts through, as our sensation-conscious conscious media show as they pounce on unethical behaviour by public figures and bodies.

If, however, we introduce a valid social philosophy to underpin both the role of government and public decision making, then market failure and public choice can be brought in as part of the process of moving from principles to their application. Centrally government is charged with ensuring the common good, which means seeing that all benefit from the economy in some reasonable way, so that gaps in what private enterprise can accomplish help mark off its role. Properly understood, this is another way of presenting the need for subsidiarity. Bring in the role of ethics to guide individual and group decision making, which is a way of invoking social justice and other social virtues, and mere logical action on the basis of preferences settles into a rightful, wider context. This is in fact a much better picture of how government determines its role in practice and how social decision making actually proceeds. Again the ideal is that a Christian ethics be more in place.

i

Chapter 10

CONCLUSION: SOCIAL ECONOMICS AND SOCIAL ECONOMY

The purpose of this book has been to try to see modern economics from the perspective of the Christian mind. Taking one's stand in an authentic and resolute way as a disciple of Christ and using the point of view that follows of the world and knowledge about it, what position does one adopt on the foundations and aims of the modern advanced economy and on the science that studies it systematically? Such an approach forces one to put aside the compartmentalization of mind so widely practiced and to set about the difficult tasks of integration, bringing together whatever truth and goodness may be found in different domains of life and knowledge about it, sifting and rejecting. Such work requires, among other essential things such as genuine religion and the habits of mind it engenders, putting in place a social philosophy flowing from Christian premises, with the interpretation it offers of community and individual life in what are conveniently called the political, social, and economic orders. General principles are posed, intermediate criteria added, and applications then struggled with. A high degree of certainty gives way to conflicts of opinion, and concrete steps will be decided only after disputes, compromises, and, one may hope, prayerful guidance.

One reason for undertaking this work of forming a different vision of economic life and science must be the sheer numbers of Christians in many societies and the importance they should presumably place on adopting an approach of mind that reflects their beliefs. A second reason, stressed in my introduction (section 1), is the possible breakdown of Western society as, and if, the framework of Judeo-Christian values continues to dissolve. The immense achievements of modern civilization become undermined if we no longer have foundational criteria to guide

175

individual and social life; equally a purely positive approach to the social sciences loses its underpinning and sense of direction. Analyses of the facts undertaken by the social sciences have uncertain potential for good if we are no longer sure of how they should be used. In this way, Christian thought becomes (for believers, at least) not merely an option to be considered along with others and classified accordingly, but an indispensable part of the solution.

But even if there is a valid case for basing a program of reform of economies and economic science on Christian thought, the vast question remains of finding its practical modalities and responding to the fact of pluralism in values and religion in modern society. Hence I conclude with some remarks on three topics: arriving at a common platform of values, revising economic science in the direction of social economics, and arriving at the policy applications of social economy.

1

Of many problems that arise concerning open advocacy of Christian thinking in relation to the economy and economic science, perhaps the most difficult is the pluralism of modern society and approaches to knowledge and decision making. Any modern context includes Christians of many persuasions, adherents to other religions, humanists, agnostics, atheists, and others with or without goodwill, so that insistence on one quite fundamental approach tends to turn off sympathy and understanding and possibilities for common action. To repeat, then, what was said at the outset, while this book has been composed from the standpoint of a Catholic Christian and a conservative interpretation of Christian premises and thought, it is not my view that only Catholic Christianity is the road to God and that it alone may serve as the basis of religiously oriented social doctrine. All true religion leads to God, and its faithful adherents may indeed arrive at authentic principles of individual and social life in the economic, political, and social orders of whatever society, even if protagonists will hold that their approach alone offers its plentitude.

This said, if Christian economists are to approach economic science with noncompartmentalized minds, setting aside the deceptions of positive theory and secular-humanist premises, their obvious choices are to attempt to draw up a Christian version of economic science—an unrealistic enterprise, as remarked (see chapter 7, section 5)—or to work within some pluralistic organisation of like-minded dissenters. Possible alternatives are social economics, institutional or evolutionary economics, or another radical grouping, such as Marxist or other reformers. The first is the obviously congenial environment, even if others offer advantages along with drawbacks, where the most awkward problem remains agreement on some minimal platform of shared values. These must constitute the premises for revising conventional economics and the starting point for recommending institutional reforms.

Accordingly the first stage of a program for common stance and action has to visualize like-minded social economists setting out from their respective and respected premises to arrive at a common platform. The tasks are not easy, but there are such achievements as statements of rights by the United Nations (1947), many governments, and other national and international agencies. Contention will hardly be absent, expecially with respect to social rights (say, the lives of the unborn or very elderly); fortunately, in the economic domain it is easier to get broad agreement on rights to work, minimal living standards, social security, industrial legislation, et cetera. Such a platform of values—secular humanists have done it (Kurtz, 1980)—constituting a loose social philosophy at some remove from their premises would then constitute the basis for a revision of economic science (social economics) and for work in the area lying between it and social ethics proper (social economy).

2

Social economics is a concept that risks being drowned in a multitude of interpretations, like the older socialism. While even liberal individualism is one form of it, via the invisible hand of Adam Smith or Chicago, social economics has commonly denoted a reaction to laissez-faire and a focus on socioeconomic institutions and common welfare. In that sense it may be traced to the reformers of the first half of the nineteenth century and to the versions of theoretical and applied economics associated with socialist and communist thought. Other strains are the Catholic social thought of the second half of the century, the solidarist doctrine of Pesch (see Mulcahy, 1952, and F. Mueller, 1977), and many reform programs of the early twentieth century (such as guild socialism, distributism, cooperatives, and corporatism). Today social economics is—at least among its protagonists[1] generally used in the sense of analysis and ad-

177

vocacy of socioeconomic institutions in the business and labor domains, governmental social security programs, international assistance, et cetera, or more simply and inclusively the study of social welfare in the economic order, though reforming economic science is also a basic concern. Further, discussions of social economics today attract specialists from mainstream economics, industrial relations, sociology, social work, social psychology, and beyond, so that they are typically interdisciplinary.

My preference, however, is to confine the term to denoting a revised economic science, while reserving ''social economy'' for the intermediate area between it and social ethics. The basic feature marking social economics off from the conventional version is the inclusion of values reflecting individual and social welfare,[2] along with the sort of modifications of methodology suggested in chapter 8. In line with earlier discussion (see chapter 7, sections 2–5), it may be defined as the science that studies human behavior in some convenient classification of economic institutions—production, exchange, distribution, et cetera—with the aim of furthering an immediate material well-being linking up with overall welfare. All other facets remain ancillary to this. The economic values in question have been summarized (see chapter 4) as basic freedoms to use one's talents, labor, and property as one wishes, while exercising responsibility toward others; such an organization of institutions as both creates a work environment respecting and enhancing the person and safeguards a hierarchy of social groupings (implying restraint on competition and mergers) and a distributional outcome where everybody receives primarily from work, but also through necessary social programs, certain minimal standards of health, habitation, and education. To put all this another way, the basic problems that must be solved in any economy—what to produce, how to produce, and how to distribute and exchange—would be solved in ways consonant with human dignity, in our lives as individuals and as members of the family, local and national society, and also the international community.

Since the values in question will certainly be grounded in some total philosophy of life and view of the person, it becomes impossible to view social economics as a quite specialized field of study, cut off horizontally and vertically from related fields. Instead, through unifying principles it connects up with behavior as studied in many social sciences. In this way their distressingly specialized studies may be drawn together. It is not merely a question of exposing and developing lateral connections, though these are important enough, but what matters more is the vertical linking from common values. For example, the economic study of consumer behavior undoubtedly should be complemented by sociological, psychological, and other aspects, so that horizontal links develop; add to this common vertical roots, and there is a far surer and more solid basis for convergence of knowledge than approaches remaining on an essentially positive plane.

As for methodology, social economics would (following the suggestions of chapter 8) take a middle road between excessively abstract and merely descriptive approaches to economic reality, use mathematical modeling with discretion, employ a wider concept of rationality, and treat the concepts of maximization and efficiency with reserve. Scientific rigor and precision would be toned down in favor of a looser, doubtless more literary, style, to reflect individual and social reality more accurately. Such suggestions point to far-reaching revisions: Consumer behaviour and welfare would be recast; the theory of the firm would move from so much unverifiable a priorism to a heavier focus on industrial organization; distributive theory would take fuller account of its ethical, social, and behavioral sides; macroeconomics would move away from its search for a quasi-physical theory of behavior of economic aggregates to more emphasis on its ethical side; just pricing and wages would become new preoccupations; and economic development and aid would be seen as central issues in world redistribution. These are a few of many instances where the central thrust would be to shift a narrowly positive approach towards an analysis linked to a wider ethical and social context. In this way, incidentally, instructors would no longer be continually confronting frustrated, rebellious classes with conjectural theories that cannot be brought into significant relation with social issues. As they well know, a large number are incapable of verification, falsification, or even satisfactory corroboration.[3]

Clearly, the challenge of such a social economics would be to come to grips with well-established pieces of economic theory, rejecting, reformulating, and refashioning as necessary. Vast work is required, where previous chapters (chapters 6 and 9) are only inadequate beginnings.

3

After revision of economic science, there remains the need for intense study of the neglected area between it and social ethics. This is the intermediate zone where one side reaches out with its analysis and factual knowledge and the other with its intermediate criteria. To this in-between field the name social economy is readily attached, about which three remarks may be made. First, this is more apt than "political economy," since the latter chiefly suggests government policy making. Clearly, however, the area between ethics and the economy must embrace the whole of socioeconomic behaviour and institutions. The internal working of firms and unions is as much a matter for consideration as their relations with overseeing government.

Second, "social economy" implies multidisciplinary investigation and integrative work. While it remains itself primarily concerned with economic applications, sociological, psychological-cultural, political, and other inputs are required. Third, ethical investigation of economic (equally sociological, psychological, political, et cetera) matters has evidently been a much neglected area (cf. Deats, 1972, chapter 1). It cannot be substituted for by merely positive inquiries purporting to explain what people do and why, while projecting normative implications for behavior to an extent Hume thought religion alone was guilty of, never science.[4] Today's secular universities appear incapable of undertaking investigations that treat ethics, not to speak of moral theology, with enough seriousness to devote anything like an adequate volume of research to its social importance. We experience instead a dearth of moral discourse on economic behavior, which contrasts strangely with former times and the volume of it usual in communist societies, where the population is constantly advised on how they should act in the social interest.

Social economy is not proposed merely as a meeting ground between an intact positive economics and the policy field, an intermediate area where values simply encounter and use positive analysis for applied ends. There is, of course, a tempting case for leaving an established positive science intact, to which may then be linked a rejuvenated political economy.[5] In a typical interpretation, the former would keep its character, to avoid confusion of values and guard communicability, while political economy consciously would adopt value premises to join analysis with policy applications. Long-standing experience, however, has made it clear that such an approach permits the scientific version of economics, with its neglect and perversion of values, to continue to hold sway in academic headquarters, where the profession may talk whole lifetimes away without any need to confront the practical consequences of their analysis. Political economy in fact never gets much beyond polite recognitions of its importance. Instead, we need social economy as an intensive area of work requiring full development in its own right, continuing on from a revised economic science.

*   *   *

But social economics and social economy must be left with these remarks, since their proper development would require another book. Instead my overriding purpose has been to seek out the implications of the central beliefs of Christianity for economic institutions and their operation in a free society and for the nature of the social science studying them in a systematic way—a simple aim but productive of enormous complexity. Can one give an acceptable statement of Christian beliefs, socioeconomic principles, and their sources that will satisfy Christians themselves; in what ways and how surely may one move to applications; to what extent must social science guide and correct ethical directives? Criticism of answers to these questions is the easy part; the alternatives proposed are more to the point.

My broad conclusions are that the foundational institutions of a free economy may be given solid if qualified justification. Personal economic freedoms, private property and enterprise, competition, and the search for benefit may all be connected up with human rights, with individual advantage qualified by social obligation. These and other principles require to be led through to applications by developing more specified criteria and by using the normal committee and compromise paraphernalia of a society that respects personal liberty and dignity. As for economic science, its nature and aims, along with its methodology, are in need of revision before harmonization with properly Christian thinking is possible, since a religious approach is confronted by systematic exclusion of its values by positivism, along with the false coin created. At a former time, we were able to live with an autonomous economic science standing on conventionally accepted bases, with value judgments modifying conclusions as their adherents chose. But the rift with Christian thought has become so sharp, the crisis of society such, that for those who put religious premises in first place it is now necessary to dissent openly and strongly.

Methodology in economics and in science generally has been extensively reexamined over the past twenty-five years. Partly these discussions have been concerned with methods of acquiring knowledge, partly with the epistemology of what we know, and partly with the

181

fundamental issue of what sure knowledge we may ever acquire. In one way, the methodology of the social sciences is more interesting than that of the physical sciences, since the former are concerned directly with human behavior. In economics, extraordinarily refined examinations have been made of the nature of economic theory, how it should be formulated, and what it may hope to accomplish. But if you read patiently through numerous writers, you soon notice that for all their intense interest in truth about economic knowledge, they have little or nothing to say on what truth may be in some absolute sense or what economic reality may finally be. If interested in a Christian approach to truth, you are painfully aware that anything that would raise theological or divine questions has no place. It is at bottom, and no further, a matter of ascertaining what reality and truth may represent for like-minded peers who agree to excise whatever smacks of religion from their discussions and to remain on an entirely humanist-secular plane.[6] To this extent, therefore, despite many impressive dissections and proposed revisions, the methodological examinations in question—indeed, the bulk of the philosophy of science—remain fundamentally incomplete and to that extent falsified. A Popper and a Feyerabend may scoff at absolutes, but without them successive relativist explanations bend and are uprooted in the first strong wind of dissent.

For finally and indispensably one must have some standard of truth, an overarching criterion to judge all that is human. Within the confines of what is created and finite, no such criterion can be found. For Christians it is Jesus alone who is the Truth, the eternal Word spoken by the Father, the one standard by which all truth and knowledge are finally measured. To the extent that the search for knowledge in the physical realm and in the social sciences disregards the Son of God, the Way between God and man, it can never properly attain its object. All the methodological and epistemological inquiries into science pursued in whatever domain finally must remain flawed to the extent they do not acknowledge in some due way the authorship of God and lordship of His Son. This is what the Christian must believe and affirm. As history tells us from the past, as it will show again, Christianity endures and what leaves it aside perishes sooner or later, since only what is divinely sustained is lasting in this world.

NOTES

Introduction

1. Spengler's early work (1926) proved only the prelude to many similar analyses.
2. Fourastié (1981) has presented several of the themes developed in this introduction; cf. also Griffiths (1982, p. 1), Vickers (1982, p. 2), and Holmes (1983).
3. Blaug (1980a, pp. 253–56) summarizes some of the assessments that have appeared. See also Bell and Kristol (1981).
4. Recent years have seen the formation of Christian groups in several countries ready to break with conventional economic science or political economy. Until perhaps twenty years ago, Christian economists seemed mostly prepared to go along with an autonomous economic science (Munby, 1956, for example).
5. Catholic (kata holos) is here taken in its original connotation to mean "integral." In the third and fourth centuries, the "catholic" group in the Christian church fought, at times desperately, Arians, Donatists, and other "heretics," before eventually prevailing and affirming its character notably in the Nicene Creed. The dying Monica rejoiced that her son, Augustine, had become a Catholic Christian (*Confessions,* IX, 10). I am not using the term "catholic" in its post-Reformation sense, as is natural for Protestant Christians.

PART 1. THE CHRISTIAN MIND

Chapter 1. Some Foundations

1. Kolakowski (1982, p. 175) argues that religious language has meaning only within a context of worship, where knowledge, understanding, and moral commitment appear as a single act.
2. Newman (1874) remains a valuable discussion of how we may approach proofs for the existence of God and our agreement with them. Kant is believed by many to have disposed of such arguments by questioning their epistemological bases, but his line of thought also undermines the possibility of all sure knowledge, including argumentation itself. Cf. also Kolakowski (1982, chapter 2).
3. In the final section of *Anna Karenina* (in Levin's conversation with the old peasant), Tolstoy expresses his anguish from failure to grasp this motive for life and his joy at finding the answer. But "ad maiorem dei gloriam" (for the greater glory of God), a phrase that has inspired generations of Christians, comes alive not as an intellectual solution but only through the Spirit of God.

4. Maslow (1968) is perhaps the best known representative of this line of thought. See McDonagh's comments (1982, pp. 29–31).
5. For example, Schillebeeckx (1979). The sort of recasting of traditional doctrines attempted by this author and others has, to all appearances, had no effect on scientific and academic opinion.
6. Literally "know beyond," meaning "change your mind for the better." Both Jesus and John the Baptist cry out, "Metanoeite" in the Greek version of their call to repentance (Matthew 3: 2; Mark 1: 15).
7. In modern society, people often speak of an "identity crisis," meaning that they are seeking a satisfactory answer to the question of who they are and what the purpose of their life is. The Christian believes that men and women realize their true identity in Jesus, Mediator between God and man and Way to the Father. This is not to deny that ill health or employment and marriage problems require practical solution and specialized treatment. Also, meditation programs, encounter weekends, personality analysis, et cetera, may indeed be helpful. But active belief in Christ is the foundation of personal stability and direction, and with this the rest can be put surely in place.
8. Giordani wrote three fascinating books in the 1930s on the social teachings of Jesus, the apostles, and the early church fathers. (See Bibliography.)
9. Some choose to study Christian social thought from the perspective of "what the church teaches" in papal and episcopal statements. While I do not question the importance of such an approach, my need to link up with economic thought requires a more analytical foundation (cf. chapter 5).

Chapter 2. Approach of Mind

1. Shaken by some event towards the end of his life, Aquinas said of his colossal *Summa Theologica*, "All that I have written seems like straw to me" (Weiskeipl, 1974, p. 321) and refused to write more. This final emptiness is typical of the greatest and the least looking back over their lives. For a recent example, see de Beauvoir (1984), recounting the end of Jean-Paul Sartre.
2. Jean-Paul Sartre is the prophet of philosophical existentialism, while McDonagh (1982, chapter 3) comments on the psychologists.
3. See Maritain (1946) for a celebrated attempt. An example from the secular domain is communist thought: Comical as the results have been, a common faith in the dialectical materialist philosophy bequeathed by Marx led Soviet intellectuals to try to integrate important branches of intellectual and cultural work (cf. Wetter, 1958). Scientists, artists, and workers are expected, just like religious adherents, to devote regular study to communist thought.
4. Barbour (1966) gives an excellent account of the relations between religion and science.
5. See Caldwell (1982, chapters 4–5) and Blaug (1980a, part 1) for summaries of the views of Popper, Kuhn, Lakatos, Feyerabend, and others on the problems of arriving at scientific truth. No little confusion now surrounds the concept and status of scientific laws and knowledge (as opposed to the cause-effect sequences we use throughout modern life).
6. "You wish to understand? Believe! . . . For understanding is the reward of faith. Therefore, do not seek to understand that you may believe, but believe that you may understand; for unless you have believed, you will not understand." In this same passage (*Commentary on St. John*, Chapter 29, section 6), Augustine remarks that "credo in Deum" means "I believe *on* God, placing my trust totally in Him." When

the great creeds were formulated, Christians did not have to contend with denials of the existence of God or gods.

7. Westhues (1982, chapter 7) offers an extended essentially negative account of how modern sociology analyzes religion. The content of physics, medicine, and economics is also largely the creation of the professionals concerned, reflecting their concepts, analysis and reasoning, though explanations and prediction of causes and effects in physical relations must convince us that much objective truth is present as well. Feyerabend (1975, p. 275) argues that "science is much closer to myth than a scientific philosophy is prepared to admit."

8. The *Instruction on Christian Freedom and Liberation,* issued by the Vatican (Rome, March 22, 1986) in part as a commentary on liberation theology, is a masterly account of Christian freedom.

9. See Weber (1905) and Tawney (1926). The thesis in question has been repeatedly discussed, pro and con. cf. part 2, note 4.

10. Wand gives an excellent summary in his abridgment of the *City of God* (1963, pp. xi–xxiii).

11. *Summa Theologica,* I, Q.I, 8 (2nd resp.). Here Aquinas is noting how faith aids reason, but the phrase recurs in his writings. See Passerin d'Entrèves (1959, p. xiii, and 1939, chapter 2) for the sense used in my text. The underlying question is the formulation of a theodicy, or vindication of Providence, before the fact of evil. For a forceful objection to the Catholic linking of nature and grace, see Dooyeweerd (1979, chapter 5).

12. The *Syllabus of Errors* of 1864 (Pius IX) was followed by that of 1907 (Piux X), plus the encyclical *Pascendi* (1907). Three years later, clergy were required to take an antimodernist oath. While modernism is a large topic, not a few propositions were condemned that would today be rephrased or even omitted. See Reardon (1970) and Vidler (1934).

13. Galileo is often cited as an originator of this approach. (See Barbour, 1966, chapter 2, section II.)

14. See Ayer (1959, introduction). His 1936 book is widely regarded as a popular and youthfully exuberant account of certain of their doctrines.

PART 2. CHRISTIAN ECONOMIC THOUGHT

Introductory Remarks

1. That is, in leading European languages; see Moon (1921), Cronin (1956 [the 1950 ed., p. 737, contains a brief bibliography]); Furfey (1942); Williams (1950); Fogarty (1957). Charles (1982) is helpful for some recent developments.

2. The most extensive defence is Calvez and Perrin (1961, chapters 1, 3), reflecting perhaps hostility to "l'église" so widespread in France.

3. There is no obvious history of Protestant socioeconomic thought. Troeltsch (1931) is a celebrated source, and Preston (1981) contains some historical material.

4. Preston (1972, chapter 1) reviews the Tawney and (more briefly) Weber theses.

Chapter 3. Social Premises

1. The statement of social and economic principles in chapters 3 and 4 is my personal rendition of the natural law tradition elaborated in many sources. Cronin (1956), Messner (1949), Rommen (1945), and Dirksen (1961) give typical accounts of it.
2. Popper (1966, Vol. 2, chapter 11) emphatically disapproves of Aristotelian intuitionism, which leads to "oracular" philosophy. Christian thought takes a middle stance between exaggerated reliance on intuitive insights and a scientific and philosophical method that insists vainly on "proving" all sure knowledge according to criteria of verification, falsification, et cetera.
3. Finnis (1980, pp. 211–16) discusses the United Nations Universal Declaration of Human Rights (1948). His book is a masterly review of the history and meaning of natural rights, marred by a resolute leaving aside of the divine dimension and by such a quantity of comment on his and other people's views that clear conclusions tend to be drowned.
4. The fact that human rights have been abused by apparently religious societies and individuals requires a discussion of the emergence of evil and its overcoming. As for the more difficult problem that various rights, now regarded as "natural" or at least universally accepted, were once passed over, see section 6 in this chapter.
5. The social ideal implanted in Christian thought is in no way falsified by the anchorite model, where some live solitary lives for religious reasons. If they do not render this mode of life social through prayer and penance for others, there is little merit in it.
6. See Giordani (1943, chapter 7; 1944, chapter 2) for some beginnings and *Familaris Consortio* (1981b) of John Paul II for a recent restatement and defence.
7. This quite innocent idea has been at times rendered suspect through being linked to authoritarian concepts of the organic state connected with fascism.
8. Pius XI gave this principle its modern prominence in *Quadragesimo Anno* (1931, para. 79). See also Calvez and Perrin (1961, pp. 121–22, 328 seq.) and Dooyeweerd (1979, p. 124 seq.)
9. See Finnis (1980, chapter 1), for a dissection of Hart, Kelsen, and others on the concept of law. His own definition (p. 276) appears to restate the traditional statement in my text, while basing itself on the "practical reasonableness" of coordinating the community's search for the goods involved (chapters 2, 3). But the attempt to avoid introducing divine ordinance is a weakness he simply cannot overcome.
10. This paragraph is based on Aquinas (*Summa Theologica*, I-IIae, Q. 90–97), but does not follow his classification closely.
11. Finnis (1980, p. 398) tells us correctly that one cannot fully understand Aquinas's "participatio legis aeternae in rationali creatura" without rounded knowledge concerning his concepts. But he omits the entire side of divine guidance and inspiration, which Aquinas certainly treated as a necessary aid to understanding (cf. Maritain, 1958, p. 48).
12. In addition to Finnis (1980), see also Passerin d'Entrèves (1951) and, for a different approach, H. Hart (1961, chapter 11). There is much more. Rushdoony (1973), in a work reflecting neo-Calvinist thought, states (chapter 13, section 3) that the Roman Catholic approach to the natural law is a subversion of divine law (namely, the Ten Commandments), derived from Roman and Greek sources.
13. Such a turning aside from the natural law (for example, see Gremillion, 1976, pp. 10 134) is a far cry from the Christian social thought of the pre-Vatican II period, which placed such heavy emphasis on it. Messner's well-known *Social Ethics* (1949) is subtitled "The Natural Law in the Modern World" and is constructed on sociophilosophical, nontheological reasoning. Such an attempt cannot be entirely satis-

factory, since religious belief enters to accept the centrality of God and the natural law as a reflection of divine law.

14. Aquinas (*Sum. Theol.* I–IIae, Q. 100, 3, resp.) and others have insisted that although some dictates of the natural law are evident to all (e.g., the prohibition on murder), many of its requirements call for the "guidance of the wise and enlightened." (The progress of children in understanding moral law is evident.)

15. Many writers have considered the problem of relating the concepts of immutable natural and divine law to our awareness of their requirements and their application to different human situations. Messner (1965, pp. 74–76) speaks of a "long evolution in moral consciousness" in relation to the immutability of natural law. Jesus' reply to his questioners on divorce (Matthew 19: 8) appears to evoke this sort of evolution. Modern "process theology," however, seems to join the older evolutionary philosophers (such as H. Spencer) in visualizing human rights themselves as subject to fundamental evolution.

16. If so many Christian societies have in the past practiced slavery, Christianity has from the beginning insisted on the equal worth of freeman and slave before God and the need for fair treatment of all in bondage. There is a crucial distinction between a sense in which the master takes himself to be in absolute control and a second in which he sees himself responsible for the welfare of the person in bondage. Christianity has always held the second view, despite the contrary arguments and actions of misguided individuals and groups. The letters of Gregory I (the Great) are instructive on this point. (See Dudden, 1905.)

17. But I cannot venture here on the famous "iniusta lex non est lex," an assertion that understandably enrages positivists; cf. Hart (1961, p. 152 seq.), Finnis (1980, pp. 363–66).

18. Pius XI, *Quadragesimo Anno*, 1931, para. 137; cf. also John Paul II, *Dives in Misericordia*, 1981, paras. 117–21. For a contrary example, Rawls (1971) exaggerates social justice as the basis of peace and order in society, leaving love as its effect and supererogatory (pp. 501, 478–79).

19. "Justitia est constans et perpetua voluntas ius suum cuique tribuendi." The *Digest* of Justinian ascribes this to Ulpian, a third-century Roman jurist; the medievalists quoted it from Isadore (d. 636). Again my approach to justice differs from the secular. The contortions of the latter trying to define justice in terms of purely human arrangements are a wonder to read (for example, Hart, 1961, chapter 8).

20. My discussion remains close to the neo-scholastic tradition, founded on Aristotle's *Nichomachaean Ethics,* Book V, and Aquinas's *Summa Theologica,* II–IIae, Q. 57–62, but with modifications. There are many excellent discussions of justice, such as Pieper (1965), del Vecchio (1952), and Finnis (1980). My division of justice into social, distributive, and commutative does not overlook the convenience of speaking of legal, international, and other forms of justice for certain purposes.

21. In the past (McKee, 1981, p. 5, footnote 10), I have included the obligation to pay taxes as part of distributive justice. As my text indicates (in section 9), I am also now, as against my earlier views, convinced by the case for recognizing contributive justice.

22. This term is adopted from Dempsey (1957), while departing from his merely equating this with social justice. That is, I guard social justice in its wider sense and use "contributive justice" in the narrow sense explained in my text. The *Pastoral Letter* (see chapter 7, section 9) of the U.S. Bishops uses social justice in the narrow sense (*Second Draft,* 1985, paragraph 75, *Third Draft,* 1986, paragraph 71).

23. I have summarized and criticized Rawls's views elsewhere (McKee, 1979); see also chapter 9, note 15.

187

Chapter 4. Economic Principles

1. Two encyclical letters of John XXIII (*Mater et Magistra* [1961] and *Pacem in Terris* [1963]; see in Gremillion 1975) contain an elaborate listing of economic rights and principles. My modest aim is to *illustrate* the derivation of principles prior to discussing the passage to applications.
2. This approach to Christian economic principles is often presented as the fact of *creation* of man by God and his consequent total dependence; cf. *Pastoral Letter on Catholic Social Teaching and the U.S. Economy, Second Draft* (1985, paragraphs 37–40) and *Third Draft* (1986, paragraphs 31–34).
3. Perroux (1964) has long described outlays on such minima as "les coûts de l'homme," arguing society's obligation to ensure their coverage. The Webbs expressed similar ideas (1911) in supporting a national minimum wage (pp. 12, 92).
4. Many biblical injunctions (cf. chapter 5, sections 1–3) and church statements could be referred to and the social benefits of property invoked. Clearly Christian thought reaches beyond mere humanism at this point and contrasts sharply with individualism.
5. Furubotyn and Pejovich (1972) survey the concept of property rights in relation to economic theory.
6. Leo XIII, *Rerum Novarum* (1981). Waterman (1982) thinks a contradiction can be developed between Aquinas and Leo on whether an individual's right to private property is from natural law or only positive law. Aquinas (II–IIae, Q. 66, 2, i) says that individual possession of property is an addition of human reason to the natural law, which for Waterman implies a human arrangement. There are, however, various instances in which Catholic thought speaks of such additions as "natural": Parents are said to have the right to educate their children in Christian schools by virtue of the natural law. Catholics see no difficulty in church authority adding specifications to more general principles of the natural law. *Rerum Novarum* is perhaps heavy-handed respecting the legitimacy of state control of areas of property, and later encyclicals have accepted openly the case for limited nationalizations of industry.
7. Waterman (1982, quoting de Sousberghe in Ryan, 1978, p. 60) also thinks that Leo XIII was influenced in his view of the natural right to private property by Locke's argument. That Locke is the most influential authority for basing entitlement to private property on the fruits of one's work seems correct (but cf. Dooyeweerd, 1973, p. 455). It is interesting that John Paul II repeats it in *Laborem Exercens* (1981, pp. 12, 14). The potential harm of Locke's argument, as indicated in my text, is its use to insist on the individual side of property owning to the neglect of social benefits. Labor, too, is social.
8. In the celebrated remark of Ambrose: "You are not making a gift of your possessions to the poor person. You are handing over to him what is his. For what has been given in common for the use of all, you have arrogated to yourself. The world is given to all, and not only to the rich." See *Populorum Progressio,* paragraph 23, plus sources, in Gremillion (1975).
9. Mother Theresa's argument (in her addresses) is that unless we give from our needs and not from our abundance, we are not really proving our love (cf. Mark 12: 41–44).
10. There are many further aspects of the right to work, such as self-realization and absence of discrimination, which space precludes my taking up and which, in any case, are not essential to my purpose.
11. The most important modern statement of these rights is *Laborem Exercens,* a letter addressed to "all men and women of good will" by Pope John Paul II in 1981. This remarkable document develops a theology and spirituality of work, affirms that the

conflict between labor and capital at this phase of history is to be solved by accepting the priority of labor over capital and the common benefits of property, and tells us that the rights of workers involve preeminently employment and just distribution. A doctrine of full employment is stated in strong terms (paragraphs 16, 18). I had hoped to include a discussion of unemployment in chapter 6, but this was passed over in favor of inflation.

12. Doubtless an instinct linked to our "fallen nature" or, to put it alternatively, one flawed by our potentiality for self-harm and evil behavior towards others.

13. Michael Novak (1982) instances similar conclusions, though (if labels must be used) my own position is more "centrist."

14. Notably *Mater et Magistra* (John XXIII (1961, paragraphs 51–57)); cf. also John Paul II's *Redemptor Hominis* (1979, paragraph 16), which declares that "the laws of healthy competition must be allowed to lead the way in the sector of trade."

15. Worland (1981) may be referred to for recent discussion of the medieval concept of just price. He wishes to link it to neo-classical competitive price, which in my view encounters the problems specified in my text.

16. The objections of most economists to the notion of just price are centrally two. First, the introduction of moral concepts into economic analysis is no part of an objective account of cause and effect; value judgments do not belong in what the economist should be doing. (This dispute is taken up in chapter 7, section 4). Second, even if one admits to the force of the moral concept, the problem is to know precisely and unambiguously what a fair price may be. But this is to set up wrongly conceived premises for "scientific" economic knowledge (cf. chapter 8, sections 1–2, and 11).

17. Danner (1982; 1983, chapters 2–3) instances the problems created for knowing just price by focusing too heavily on various senses of value.

18. Many have echoed a similar idea. The old socialist slogan "from each according to his abilities, to each according to his needs" hints partly at it. Also, a cunning proposal of the Carter Tax Commission (1966) in Canada had progressively wealthier persons keep a steadily larger amount of their income for their basic needs, before arriving at the "discretionary" or less basic portion that would be the proper subject for graduated taxation.

19. It is worth emphasizing that prudence, itself a key cardinal virtue, enters to regulate the practical application of justice. In this respect, I make mine all Pieper (1965, p. 3 seq.) has to say.

20. Cf. von Hayek (1976, Vol. 2, chapter 9); Beauchamp (1982); Donaldson (1982); Meade (1975b). There is one tempting way in which "distributive justice" may be applied to the just distribution of property: If you take the view that all property has its social side—nobody produces merely as an individual, and society always has some claim on the fruits of work—you may interpret this part as "common property" requiring to be appropriately distributed (cf. Worland, 1967, pp. 238–41). However, using distributive justice in this corrective sense makes it a further modifier of an initial distribution of income and wealth brought about by commutative justice, taxes and the allocation of public goods, and decisions to spend and save over time. Hence it is better to stay with the sense of distributive justice given in my text.

Chapter 5. Alternative Routes

1. Almost every page of Aquinas's *Summa Theologica* discusses biblical citations for and against the question being debated, as well as citing early authorities of the

church. The evangelically inclined may find Aquinas's procedures more to their liking than perhaps supposed.

2. The number of distinct texts of the Bible seems to be at least fifty, as the result of successive revisions published over the last 40 years. *The Jerusalem Bible* (1966 New York: Doubleday,), related to *La Bible de Jérusalem* (Paris: Cerf, 1956), is the general source of references used in this book.

3. Preston (1981, pp. 44, 60) is of the same opinion. Chilton (1982) offers many illustrations of the use of different and differently interpreted quotations to derive opposing views on economic analysis and policy.

4. Notably *Populorum Progressio (On the Development of Peoples,* 1967), *Gaudium et Spes (Pastoral Constitution on the Modern World,* 1965) and *Laborem Exercens (On Human Labour,* 1981); see in Gremillion, 1976. See Hehir (in Houck and Williams, 1983) on the changed presentation of papal teaching.

5. The sorts of topics usually raised belong to the judgmental and reforming stages of social principles, whereas their foundation and methodology of application are rather my concern. While the criticisms and recommendations typically given contain their degree of truth, many popular treatments (Goulet, 1971 and 1974, for instance; and Monsignor Gremillion, 1976, chooses to write on much the same level) are superficial.

6. The Latin American Episcopal Council, CELAM, met in Medellin, Colombia, in 1968 and issued a number of statements on the church and Latin America. See notably "Poverty of the Church" in Gremillion (1976) or more fully two volumes, *Position Papers* and *Conclusions,* issued by CELAM in 1970 and published by the United States Catholic Conference.

7. The finest analysis of contemporary Christian poverty I know is Delfieux (1981, chapter 6).

8. Dorr (1984) has scrutinized one hundred years of Vatican social teaching ("official" documents, in sum) to trace modern emphasis on an option for the poor. He finds that prior to Vatican II, papal statements showed a special concern for the poor but combined this with support for an established order, mostly through fear of socialist upheaval. After Vatican II and the Medellin statements (see note 6), Paul VI was fairly into the approach reformers now find necessary, as also John Paul II, if more circumspectly. Father Dorr has, however, little to say in direct analysis of what an option for the poor may mean (as he acknowledges, p. 4), and simply draws the repeated inference that "structural" changes are required to alter the lot of the poor. What reforms of institutions and structures may be required to cope with the problems of the poor and marginalized is, of course, a vital issue, but lying beyond my scope.

9. Citing Gelin (1964), Gutierrez (1973, chapter 13) says that two main lines of thought on poverty stand out in the Bible, namely that it is a scandalous condition and that it is a kind of spiritual childhood, meaning a total openness to and dependence on God. The first cannot be the Christian ideal, he declares, and the second is partial and insufficient, for it must be completed by a readiness to accept material poverty as an act of solidarity with the poor and protest against poverty. When poverty is overcome, the Kingdom begins (and this is the best interpretation of Luke 6: 20: "Blessed are the poor, for the Kingdom of God is theirs"). The third challenge held out by Gutierrez, I should say, is an ideal for those whose hearts are able to bear it, rather than an obligation to be placed on all Christians.

10. For instance, Gutierrez (1973); Boff (1979); Segundo (1978); Gibellini (1979).

11. Gutierrez (1973, chapter 1; 1979, p. 22, in Gibellini). "Praxis" means accepted practice or customary modes of living, and its liberation style may go on to reinterpret Christianity, the liturgy, the church, and other fundamental domains. This may be

190

accompanied by aspersions on "pietistic" interpretation of Scripture, "uninvolved" living, the romantic and brief revival of neo-scholasticism, and the resemblance of conservative theology to ideal Greek thought, more interested in polished analysis than action and authenticity. Gutierrez (1973) contains much admirable material alongside what many dissent from.

12. In late 1984 the Sacred Congregation for the Doctrine of the Faith issued a statement condemnatory of Marxist trends in liberation theology. (See Bibliography.) Father Gutierrez likes to tell the following pleasantry during his public addresses: "European theologians think in the morning and act in the afternoon; we liberation theologians act in the morning and think in the afternoon." After the laughter, his listeners are uncomfortably reminded of Marx's approach.

13. *Pastoral Letter on Catholic Social Teaching and the U.S. Economy,* issued as a *First Draft* in November 1984 by the U.S. Catholic Conference (Washington). My comments are based on the *Second Draft,* of October 1985. A *Third Draft* was issued in June 1986 (a final version being scheduled for November), now titled *Economic Justice for all.* No modifications to the brief remarks of my text are called for.

14. See *Toward the Future* (1984), a lay letter on Catholic social thought and the U.S. economy, evidently composed to counteract trends in the Bishops' statement. (See note 13.) W. Simon and M. Novak headed the privately constituted commission.

15. Cf. Paul VI's *Octogesima Adveniens* (1971, paragraphs 3–4). (See in Gremillon, 1976.)

16. See the exchange between Waterman (September 1983) and Wilkinson (March 1984) in *Canadian Public Policy.*

17. Mother Theresa repeatedly remarks in her addresses that without prayer and contemplation, the work of her Sisters in caring for the destitute would be the same as that of social workers (with no disparagement intended).

Chapter 6. Wages and Inflation

1. "Economic theory" means a fairly developed hypothesis, or chain of hypotheses, linking cause(s) and effect(s). Developed initially by induction from observed facts and presumably tested, it is often stated deductively by posing assumptions approximating reality. "Analysis" is a less settled term, sometimes used equivalently to "theory" and sometimes indicating the work of sifting facts and hypotheses.

2. Firms beyond quite moderate size do not normally employ the notion of marginal revenue product, since they cannot identify it. Consequently their demand for factors proceeds along other lines, say, simply the need for more labor of a certain type. The economic theory in question states an ideal solution to the problem, which on a priori grounds is presumed to correspond to that found in an experiential way.

3. See chapter 5, sections 2–3, *Rerum Novarum* (1891), and *Laborem Exercens* (1981, paragraph 19).

4. I intend a less rigid division than the well-known statement of Ricardo (1821, chapters 1–2). Some invoke Scripture (e.g. Vickers 1982, pp. 96–97).

5. See Cronin (1956, p. 206 seq.); Dirksen (1961, p. 196 seq.); Piux XI *(Quadragesimo Anno,* paragraph 71); and John Paul II *(Laborem Exercens,* paragraph 19).

6. See, for example, Nicholson (1983, p. 18): "St. Thomas Aquinas believed value to be divinely determined," which is a strange reading of his *Summa Theologica,* II–IIae, Q. 77.

7. In a brave book (1967), Worland tried to link welfare economics closely with scho-

lastic philosophy (meaning Aquinas). Each complemented the other. Notably, welfare economics needs a criterion of just distribution to arrive securely at productive efficiency, while scholastic philosophy needs the other to relate just price in a technically successful way with distributive justice (meaning just distribution of income and wealth; cf. chapter 4, note 20). Merely one objection to Worland's aim is that the concepts of economic justice introduced would become as applicable to actual life as welfare economics, which is nil given its premises and technical weaknesses.

8. Really, any discussion of inflation should be conducted in tandem with an analysis of the consequences for unemployment of rising and falling rates of price increase. But I cannot work that kind of analysis into this brief treatment.

9. The Phillips curve (see Phillips, 1958) links falling unemployment with rising wage rates (or prices).

10. Friedman's work (chiefly 1963) led to numerous investigations of such relations with uncertain outcome.

11. See Kantor (1979) and Maddock and Carter (1982) for useful surveys and bibliographies.

12. Whether Smith may have had a merely physical or a providential concept of the invisible hand is a matter over which scholarly ink has flowed. The point can only be a matter for speculation in the light of the earlier and later writings Smith left.

13. The doctrine of solidarism originally propounded by Pesch (over 1904–23; see Mulcahy, 1952) is reechoed today as a call for solidarity in economic relations (cf. chapter 10, section 2). Perhaps "union for common good" would be a more natural English expression.

14. It is commonly said that the decision of the Canadian government to index personal exemptions for income tax in 1974 was aimed at wage demand restraint. There is little indication it had any success.

15. By the mid-1980s, a triple problem has replaced the inflation emphasized in my text, namely unemployment–public deficit–potential inflation. Enormous deficits in many countries stand in the way of government stimulation to lessen unemployment, while mere demand expansion risks reviving the inflation damped down by oil price decreases. The reader will perceive, however, that these related problems call for the same moral awareness and cooperation to attack them effectively.

PART 3. ECONOMIC SCIENCE AND THE CHRISTIAN MIND

Chapter 7. The Setting of Economic Science

1. This remark is usually ascribed to Jacob Viner.

2. The question of the formal purpose of economic science is not to be confused with that of economics as an art (cf. J. N. Keynes, 1890, chapter 2, note 13). The economist may act as practical adviser, invoking the usual things arising in management—prudence, use of different fields, flair, et cetera. Such a study of the economist in action, of the application of economics in effect, is distinct from that of the orientation of the science itself.

3. Blaug (1980a, chapter 5) surveys the history of this question, but feels no need to

conclude other than declaring that hypothesis testing is the way to weed out political and social prejudices (p. 156). Method is what really matters, according to Blaug.

4. The first step of moral philosophers in arriving at some concept of the good shows repeatedly that faith or primary intuition of some sort is necessarily involved; cf. Finnis (1980, chapters 3–4).

5. The books of Becker, Buchanan, and Friedman cited in the bibliography are ready illustrations. Kolakowski (1982, p. 84) affirms the statement of my text.

6. Of course, there are the other interpretations of "original sin," cf. Tresmontant (1980, chapter 8), and John Paul II stresses work as imitating the creative act of God (*Laborem Exercens,* paragraphs 4, 9).

7. For instance, Ropke (1963), von Mises (1963), von Hayek (1944, 1960, 1973–79), and Friedman (1962, 1981).

8. Pareto notes (1968, Vol. 12, para. 2133) that when one passes to society and sociology from pure economics, wider criteria may correct the economic maximum. In pure economics, one may refer only to the maximum of ophelimity (an invention of Pareto) *for* a group, not *of* a group, whereas in sociology (as he uses the term) it is permissible to speak of a maximum of utility both for and of a group. (I have translated Pareto's *collectivité* as *group*.)

Chapter 8. Methods of Analysis

1. Some well-known studies of economic methodology are: Blaug (1980a), Caldwell (1982), Boland (1980), and Machlup (1978). These are the tip of the iceberg.

2. If my text casts aspersions here and there on Platonic reality and knowledge (cf. *Republic,* Book 7), I do not forget the ethical tone that pervades Greek philosophy in general and the writings of Plato in particular.

3. For example, Debreu (1959, a work that had much to do with his being awarded the Nobel Prize in Economics for 1983) and Morishima (1976).

4. Cf. Davis and Hersh (1981—for example, chapter 2, The Ideal Mathematician). The limits of such creation I leave to wiser minds.

5. For example, it is impossible to draw squares on three sides of a given right-angled triangle where that on the hypotenuse precisely equals the sum of the other two. Proofs of the proposition are accurate (where the question of a mathematical "proof" is interesting enough), but real instances never correspond exactly. Even more in applied mathematics, representations of phenomena never do more than approximate the reality. Thus Davis and Hersh (1981, chapter 3) refer to mathematical propositions as models.

6. See, for example, Tower (1981, Vols. 1–4, *Microeconomics and Macroeconomics)* and Varian (1978).

7. Simon has long utilized the concept of "bounded rationality" (see 1957, p. 198), by which he means that the mind can exercise rational choice over only a limited range of considerations, as opposed to an assumption common in economic theory that a utility or profit maximizer may have perfect knowledge of the possibilities open. But Simon has never (to my knowledge) defined what he means by rational or reasonable, and his work after nearly fifty years (cf. 1983, p. vii) remains inconclusive.

8. As Aquinas puts it, "the first rule of reason is the natural law" (*Sum. Theol.* I–IIae, Q. 95, 2; see also Qs. 90–94).

9. Arrow (1963; cf. also 1973 and 1974). The four conditions are: transitivity of choices, which may be put into any order by the individuals concerned; the order must not

be altered if any choice drops out; the social valuation reflects individual valuations; and nondictatorship. The theorem is reproduced in many texts (e.g. Abrams, 1980, chapter 3; Due and Friedlander, 1981, chapter 3).

10. "If reason is like an organon constituted *a priori*, one may wonder how reason chances to fit in with the real. But if reason is not constituted *a priori*, if the principles of reason are in fact drawn from the real itself through our knowledge of the real, in that case no surprise is necessary that accord exists between reason and the real. . . . Rationality is not an order or a structure constituted *a priori*, but a relation between the human mind and the real." (Tresmontant, 1966, pp. 161–62).

11. The widespread practice of freezing all other circumstances ("ceteris paribus") in cause-effect theorems means that their verification (or falsification) is virtually impossible. The alternative of general equilibrium analysis, where no variables are restrained, poses even more baffling problems for verification and prediction. (Economic theory repeatedly uses the concept of equilibrium, meaning a balancing of forces. Its limitations are blatant, but no alternative is in sight, since the physics model requires to be abandoned first.)

12. The sense of "contemplation" of knowledge—the original sense of "theoria" in Aristotle—intended here is distinct from demonstrations or affirmations that certain effects follow given causes.

13. Cf. Howard and King (1975, chapter 2); see also Blaug (1980b) and Tool (1982, 1983).

14. Cf. Lutz (1985) and Hill (1983). See chiefly Peirce (1931), James (1890), and Dewey (1939).

15. Cf. Lutz (1985) and Tool (1977). See Ayres (1944).

16. Throughout his life Newman remained convinced that finally most people are persuaded to hold the views they do, certainly on fundamental questions, through an assemblage of considerations bearing on them, rather than by some single shattering line of proof (cf. Lash, 1978, p. 5). Which implies, incidentally, that the "setting" of the Christian mind—belief, prayer, and place of will before intellect—is important for its questioning of the limited methodology dominant in neoclassical theorising.

Chapter 9. Welfare Economics and Social Economy

1. Some sources on theoretical welfare economics are: Little (1957), de Graaff (1957), Nath (1969), and Winch (1971).

2. This maximization device is widely used in economics: here, when the extra returns per final dollar of outlay on factors of production are equalized, we have their most efficient allocation to resources.

3. Cf. Marshall (1920, Book 3, chapter 6) and Pigou (1930, Part 1, chapters 1–2).

4. See, for example, Gould and Ferguson (1980, chapters 15–16) and Henderson and Quandt (1958, chapter 7).

5. Briefly: (i) The reasoning suffers from circularity, since given distribution must be assumed to help determine consumer preferences, whereas introducing production means they cannot be so taken. Production gives rise to factor payments = income distribution, so that altering production means different incomes and preferences. (ii) Private and social efficiency is assumed when achieving both is an enormous problem. (iii) The perfectly competitive organization of industry supposed does not exist. (iv) A technical difficulty (Lipsey and Lancaster, 1956–57) is that the Pareto optimum is unknowable unless it is determined at once from an inferior position.

194

If we move in a series of steps, say by dismantling tariffs on trade, the first best outcome alters with each adjustment, since resources are reallocated continually.

6. In microeconomic theory, a consumer "reveals his preferences" by his actual purchases, which presumably correspond to the tangency points of supposed indifference curves and budget lines. The concept of revealed preference (introduced by Samuelson in the 1930s; see Wong, 1978) may be used to infer the shape of an indifference map or instead to present an alternative way of deducing consumer behavior.

7. The embarrassingly egotistic premises of Pareto reasoning have long been apparent, so that various attempts have been made to reshape them to take account of the welfare of others. Hochman and Rodgers (1969) applied the concept of the Pareto optimum to distribution by supposing the utility of Mutt, a richer person, to depend on that of Jeff, a poorer, and vice versa, and proceeding to certain tax-transfer maximization exercises. Some obvious objections are that the approach does not break away from egotism, since redistribution is made to depend on self-interest, and the root question of the good of individuals and how it connects up with that of others is buried in the procedural study of a problem, the solution of which is implicit in the assumptions adopted. See McKee (1980) for further discussion, and cf. chapter 7, section 8.

8. Public goods could be efficiently priced to individual consumers only if each honestly revealed the strength of his preference for them. Because they are approximately equally available to all (I may use the park bench as freely as you), we have an incentive to understate our desire and "free ride" on what is paid for by others. Hence a system of taxation must replace market purchase.

9. In a prominent example, Buchanan (1975, chapters 2–5) sketches how nonidealistic self-interested behavior is to lead to the constitutional contract or rules for behavior, the postconstitutional contract or the institutions of the private economy and what is encompassed by the theory of public goods, and the continuing contract or changes in the status quo.

10. A summary of these hypotheses is given in Bird (1970, part 2). Their meaning is noted in the text, apart from the productivity thesis of Baumol (1967), which argues that public costs will rise to reflect rising labor productivity and earnings in the private sector. Since government is more labor-intensive, the need to match private earnings approximately will cause public outlays to rise as a proportion of national product.

11. Borcherding (1977, p. 56) estimates that about one-half of the growth of government can be ascribed to measurable economic forces (increased affluence and population), "other" influences accounting for the rest.

12. The classic discussions of social contract occurred in the seventeenth and eighteenth centuries (Hobbes, Rousseau), but faded in the following century before the organic theory of the state, influenced by Hegelian thinking, and a realization of the fantasies of naturalist thinking. There is no need for me to raise these earlier discussions, since the modern theory of social contract belongs rather to secular-humanist, post-Christian currents.

13. Thus D. Mueller (1976, p. 395) begins his survey of economists on public choice theory.

14. See Abrams (1980, chapter 6) or Nicholson (1983, chapter 6). There are a number of variants of the rules of the prisoners' dilemma and other logical choice games.

15. Rawls (1971) constructs his program for achieving social justice by supposing an intuitive (he doubtless prefers to term it rational) perception of primary goods (liberty, equality of opportunity, income, self-respect) and using social contracting to construct

a "full theory of the good." Each person is imagined to choose from behind a veil of ignorance as to how life will treat him, so that he opts for such a structure of institutions as will mostly benefit him should his supposedly unforeseen outcome in life go badly for him. A curious amalgam results of an Aristotelian view of the virtuous man and the rational calculus typified by welfare economics. (See McKee, 1979).

16. The concept of "merit" goods was introduced by R. Musgrave (1959, chapter I). Education services, for example, could be provided only to those willing to pay for them, but they are socially so important in modern society that everybody should receive some minimum level. Hence such merit "public" goods, or collective goods in an older terminology, should be provided for by taxation.

Chapter 10. Conclusion: Social Economics and Social Economy

1. Representative views may be found in the *Review of Social Economy*, the *International Journal of Social Economics*, and to some extent in the *Journal of Economic Issues* (primarily institutionalist) and the *Review of Radical Political Economics* (typically Marxist). Ischbolding and Sharp (1980) have tried to define social economics from the point of view of cognitive systems theory, and Pettman (1977) favors a systems theory approach to social and economic phenomena.

2. Though founded on values and drawing them from social ethics, social economics would emphatically retain its independence (though not absolute autonomy). However possible seventy or eighty years ago, today the vast corpus of economic analysis and knowledge built up cannot conceivably be viewed as "a branch of moral science." Cf. Antoine (1921, p. 9), Devas (1907), and even a remark of J. M. Keynes: "Economics is essentially a moral science and not a natural science" (quoted in *Journal of Post-Keynesian Economics*, Fall 1978, p. 6), though doubtless he was not thereby questioning accepted views of its autonomy.

3. Blaug (1980a) devotes his part 2 to a methodological appraisal of the neoclassical research program, commenting on the validity of a number of neoclassical theories. See also Boland (1982).

4. Echoing Hume (1740, Book 3, section 1), it is often stressed that one cannot get logically from what is to what ought to be, and vice versa. In terms of deduction this is correct, since the crossover requires insertion of moral premises. In actual life this is precisely what we do, inserting the assumptions necessary to get from, say, the facts of child abuse to moral judgments and injunctions.

5. Cf. Goodhart (1980, p. viii) and no less than Robbins (1981). See also Phelps (1985).

6. Vatican II (1962–65) made several appeals (notably in *Gaudium et Spes)* to scientists and intellectuals to take notice of better formulated religious truths reexpressed in modern thought and language. Largely their appeals have fallen on deaf ears. Only a Theophilus (one who loves God; Luke 1:4) takes religious truth seriously.

BIBLIOGRAPHY

BOOKS AND ARTICLES

Abrams, P. *Foundations of political analysis.* New York: Columbia, 1980

Antoine, C. *Cours d'économie sociale.* Paris: Alcan, 1921.

Aquinas, St. Th. *Summa Theologica:* London: Blackfriars, with Eyre and Spot-tiswoode, 1967–74.

Aristotle, *Nichomachaen ethics.* Translated by J. Thomson. New York: Penguin, 1955.

Arrow, K. *Social Choice and Individual Values.* New York: Wiley, 1963.

———. "Values and Collective Decision-Making." In *Economic Justice,* edited by E. Phelps. New York: Penguin, 1973.

———. "General Economic Equilibrium." *American Economic Review* (June 1974).

Ayer, A. J. *Language, Logic and Truth.* New York: Dover Publications, 1950.

———. (ed.) *Logical Positivism.* Glencoe, Ill. Free Press, 1959.

Ayers, C. *The Theory of Economic Progress.* Chapel Hill: University of North Carolina Press, 1944.

Barbour, I. *Issues in Science and Religion.* London: SCM Press, 1966.

Bator, F. "The Simple Analytics of Welfare Maximisation." *American Economic Review* (March 1957).

Baum, G. *The Priority of Labour.* Ramsay, N.J.: Paulist Press, 1982.

——— and D. Cameron. *Ethics and Economics.* Toronto: Lorimer, 1984.

Baumol, W. "Macroeconomics of Unbalanced Growth." *American Economic Review* (June 1967).

Beauchamp, T. "The Ethical Foundations of Economic Justice." *Review of Social Economy* (December 1982).

Beauvoir, de, S. *Adieu: A Farewell to Sartre.* New York: Pantheon Books, 1984.

Becker, G. "Theory of Social Interactions." *Journal of Political Economy* (November-December 1974).

————."Altruism, Egoism, and Genetic Fitness: Economics and Sociobiology." *Journal of Economic Literature* (September 1976).

————. A Treatise on the Family. Chicago, Ill.: University of Chicago Press, 1981.

Bell, D., and I. Kristol (eds.). *The Crisis in Economic Theory*. New York: Basic Books, 1981.

Bell, J. F. *A History of Economic Thought*. New York: Ronald, 1967.

Beveridge, W. *Full Employment in a Free Society*. London: Allen and Unwin, 1944.

Bird, R. *Growth of Government Spending in Canada*. Toronto: Canadian Tax Foundation, 1970.

Blamires, H. *The Christian Mind*. Ann Arbor, Michigan: Servant Books, 1978.

Blaug, M. *The Methodology of Economics*. Cambridge, U.K.: Cambridge University Press, 1980a.

————. *A Methodological Appraisal of Marxian Economics*. Amsterdam: North-Holland, 1980b.

Boland, D. *The Foundations of Economic Method*. London: Allen and Unwin, 1982.

Boff, L. *Jesus Christ Liberator*. Maryknoll, N.Y.: Orbis, 1979.

Borcherding, T., (ed.). *Budgets and Bureaucrats*. Chapel Hill: University of North Carolina Press, 1977.

Buchanan, J. *The Limits of Liberty*. Chicago, Ill.: University of Chicago Press, 1975.

Caldwell, B. *Beyond Positivism*. London: Allen and Unwin, 1982.

Calvez, J., and J. Perrin. *The Church and Social Justice*. Chicago, Ill.: Regnery, 1961.

Carrel, A. *Man the Unknown*. London: Universe Books, 1961.

Charles, R., with D. Maclaren. *The Social Teaching of Vatican II*. Oxford, U.K.: Plater Publications, 1982.

Chilton, D. *Christians in an Age of Guilt Manipulators*. Tyler, Tex.: Institute of Christian Economics, 1982.

Cronin, J. *Catholic Social Principles*. Milwaukee, Wis.: Bruce, 1950.

————. *Social Principles and Economic Life*. Milwaukee, Wis.: Bruce, 1956.

Danner, P. *An Ethics for the Affluent*. Lanham, Md. Univ. Press of America, 1983.

————. "Personalism, Values and Economic Values." *Review of Social Economy* (October 1982).

Davis, P., and R. Hersh. *The Mathematical Experience*. New York: Houghton Mifflin, 1981.

Deats, P. *Towards a Discipline of Social Ethics*. Boston, Mass.: Boston University Press, 1977.

Debreu, G. *Theory of Value*. New York: Wiley, 1959.

198

Delfieux, P.-M. *Jerusalem Livre de Vie*. Paris: Cerf, 1981.

Dempsey, B. "The Range of Social Justice." St. Louis: *Social Order* (January 1957).

Denison, E. *Accounting for Slower Economic Growth*. Washington, D.C.: Brookings, 1979.

Desai, M. *Marxian Economics*. Oxford, U.K.: Blackwell, 1979.

Devas, C. *Political Economy*. London: Longmans Green, 1907.

Dewey, J. *Theory of Valuation*. Chicago, Ill.: University of Chicago Press, 1939.

Dirksen, D. *Catholic Social Principles*. St. Louis, Mo.: Herder, 1961.

Donaldson, T. "What Justice Demands." *Review of Social Economy* (December 1982).

Dorr, D. *Option for the Poor: A Hundred Years of Vatican Social Teaching*. Maryknoll, N.Y.: Orbis, 1984.

Dooyeweerd, H. *Roots of Western Culture*. Toronto: Wedge Publishing, 1979.

Downs, A. *Inside Bureaucracy*. Boston, Mass.: Little Brown, 1966.

Dudden, F. *Gregory the Great*. London: Longmans Green, 1905.

Due, J., and A. Friedlander. *Government Finance*. Homewood, Ill.: Irwin, 1981.

Ferree, W. *The Act of Social Justice*. Dayton, Oh.: Marianist Publications, 1951.

Feyerabend, P. *Against Method*. London: NLB, 1975.

Fisher, I. *The Theory of Interest*. New York: Macmillan, 1930.

Fogarty, M. *Christian Democracy in Western Europe, 1820–1953*. South Bend, Ind.: Notre Dame 1957.

Finnis, J. *Natural Law and Natural Rights*. Oxford, U.K.: Oxford University Press, 1980.

Fourastié, J. *Ce que Je Crois*. Paris: Grasset, 1981.

Friedman, M. *Capitalism and Freedom*. Chicago, Ill.: University of Chicago Press, 1962.

———. *Free to Choose*. New York: Avon, 1981.

Friedman, M., and A. Schwartz. *A Monetary History of the Unites States, 1867–1960*. Princeton, N.J.: Princeton University Press, 1963.

Furfey, P. *A History of Social Thought*. New York: Macmillan, 1947.

Furubotyn, E., and S. Pejovich. "Property Rights and Economic Theory." *Journal of Economic Literature* (December 1972).

Galbraith, J. *The New Industrial State*. New York: Houghton Mifflin, 1967.

Gelin, A. *The Poor of Yahweh*. Collegeville, Minn.: Liturgical Press, 1964.

Gibellini, R. *Frontiers of Latin American Theology*. Maryknoll, N.Y.: Orbis, 1979.

Giordani, I. *The Social Message of Jesus*. Paterson, N.J.: St. Anthony Guild, 1943.

———. *The Social Message of the Early Church Fathers*. Paterson, N.J.: St. Anthony Guild, 1943. (Note: *The Social Message of the Apostles* has not been translated and published in English as of this printing.)

Goodhart, C. *Money, Information and Uncertainty*. London: Macmillan, 1975.

Goudzawaard, B. *Capitalism and Progress*. Toronto: Wedge Publishing, 1978.

Gough, J. *The Social Contract*. Oxford, U.K.: Oxford University Press, 1957.

Gould, J., and C. Ferguson. *Microeconomic Theory*. Homewood, Ill.: Irwin, 1980.

Goulet, D. *The Cruel Choice—A New Concept in the Theory of Development*. New York: Athenaeum, 1971.

―――. *A New Moral Order: Studies in Development Ethics and Liberation Theology*. Maryknoll, N.Y.: Orbis, 1974.

Graaff, de V., J. *Theoretical Welfare Economics*. Cambridge, U.K.: Cambridge University Press, 1957.

Gremillion, J. *The Gospel of Peace and Justice*. Maryknoll, N.Y.: Orbis, 1976.

Griffiths, B. *Morality and the Marketplace*. Maryknoll, N.Y.: Hodder and Stoughton, 1982.

Guardini, R. *The Virtues*. Chicago, Ill.: Regnery, 1967.

Gutierrez, G. *A Theology of Liberation*. Maryknoll, N.Y.: Orbis, 1973.

Hagerty, C. *The Holy Trinity*. North Quincy, Mass.: Christopher Publishing, 1976.

Hart, H. L. A. *The Concept of Law*. Oxford, U.K.: Oxford University Press, 1961.

Hayek, von, F. *The Road to Serfdom*. Chicago, Ill.: University of Chicago Press, 1944.

―――. *The Constitution of Modern Liberty*. Chicago, Ill.: University of Chicago Press, 1960.

―――. *Law, Legislation and Liberty*, 3 vols. Chicago, Ill.: University of Chicago Press, 1973, 1976, 1979.

Head, J., and R. Bird. *Modern Fiscal Issues*. Toronto: University of Toronto Press, 1972.

Henderson, J., and R. Quandt. *Microeconomic Theory*. New York: McGraw-Hill, 1958.

Hicks, J. *Value and Capital*. Oxford, U.K.: Oxford University Press, 1939a.

―――. "Foundations of Welfare Economics." *Economic Journal* (1939b).

Hill, L. "Social and Institutional Economics." *Review of Social Economy* (December 1978).

―――. "The Pragmatic Alternative to Positive Economics." *Review of Social Economy* (April 1983).

Hirsch, F. *The Social Limits to Growth*. Boston, Mass.: Harvard University Press, 1976.

―――. and J. Goldthorpe. (eds.). *The Political Economy of Inflation*. Boston, Mass.: Harvard University Press, 1978.

Hirshleifer, J. "Shakespeare vs. Becker on Altruism." *Journal of Economic Literature* (June 1977).

200

Hochman, H., and J. Rodgers. "Pareto Optimum Redistribution." *American Economic Review* (September 1969).

Holmes, A. *Contours of a World View*. Grand Rapids, Mich.: Eerdmans, 1983.

Houck, J., and F. Williams (eds.). *Co-Creation and Capitalism*. Lanham, Md.: University Press of America, 1983.

Howard, M., and J. King. *The Political Economy of Marx*. New York: Longman Group, 1975.

Hume, D. *A Treatise on Human Nature*. 1740. Reprint, Oxford, U.K.: Oxford University Press, 1888.

Hutchinson, T. *The Significance and Basic Postulates of Economic Theory*. 1938. Reprint. New York: Kelley, 1960.

Irenaeus. *Adversus Haereses*. Cambridge, U.K.: Cambridge University Press, 1857.

Ischboldin, B., and J. Sharp. "Cognitive Systems Theory." *International Journal of Social Economics, No. 6* (1980).

James, W. *Principles of Psychology*. New York: H. Holt, 1890.

John-Paul II. *Laborem Exercens*. Rome, 1981.

———. *Familiaris Consortio*. Rome, 1981.

Kantor, B. "Rational Expectations and Economic Thought." *Journal of Economic Literature* (December 1979).

Keynes, J. M. *Essays in Biography*. London: Macmillan, 1924. Reprint, New York: 1933.

———. *The End of Laissez-Faire*. London: Hogarth Press, 1927.

———. *General Theory of Employment, Interest and Money*. London: Macmillan, 1936.

Keynes, J. N. *The Scope and Method of Political Economy*. London: Macmillan, 1890.

Klamer, A. *The New Classical Macroeconomics*. Brighton, U.K.: Wheatsheaf, 1980.

Klein, P. "American Institutionalism." *Journal of Economic Issues* (June 1978).

Knox, R. *Enthusiasm*. Oxford, U.K.: Oxford University Press, 1950.

Kolakowski, L. *Religion*. Oxford, U.K.: Oxford University Press, 1982.

Kuhn, T. *The Structure of Scientific Revolutions*. Chicago, Ill.: University of Chicago Press, 1970.

Kurtz, P. *A Secular Humanist Declaration*. Buffalo, N.Y.: Prometheus Books, 1980.

Lakatos, I. *The Methodology of Scientific Research Programmes*, Vol. 1. Cambridge, U.K.: Cambridge University Press, 1978.

Lamont, C. *The Philosophy of Humanism*. New York: Frederick Ungar, 1965.

Lange, O., and J. Taylor. *On the Economic Theory of Socialism*. 1939. Reprint, New York: Kelley, 1970.

Lash, N. *Newman on Development*. Shepherdstown, W.V.: Patmos Press, 1978.

Leo XIII. *Rerum Novarum*. Rome, 1891.

201

Leibenstein, H. *Beyond Economic Man*. Boston, Mass.: Harvard University Press, 1980.

Lipsey, R., and K. Lancaster. "General Theory of the Second Best." *Review of Economic Studies* (1956–57).

Lipsey, R., G. Purvis, and P. Steiner. *Economics*. 5th Canadian Ed. New York: Harper and Row, 1985.

Little, I. *A Critique of Welfare Economics*. Oxford, U.K.: Oxford University Press, 1957.

Locke, J. *Two Treatises of Government*. 1690. Reprint. New York: Mentor, 1963.

Lowe, A. *On Economic Knowledge*. New York: Harper and Row, 1965.

Lucas, R. "An Equilibrium Model of the Business Cycle." *Journal of Political Economy* (December 1975).

Lutz, M. "Pragmatism, Instrumental Value Theory, and Social Economics." *Review of Social Economy* (October, 1985).

Machlup, F. *Methodology of Economics and Other Social Sciences*. New York: Academic Press, 1978.

Madden, M. *Political Theory and Law in Mediaeval Spain*. Fordham, N.Y.: Fordham University Press, 1930.

Maddock, R., and M. Carter. "A Child's Guide to Rational Expectations." *Journal of Economic Literature* (March 1982).

Maritain, J. *The Things Which Are Not Caesar's*. London: Sheed and Ward, 1930.

———. *Humanisme Intégral*. Paris: Aubier, 1936.

———. *The Range of Reason*. New York: Scribner's, 1942.

———. *Les Degrés du Savoir*. Paris: Desclée de Brouwer, 1946.

———. *The Person and the Common Good*. New York: Scribner's, 1947.

———. *St. Thomas Aquinas*. New York: Meridian, 1958.

———. *De l'Eglise du Christ*. Paris: Desclée de Brouwer, 1970.

McCloskey, D. "The Rhetoric of Economics," *Journal of Economic Literature* (June 1983).

McDonagh, J. *Christian Psychology*. New York: Crossroads, 1982.

McKee, A. "Labour Earnings Identity." Université Laval: *Industrial Relations,* (December 1973).

———. "From a Theory of Justice to its Implementation." *Review of Social Economy* (April 1979).

———. "The Pareto Optimum." *International Journal of Social Economics,* No. 7 (1980).

———. "What is Distributive Justice?" *Review of Social Economy* (April 1981a).

———. "Inflation, the Moral-Behavioural Aspect." *International Journal of Social Economics,* No. 4 (1981b).

202

————. "Market Failure and the Place of Government in Social Economy." *Review of Social Economy* (April 1984a).

————. "Social Economy and the Theory of Consumer Behaviour." *International Journal of Social Economics*, No. 3/4 (1984b).

Marshall, A. *Principles of Economics.* London: Macmillan, 1920.

Martin, D., J. Mills, and W. Pickering. *Sociology and Theology,* Brighton, U.K.: Harvester, 1980.

Maslow, A. *Towards a Psychology of Being.* Princeton, N.J.: Van Nostrand, 1968.

Meade, J. "The Meaning of Internal Balance," *Economic Journal* (September, 1978).

————. *The Just Economy,* Vol. 1 of *Principles of Political Economy.* London: Allen and Unwin, 1975.

Messner, J. *Social Ethics.* St. Louis, Mo.: Herder, 1965.

Mill, E. *The Economics of Environmental Quality.* New York: Norton, 1978.

Mill, J. S. *On Liberty.* 1859. Reprint. Oxford: Oxford University Press, 1971.

Mises, von, L. *The Free and Prosperous Commonwealth.* Princeton, N.J.: Van Nostrand, 1963.

Mishan, E. *Cost-Benefit Analysis.* New York: Praeger, 1966.

————. *Growth as the Price We Pay.* London: Staples, 1969.

Moon, P. *The Labor Problem and the Social Catholic Movement in France.* London: Macmillan, 1929.

Morishima, M. *The Economic Theory of Modern Society.* Cambridge, U.K.: Cambridge University Press, 1976.

Mueller, D. "Public Choice: A Survey." *Journal of Economic Literature* (June 1976).

Mueller, F. "Social Economics: The Perspective of Pesch and Solidarism." *Review of Social Economy* (December 1977).

Mulcahy, R. *The Economics of Heinrich Pesch.* New York: Henry Holt, 1952.

Munby, D. *Christianity and Economic Problems.* London: Macmillan, 1956.

————. *God and the Rich Society.* Oxford, U.K.: Oxford University Press, 1961.

Musgrave, R. *The Theory of Public Finance.* New York: McGraw-Hill, 1959.

————. "National Economic Planning: The U.S. Case." *American Economic Review* (May 1978).

Nath, S. *A Reappraisal of Welfare Economics.* New York: Kelley, 1969.

Netzer, D. *Economics and Urban Problems.* New York: Basic Books, 1974.

Newman, J. *The Grammar of Assent.* London: Burns, Oates, 1874.

Nicholson, W. *Intermediate Microeconomics and its Application.* Hinsdale, Ill.: Dryden, 1983.

Niskanen, W. *Bureaucracy and Representative Government.* Chicago, Ill.: University of Chicago Press, 1971.

North, G. *Introduction to Christian Economics*. Nutley, N.J.: Craig Press, 1973.

Novak, M. *Towards a Theology of the Corporation*. New York: Simon and Shuster, 1981.

———. *The Spirit of Democratic Capitalism*. New York: Simon and Shuster, 1982.

O'Brien, G. *An Essay on Mediaeval Economic Teaching*. London: Longmans, Green, 1920.

Pareto, V. *Cours d'économie politique*. 1896. Reprint. Geneva: Droz, Vol. 1, 1964.

———. *Manuel d'économie politique*. 1906. Reprint. Geneva: Droz, Vol. 7, 1966.

———. *Traité de sociologie générale*. 1917. Reprint. Geneva: Droz, Vol. 12, 1968.

Parkin, M. *Modern Macroeconomics*. Scarborough, Ontario: Prentice Hall, 1982.

Passerin d'Entréves, A. *The Mediaeval Contribution to Political Thought*. Oxford, U.K.: Oxford University Press, 1939.

———. *Natural Law*. London: Hutchinson, 1952.

———. (ed.). *Aquinas: Selected Political Writings*. London Macmillan, 1959.

Pierce, C. *Collected Papers*. Edited by C. Hartshorne and P. Weiss. Boston, Mass.: Harvard University Press, 1931.

Pemberton, R., and D. Finn. *Toward a Christian Economic Ethic*. Minneapolis, Minn.: Winston, 1985.

Perroux, F. *L'économie du XXᵉ siecle*. Paris: Presses Universitaires de France, 1964.

Pesch, H. *Lehrbuch der Nationalokonomie*. Frieburg, 1904–23.

Pettman, B., (ed.) *Social Economics—Concepts and Perspectives*. Bradford, U.K.: MCB Publications, 1977.

Phillips, A. "Unemployment and Change in Money Wage Rates." *Economica* (November, 1958).

Pieper, J. *The Four Cardinal Virtues*. South Bend, Ind.: Notre Dame, 1965.

Pigou, A. *The Economics of Welfare*. London: Macmillan, 1932.

Pius XI. *Quadragesimo Anno*. Rome, 1931.

Pokorny, D. "Smith and Walras: Two Theories of Science." *Canadian Journal of Economics* (August, 1978).

Polanyi, M. *Personal Knowledge*. Chicago, Ill.: University of Chicago Press, 1958.

———. *Science, Faith and Society*. Chicago, Ill.: University of Chicago Press, 1964.

Popper, K. *The Logic of Scientific Discovery*. 1934. Reprint. New York: Basic Books, 1959.

———. *The Open Society and its Enemies*. Vol. 2. Princeton, N.J.: Princeton University Press, 1966.

Preston, R. *Religion and the Persistence of Capitalism*. London: SCM Press, 1979.

———. *Explorations in Theology*. Vol. 9 London: SCM Press, 1981.

Prigogine, I., and I. Stengers. *Order Out of Chaos*. New York: Bantam Books, 1984.

Rapoport, A. *Fights, Games and Debates*. Ann Arbor, Mich.: University of Michigan Press, 1961.

Rawls, J. *A Theory of Justice*. Oxford, U.K.: Oxford University Press, 1971.

Reardon, B. *Roman Catholic Modernism*. Stanford, Cal.: Stanford University Press, 1970.

Ricardo, D. *Principles of Political Economy and Taxation*. London, 1821.

Robbins, L. *An Essay on the Nature and Significance of Economic Science*. London: Macmillan, 1935.

———. "Economics and Political Economy." *American Economic Review* (May, 1981).

Rommen, H. *The State in Catholic Thought*. St. Louis, Mo.: Herder, 1945.

Ropke, W. *A Humane Economy: The Social Framework of the Free Market*. Chicago, Ill.: Regnery, 1960.

———. *The Economics of the Free Society*. Chicago, Ill.: Regnery, 1963.

Ruether, R. *Liberation Theology*. Ramsey, N.J.: Paulist Press, 1972.

Rushdoony, R. *The Institutes of Biblical Law*. Nutley, N.J.: Craig, 1973.

Ryan, M. *Christian Social Teaching*. St. Peter's Seminary, London, Ontario, mimeo.

Samuels, W. *The Economy as a System of Power*. Vols. 1 and 2. New Brunswick, N.J.: Transaction Books, 1979.

Samuelson, P. *The Foundations of Economic Analysis*. Boston, Mass.: Harvard University Press, 1947.

Say, J. B. *Treatise on Political Economy*. 1803.

Schillebeeckx, E. *Jesus, an Experiment in Christology*. New York: Seabury Press, 1979.

Schumacher, E. *Small Is Beautiful*. Cambridge, U.K.: Cambridge University Press, 1973.

Schumpeter, J. *History of Economic Analysis*. Oxford, U.K.: Oxford University Press, 1954.

Schweitzer, A. *The Quest of the Historical Jesus*. 1906. Reprint, London: Macmillan, 1973.

Segundo, J. *Hidden Motives of Pastoral Action*. Maryknoll, N.Y.: Orbis, 1978.

Self, P. *The Econocrats and the Policy Process*. London: Macmillan, 1975.

Sen, A. *Choice, Welfare and Measurement*. Boston, Mass.: MIT Press, 1982.

Shackle, G. *Epistemics and Economics*. Cambridge, U.K.: Cambridge University Press, 1972.

Shils, E., and H. Rinch (eds.). *The Methodology of the Social Sciences* Glencoe, Ill.: Glencoe Free Press, 1949.

205

Sider, R. *Rich Christians in an Age of Hunger*. Downer's Grove, Ill.: Intervarsity Press, 1977.

Silk, L. *The Economists*. New York: Basic Books, 1976.

Simon, H. *Models of Man*. New York: Wiley, 1957

———. *Reason in Human Affairs*. Stanford, Cal.: Stanford University Press, 1983.

Skinner, B. F. *Beyond Freedom and Dignity*. New York: Knopf, 1971.

Sleeman, J. *Economic Crisis—A Christian Perspective*. London: SCM Press, 1976

Smith, A. *The Wealth of Nations*. 1776. Reprint. (Ed. J. Bullock, New York: Collier, 1909.

Spengler, O. *Decline of the West*. New York: Knopf, 1926.

Stamp, J. *Wealth and Taxable Capacity*. 1922. Reprint. Freeport, N.Y.: Books for Libraries Press, 1971.

Storkey, A. *A Christian Social Perspective*. London, U.K.: Intervarsity Press, 1979.

Tawney, R. *Religion and the Rise of Capitalism*. New York: Harcourt Brace, 1926.

Temple, W. *Christianity and the Social Order*. 1942. Reprint. New York: Seabury Press, 1977.

Tool, M. "A Social Value Theory in Neo-Institutionalist Economics." *Journal of Economic Issues* (December 1977).

———. *The Discretionary Economy*. Boulder, Col.: Westview Press, 1985.

———. "Social Value Theory of Marxists." *Journal of Economic Issues* (December 1982–January 1983).

Toulmin, S. *The Return to Cosmology*. Berkeley: University of California, 1982.

Tower, E. *Economics Readings Lists, Course Outlines, Exams, Puzzles and Problems*. Durham, N.C.: Eno River Press, 1981.

Tresmontant, C. *Comment se pose aujourd'hui le problème de l'existence de Dieu*. Paris: Seuil, 1966.

———. *Problèmes du Christianisme*. Seuil, 1980.

Troeltsch, E. *The Social Teaching of the Christian Churches*. London: Macmillan, 1931.

Van Til, C. *Common Grace*. Philadelphia, Pa.: Presbyterian and Reformed Press, 1954.

———. *A Christian Theory of Knowledge*. Philadelphia, Pa.: Presbyterian and Reformed Press, 1969.

Varian, H. *Microeconomic Analysis*. New York: Norton, 1978.

Vecchio, del, G. *Justice*. Edinburgh. Edinburgh University Press, 1956.

Vickers, D. *A Christian Approach to Economics and the Cultural Condition*. Smithtown, N.Y.: Exposition Press, 1987.

Vidler, A. *The Modernist Movement in the Roman Church*. Cambridge, U.K.: Cambridge University Press, 1934.

206

Viner, J. *Religious Thought and Economic Society,* Edited by J. Melitz and D. Winch. Durham, N.C.: Duke University Press, 1978.

Wand, J. *The City of God.* Oxford, U.K.: Oxford University Press, 1963.

Walras, L. *Elements d'économie politique pure.* Paris: Sirey, 1874.

Waterman, A. ''John Locke's Theory of Property and Christian Social Thought.'' *Review of Social Economy* (October 1982).

———. ''The Catholic Bishops and Canadian Public Policy.'' *Canadian Public Policy* (September 1983).

——— ''Religious Belief and Political Bias.'' In *In Morality of the Market,* Edited by L. Block, G. Brennan, and K. Elzinga, Vancouver: Fraser Institute, 1985.

Webb, S. and B. *The Prevention of Destitution.* London: King, 1911.

Weber, M. *The Protestent Ethic and the Spirit of Capitalism.* 1905. Reprint. London: Allen and Unwin, 1930.

Weingraub, S. ''A Tax-Based Incomes Policy.'' *Journal of Economic Issues* (1971).

Weiskeipl, L. *Friar Thomas d'Aquino.* New York: Doubleday, 1974.

Westhues, K. *First Sociology.* Toronto: McGraw-Hill, 1982.

Wetter, G. *Dialectical Materialism.* London: Routledge and Paul, 1958.

White, R., and C. Hopkins. *The Social Gospel.* Philadelphia, Pa.: Temple, 1976.

Wilken, R. *The Christians as the Romans Saw Them.* New Haven, Ct.: Yale University Press, 1984.

Wilkinson, B. ''The Catholic Bishops and Canadian Public Policy: A Comment.'' *Canadian Public Policy* (March 1984).

Williams, J. *Canadian Churches and Social Justice.* Toronto: Lorimer, 1984.

Williams, M. *Catholic Social Thought.* Ronald, 1950.

Winch, D. *Analytical Welfare Economics.* Harmondsworth, U.K.: Penguin, 1971.

Wogaman, J. *The Great Economic Debate.* Philadelphia, Pa.: Westminster Press, 1977.

Wong, S. *Foundations of Paul Samuelson's Revealed Preference Theory.* London: Routledge and Paul, 1978.

Worland, S. *Scholasticism and Welfare Economics.* South Bend, Ind.: Notre Dame University Press, 1967.

———. ''Exploitative Capitalism.'' *Social Research* (Summer 1981).

REPORTS

Carter Tax Commission. *Report of Royal Commission on Taxation.* Ottawa, 1966.

Pastoral Letter on Catholic Social Teaching and the U.S. Economy. U.S. Catholic Conference, Washington, D.C. (*First Draft,* 1984; *Second Draft,* 1985). The Third Draft, entitled *Economic Justice for All,* was issued in June 1986.

Position Papers and Conclusions. Medellin Conference 1968. CELAM. Washington, D.C.: U.S. Catholic Conference, 1970.

Toward the Future: Catholic Social Thought and the U.S. Economy. New York: American Catholic Committee, 1984.

Vatican. *Congregation for the Doctrine of the Faith: Instruction on Christian Freedom and Liberation.* 1986. Text in *Osservatore Romano,* English edition, April 14, 1986.

Vatican. *Congregation for the Doctrine of the Faith: Instruction on Liberation Theology.* Osservatore Romano, English edition, September 10, 1984.

Vatican Council II. *The Conciliar and Post-Conciliar Documents.* Edited by A. Flannery. Collegeville, M. Liturgical Press, 1975.

INDEX

210

211

unions, 65, 104, 113, 115
United Nations, 177, 187
U.S. Bishops, *Pastoral Letter,* 88, 95–6, 98–9, 189, 192

Values, and economic science, 127–9
Vatican II, 91
Vickers, D., xviii, 43, 87
Vincent de Paul, 93
virtues, 51

Wage theory, 102–5

Wagner's law, 166
Walras, L., 128, 138
Waterman, A., 100, 189, 190, 193
Weber, M., 126, 128, 186
Weintraub, S., 115
welfare economics, 157–62
Western society, decline, 6
Wilken, R., xvi, 28
Winch, D., 161, 196
Worland, S., 165, 190–1, 193
world, this material, 28

FUNDERBURG LIBRARY

MANCHESTER COLLEGE